Children
Who Soil

ANN BUCHANAN
IN COLLABORATION
WITH
GRAHAM CLAYDEN

Children
Who Soil
Assessment and
Treatment

JOHN WILEY & SONS
Chichester · New York · Brisbane · Toronto · Singapore

Other Wiley Editorial Offices

John Wiley & Sons, Inc., 605 Third Avenue,
New York, NY 10158-0012, USA

Jacaranda Wiley Ltd, G.P.O. Box 859, Brisbane,
Queensland 4001, Australia

John Wiley & Sons (Canada) Ltd, 22 Worcester Road,
Rexdale, Ontario M9W 1L1, Canada

John Wiley & Sons (SEA) Pte Ltd, 37 Jalan Pemimpin #05-04,
Block B, Union Industrial Building, Singapore 2057

Library of Congress Cataloging-in-Publication Data

Buchanan, Ann.
    Children who soil : assessment and treatment / Ann Buchanan, in collaboration with
Graham Clayden.
        p.   cm.
    Includes bibliographical references and index.
    ISBN 0-471-93479-8 (paper)
    1. Fecal incontinence in children.   I. Clayden, Graham.   II. Title.
    [DNLM: 1. Fecal Incontinence—in infancy & childhood.   WI 600 B918c]
    RJ456.F43B73   1992
    618.92′849—dc20
    DNLM/DLC
    for Library of Congress   92–15864
                                                                                          CIP

British Library Cataloguing in Publication Data

A catalogue record for this book is available from the British Library

ISBN 0-471-93479-8

Typeset in 11/13 pt Photina by Alden Multimedia Ltd, Northampton
Printed and bound in Great Britain by Biddles Ltd, Guildford and King's Lynn

CONTENTS

PREFACE

The aim of this book is to give practical information to child-care professionals, both medical and non-medical, who may in one way or another be involved in the treatment and management of soiling children. The book is based on six years of doctoral research by the author, involving a pilot study of children who soiled and a research study of soiling children, as well as post-doctoral involvement with other children and their families with soiling problems (Buchanan 1990). This book is written in collaboration with Dr Graham Clayden, Honorary Consultant Paediatrician at St Thomas's Hospital in London. Dr Clayden advised the author during the original study. They have since been involved in joint work with soiling children and their families.

The author's original research project involved 66 soiling children. This included a study of soiling children treated by a local paediatric department, and further study of soiling children treated by a traditional child psychiatric clinic, and finally a study of soiling children treated by an experimental 'whole child' approach which sought to incorporate treatment of the psychological, physical and social aspects of the problem. The author, a behaviourally trained social worker, was the key therapist, working under medical supervision. The research validated the benefits of an integrated 'whole child' approach for soiling problems (Buchanan 1990).

The book is designed both for the busy professional who wants, in the shortest possible time, to assimilate the essentials of the 'whole child' approach for assessing and treating the soiling child, and for those practitioners who require a more comprehensive research résumé. To meet the differing needs of readers, the book is therefore in four parts. Part I includes an extensive review of international literature on the subject, covering both causation theories and treatment studies. Part II is the practical part of the book: how to assess the 'whole child' and his family, and the treatment and management of the problem, using the 'whole child' approach. Part II stands on its own and will give the busy professional the basic information he needs to help a soiling child and his family. For those who wish to know more, Part III takes a wider look at the associated problems of soiling children. In this section Dr Clayden has written an important chapter on neurological disorders associated with soiling. There is also a chapter on the relationship between soiling and sexual abuse. Finally the Afterword looks at the wider implications from the research and suggests ways of setting up specific services for the soiling child.

The book is dedicated to the many children and their families who took part in the original research study, without whom this book would not have been possible, and who in effect taught the author all she knows.

Ann Buchanan
University of Southampton
December 1991

ACKNOWLEDGEMENTS

This book would not have been possible without the help, support and cooperation of, firstly, the many children, their families and the professionals who took part in the original study and, secondly, those who supported the writing of the book.

For inspiration and help beyond the course of duty I should like to thank Dr Graham S. Clayden, who not only advised and supported the original research, but also responded to my invitation to collaborate in writing this book; Daphne Shepherd, my doctoral supervisor and her (now my) colleagues at Southampton University; Phyllis Trafford, who agreed to my undertaking the original research; Alice Sluckin, and Alec Webster who shared their research experience in this area; and the many professionals in England and the United States who wrote discussing their findings, including, Dr Levine (USA), Dr Bentley (Scotland) and Dr Read (UK), Dr Hobbs (UK), Dr Naomi Richman (UK).

For active involvement during the study I should like to acknowledge the help of Dr Cyril Williams, consultant child psychiatrist, who sadly died during the course of the study, and Dr Robert Wilkins, who gallantly agreed to take his place, as well as the paediatric department of the Royal Berkshire Hospital, especially Dr Stone (retired), and Dr Mann. I should also like to acknowledge the help of the many general practitioners, community physicians, health visitors and others who referred cases for the project. Most important of all, I should like to thank all the children and families who agreed to take part and continued with 'Mrs Pooh', as I became known, even when things did not improve.

For help in bringing this book together I should like to acknowledge my gratitude to the publishers and authors who agreed to extracts from their works being reproduced here, especially Oxford University Press for permission to reproduce the *Information Booklet for Children and Parents*. I should also like to acknowledge the help of Wendy Hudlass and Lewis Derrick of John Wiley & Sons.

Finally, this book would not have been possible without the support of my husband, and my three children, Katie, Tessa and Helen.

PART I   Background

CHAPTER 1   Profile of the problem

When I first got to Groton I had led so sheltered a life and was so shy that I was afraid to ask where the bathroom was. Hard as it may be to believe, I did what had to be done in my pants or in the bushes. I suppose I was surrounded by foul smells. Holding back as long as I could, I started to suffer stomach pains. Not knowing the cause, school officials suspected homesickness (well I was homesick, at home I knew where the bathrooms were) and asked my parents to take me home for a few days to ease my adjustment. (James Roosevelt: 'My parents: a differing view'; from Levine 1982)

A child with a soiling problem is one of the more difficult conditions that confronts child care professionals, be they doctors, nurses, social workers, psychologists, paediatricians or child psychiatrists. Parents are often distressed. Family relationships are strained. There are feelings of anger, frustration, disgust and shame evoked by their soiling offspring. The soiling child, by the very nature of his problem, is hard to love. The guilt in such parents can be painful. In effect these parents have broken a universal taboo—in failing to toilet train their child, with all the contingent associations of 'being dirty' and risks to health both for the child and even for others, they have rendered him unacceptable, an outcast in his community.

For the child it is hard to imagine a social or physical problem which is more devastating to his sense of personal worth and dignity than the inability to control the most basic of human functions. A child who soils lives in constant fear that he may lose control of his bowels and that at any moment he will be exposed to the fury of his parents or the taunts of his peers. As James Roosevelt, he hopes by 'holding on' to solve his difficulty, but the result is only stomach aches and further soiling. Whatever course he takes he loses.

Small wonder, therefore, that the consequences of soiling can have far reaching effects on a child's social and emotional development. What child, for example, wants to sit next to another who smells? The soiling problem may seriously inhibit the child's ability to make friends. But it is not only the child who is affected. Indeed what mother wants to take her eight year old child to visit a friend knowing that at any moment he could fill the room with the smell of putrid faeces? Or indeed what parent wants to risk inviting others back to her house, which despite every precaution stinks of defaecation? The very presence of a soiling problem restricts the child's and the parent's social interaction.

Given the problems, it is not surprising that many soiling children develop strategies for withdrawal from social situations, avoiding school outings and family holidays or becoming reluctant even to go to school; nor is it surprising that some develop 'don't care attitudes' which further infuriate their parents. These attitudes are a reaction to trying to control a problem which they have in effect learnt they cannot control.

A Not Uncommon Problem

Most families have never heard of another child with a soiling problem. 'I thought my child was the only one with this difficulty' is a common cry at an initial interview. Although around 97% of all children entering primary school at five years will have achieved bowel control (Bellman 1966), this of course means that three in every 100 children will be soiling. Even at 10–12 years of age more than one boy in every 100 will still be soiling (Rutter et al. 1970). There are suggestions that the numbers may even be higher (Buchanan 1990). Because of the shame attached to the condition, it is perhaps understandable that parents are reluctant to admit their children has a difficulty. It is a family 'secret'. But the very secrecy places additional stresses on the child and his family. Whereas the community will respond positively to a mother who shares her concern about her diabetic or asthmatic child, there is likely to be less sympathy for a child who soils himself.

A Problem that is Difficult to Treat

Despite the emotions and distress evoked by a soiling child, when eventually the child emerges from the hidden recesses of the home and comes with his parents to ask for help, the helping professions can often find the condition remarkably resistant to treatment. Whether the child goes to his health visitor, his general practitioner, his local paediatric department, or to local child psychiatric or psychological services, or Social Services department, there is a fair chance that the condition will continue with short periods of respite for many years (Buchanan 1990). Even studies in specialist referral centres report treatment successes in only two-thirds of cases (Taitz et al 1986, Berg & Vernon-Jones 1964); that is if the child and his family manage to gain a referral to these centres. There is also a probability that the soiling child and his family will move from professional to professional, agency to agency throughout middle childhood seeking the elusive cure (Buchanan 1990). As such it is an expensive disorder to treat.

But despite being a problem which causes great distress, is relatively common, is often resistant to treatment, and is costly in professional treatment time, there has been comparatively little research. In many ways soiling is the 'Cinderella' of childhood disorders, meriting little research, and a hotchpotch approach to treatment which does little to help the soiling child, his family or scarce professional budgets. There have to be better ways of dealing with the problem.

A Problem that Cannot be Seen in Isolation—Associated Difficulties

One of the challenges of treating any childhood complaint is that nothing happens in isolation. The soiling child is no exception. While struggling to control his soiling, he will collect a myriad of associated or secondary problems. Physically his growth and development may be affected; emotionally his self-esteem suffers; his relationships within the family can be stressed to the extent of possible physical abuse; his peer group relationships are strained; underachievement in school is not unusual; behavioural problems are very common. The greater the stresses his family are under, the worse his problem is likely to be. There can also be associations with sexual abuse. Not surprisingly, what might present as a simple defaecation disorder, can go on to affect every aspect of the child's development and later life opportunities.

The Definition of a Soiling Child

In this book 'a soiling child' or a 'soiler' refers to any child over the age of four and under the age of 16 who has regularly soiled his pants and/or bed. The definition is deliberately broad and is intended to include *all* children with a soiling problem regardless of whether the soiling is felt to be related to physical or psychological factors. Two groups, however, are excluded from the above definition. Firstly, those children who in a moment of anger randomly place their faeces, as opposed to dirty pants, in places likely to offend are excluded.

Secondly, children whose soiling is connected with neurological disorders, for example spina bifida, and severe mental handicap, are also not included in this definition. The exception to this is an important chapter by Dr Graham Clayden on neurological disorders and faecal incontinence in Part III of the book (Chapter 11). The basis for the above definition is discussed in detail in Chapter 6. Enough to say here is that one of the questions the original research sought to answer was whether there was a clear divide between psychological soilers, who have been called 'encopretics' and who have traditionally been treated by the psychiatric services, and soiling children, whose problem is felt to be physically based and who have traditionally been treated by the paediatric service.

The Aim of the Book

The aim of this book is to help the 'helpers' to help. It makes no claims to have found the 'treatment of choice', but rather seeks to suggest ideas and give practical tips which may inspire more effective treatment for soiling children. It would not have been possible without the many children and families who took part in the original research project. During the study the author came to know many children with soiling problems and their families. Home visits took place when times were good and times were bad. If this book assists the caring professionals to help others with soiling problems (and their families) to cry less and laugh more over 'me bowels', it will have achieved its aim. As Walker (1985) says 'problems over "me bowels" have been with us since time immemorial' and are 'here to stay concerning as they do the intestinal tract . . . a mirror wherein is reflected the status of bodily activities in general, from eating and drinking and states of disease' (Walker 1985).

SUMMARY

Soiling is a problem which causes great distress to the child and his family. It is a problem which is not uncommon, affecting nearly one in every 100 children aged 10–12, and many more at younger ages. It is a problem which is difficult to treat. Even at specialist referral centres around a third of soiling children prove resistant to treatment.

It is also a problem with many associated difficulties: physical problems, medical and development concerns, emotional and psychological difficulties, strained family and peer group relationships, educational problems, social difficulties.

Because of the stresses involved many children may be at risk of physical abuse. In some cases the possibility of child sexual abuse may have to be considered.

Soiling is therefore a problem that cannot be seen in isolation. It necessitates a 'whole child' approach in assessment, treatment and management.

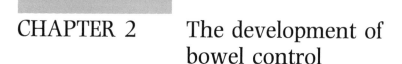

CHAPTER 2   The development of bowel control

Nanny made as much of an issue over my bowel movements as over what and how much I ate . . . I was put on the 'article' and told to do Number Two as soon as I had finished my long breakfasts. If I said I didn't want to, I was told I must 'try' and would be left sitting for up to half an hour or more . . . what a relief, what triumph when I could shout, 'done it, Nanny!'. What a worry when I could not, as this meant I would have to have Syrup of Figs in the evening . . . an extra worry was my belief in what Nanny said that not 'doing it' was alarmingly bad for me. (Lady Anne Hill in *The Rise and Fall of the British Nanny*, Gathorne-Hardy 1972, p. 263)

Don't let ten o'clock in the morning pass without making baby's bowels move if they have not moved in the previous twenty hours. (Truby King 1913)

Learning not to soil within the immediate living area is expected of all infants in every human social group that has been observed. One of the most important socialisation tasks that a mother has to undertake in any culture is to teach her young infant to respect this universal taboo. In most cultures this training has been successfully undertaken by the age of four. It is interesting that this training is not confined to human beings. Many animals train their young to excrete away from the immediate living area. This was demonstrated by Laird's study of young pigs (1973) but can also be observed in domestic cats and dogs.

Age of Bowel Control

As will be seen later, cross cultural studies show a remarkable consistency in the age a child achieves bowel control, which suggests that maturational factors may be as important as training techniques. In an epidemiological survey in Sweden, Bellman (1966) surveyed 8863 children between the age of seven and eight in their first year of school using a parent questionnaire. She found that bowel control seemed as a rule to be established and stabilised during the child's fourth year,

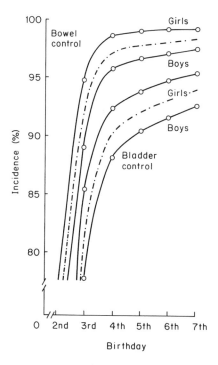

Figure 1. Incidence of bowel and bladder control between the second and seventh birthdays (from Bellman 1966, 'Studies in encopresis', with permission)

and as can be seen from Figure 1, over 97% of boys and 99% of girls achieved bowel control by the age of seven. More general studies in England examining child care practices and the extent of psychological problems in children, which will be examined in the next chapter when we consider children who fail to gain bowel control, report similar findings.

Normal Bowel Function

Normal bowel function in humans is a complicated process involving both a voluntary and an involuntary action. Given this, it is remarkable that most children do manage to gain control of their bowels, for it is only by gaining control over the voluntary process that the child is able to defaecate at the right place and time. As can be seen from Figure 2, in the main the colon serves as a reservoir for the residual

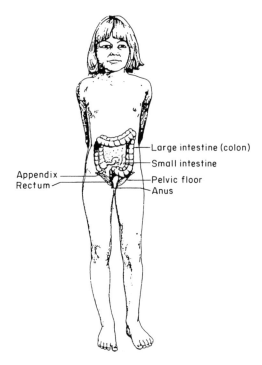

Large intestine (colon)
Small intestine
Appendix
Rectum
Pelvic floor
Anus

Figure 2. The lower bowel in children (reproduced from Morgan 1981 by permission of the author and Butterworth-Heinemann Ltd)

matter in the diet. The contents of the colon are concentrated through the resorption of liquid.

In a normal bowel, waves of contractions pass along the colon a few times each day and move relatively large masses of concentrated matter into the rectum. This elicits the sensory nerve impulses from the rectum to the spinal cord, which produces the urge to defaecate. Whether to defaecate or not is the voluntary decision. Children who have been successfully bowel trained can generally choose the time and place. If defaecation is to take place the abdominal muscles contract at the same time as the external sphincter, the anus, relaxes. Voluntary straining can increase the pressure in the rectum to stimulate defaecation. To postpone defaecation there is a voluntary tightening of the external sphincter and if necessary the perineal muscle too. When defaecation is postponed the rectum adjusts to its increased content and the urge to defaecate often disappears though the faeces are retained. The next stimulus to defaecate may not arise until further faecal matter is carried down to the rectum by mass movement, probably several hours later. In 'normal' bowel function, there are considerable variations in the need to defaecate. Bowel movements can occur in healthy children and adults, several times a day, several times a week, or only a few times a month. Pinkerton (1958) reported cases of young children going through prolonged periods without evacuation and continuing to enjoy good health, eating normally and showing abundant energy throughout. In contrast to this, bowel movements can also occur at very frequent intervals, even though the bowel is empty, in certain inflammatory or toxic conditions—the symptom known as diarrhoea.

The effect of emotions on bowel movements

There is considerable evidence that a person's emotional state can affect the process of the bowel function. Kohler (1925) in *Mentality of Apes* notes that the sight of big animals so frightened his chimpanzees that it had an immediate laxative effect on them. In man there is the well-known examination diarrhoea and the violent effect on the bowel in the face of extreme fear. It is also felt that the colon and rectum may be stimulated by gastric reflexes at meal times. Friedman & Snape (1946) have shown that in patients who have had a colostomy, the mucosa of the colon reddens and swells even at the sight and smell of food. It is felt this may be a conditioned response as in Pavlov's salivating dog. Depression is also associated with constipation, particularly in adults and the elderly (Brocklehurst & Kahn 1969, Preston et al 1984). This is illustrated by the study of Grace et al (1951), who quoted an interesting case of a 31 year old Finnish physician who became depressed on arrival in the USA. During his depression, observations by barium meal technique showed no change in the size and shape of his bowel after a meal. However, later when he was recovered from his depression, the large bowel showed marked shortening and narrowing after taking a meal. It is understandable that any emotional state which slows down the body's metabolic processes is likely to affect the bowels, but it is interesting that physical changes can actually be observed. How far these findings showing a relationship between depression and constipation in adults can reliably be applied to children is not known. In a recent paper Kazdin & Petti (1982) reviewed a number of scales measuring depression in children. Although most scales cover symptoms described variously as 'does your child worry about aches and pains', few if any specifically consider constipation as a possible indicator of depression.

The role of diet

Diet also has a role in the frequency and size of motions. For example, in undeveloped countries where it has been noticed that the faeces are larger and heavier, it is assumed that this is related to the large quantities of fibrous foods in the diet. It has also been shown that the amount of liquid in the diet and the actual balance within the diet is important. A poor diet or insufficient food can lead to constipation and failure to thrive. The whole subject of diet and its relationship to bowel disorders is a developing area of study. Its role in the causation of soiling will be considered in the next chapter, but some of the more controversial literature on its role in a wide range of behaviour disorders in children will be examined in Chapter 10.

Bowel Training in other Cultures

Although normal bowel function is a complicated process, most children in all cultures are successfully toilet trained. It is interesting to take a cross cultural perspective to gain some understanding of how children in different cultures are trained (Table 1). The following has been extracted from a study of six cultures by Whiting (1963).

A Guisli community in Kenya

Nyansongo is a Guisli community in the white highlands of Kenya. Families live in thatched round structures with walls and floors of mud and wattle with no latrine. At around 26 months, which is often around the birth of another sibling, the mother takes a child to a bush or field some distance from the house and demonstrates what to do. After several demonstrations, and when she feels he has had enough instruction, she will cane him for daytime defaecation in the house or yard but not for night-time infractions. At this stage the child ordinarily wakes his mother and she puts him in the corner of the house or yard and then sweeps up the faeces in the morning. Finally the child is punished for defaecating in the house at night too, as he is supposed to

Table 1. Cross cultural perspective on bowel training

Culture	Level of development	Age at start of training	Method used (clothing during training)	Age when most children successfully trained
Nyansongo	Kenyan community very primitive	26.7 months	Modelling Steps to proficiency Punishment (Minimum clothing)	2–3 years No latrines
Rajputs	Indian farming community Purdah system Primitive latrines	As soon as walking	Modelling Clueing with 'sizzle' noise for urination Steps to proficiency (Trousers with crotch cut out)	2 years
Taira	Japanese rural community Wooden huts Working mothers Grandmother/sibling care in second year	10 months	Placing child on a pot Time schedule Verbal reinforcement Self-training (Swaddling during first year)	2–3 years
Orchard Town	Westernised urban community	First year	Placing child on a pot Time schedule U.S.A. Soapsticks, suppositories, enemas Punishment Verbal reinforcement Rewards (Nappies)	2–2½ years

Adapted from Whiting, B.B. (ed.) (1963) *Six Cultures. Studies in Child Rearing. Laboratory of Human Development*, John Wiley & Sons, New York & London.

perform his elimination in the daytime or to wake up someone to accompany him outside at night. The amount of time mothers spend on this training ranges from one week to one year, but most take around one month. Some mothers who trained quickly attribute it to the fact that they were 'serious' about it and punished severely for infractions.

The Rajputs of Kalapur in India

Living some 90 miles north of Delhi and close to the foothills of the Himalayas are an old warrior ruling race turned farmers and landowners. The women live in a purdah system and their lives go on within enclosed courtyards. Homes have latrines but there is also a drain in one corner of the courtyard. It is to this drain that the child is led as soon as he can walk to urinate or defaecate. Adults make a 'sizzle' sound to encourage urination. When the mother sees him squatting to defaecate she encourages him to go by himself to the latrine or the cattle compound inside the courtyard. Most children learn to eliminate in the proper spot during their second year. Since children ordinarily wear only shirts they have no clothes to remove for elimination. During the winter a child who is not toilet trained wears trousers with the crotch cut out—the very opposite of a nappy.

*Taira, an Okinawan village southwest of
the Japanese island of Kyushu*

The Tairans wear simple Western dress and live in simple wooden houses. Mothers return to work in the fields when the child is some three or four months old and only return at intervals to feed the child. Babies are left in the care of grandparents and older siblings. Babies are heavily swaddled and although care is taken to keep them clean in the first year, thereafter they are often left for long periods in wet nappies. From the age of about 10 months and when she is at home, the mother tries to anticipate urination or an impending bowel motion from the child's facial expressions. She will then hold the child in a sitting position encouraging him to urinate or eliminate. If the child is successful she praises and hugs him, but does not punish him for dirtying his nappies. Sometimes a mother will develop a sort of mental clock for 'trying' this routine. But the mother does not instruct the older sibling who may have the care of the child during the day to continue the system. Eventually most children train themselves with the minimum of instruction.

Orchard Town, New England, USA

This is a community which embodies all the New England virtues of self-respectability and self-reliance. Spoilt behaviour, laziness, rebelliousness, discipline problems and lack of appetite are traits, which in various degrees are thought to be emphasised by the parental treatment of the child. The process of toilet training includes giving the child the 'idea' by sitting him on a potty or toilet, grunting and running water, waiting for his 'regular' time or putting him on the toilet just after urination or defaecation. The idea is often expressed that the mother should not force the child in any way. Forcing in toilet training is considered to be responsible for making a child 'rebellious'. In practice the mothers seemed to use a variety of techniques to train their children.

Girls were easier to train than boys and were generally completely trained by two or two and a half years. Parents felt very responsible about lack of success in toilet training. If the child was slow in learning, they felt they had started toilet training too late or too early. At other times they worried that they had been too strict. Mothers said that they were more relaxed with later children. It was the mother who wavered between leniency and strictness who tended to be least successful in toilet training.

Training methods employed by the New England mothers:

- Putting on a pot at regular times after the child is able to sit up.
- Use of a soapstick, suppositories or enemas at regular times (one in four mothers use them).
- Occasional spanking.
- Shaming the child.
- Rubbing the child's nose in the faeces.
- Praising for proper performance.
- Lifting at night.
- Rewards.

(From Whiting (ed.) (1963) *Six Cultures. Studies in Child Rearing.*)

It is worth noting that in all these cultures toilet training appears to be the function of the mother. This suggests that it is expected to occur at an early age when the mother has the principal charge of the infant and that it may also be seen as an extension of the mother's other primary functions.

The overriding message from this cross cultural analysis is that whatever method of toilet training is used most children learn bowel control at roughly the same age. This is an interesting finding because in the next chapter, which looks at the causes of soiling in children, some authorities have suggested that it is the method of training the child which brings about the soiling problem.

Development of Present Day Attitudes to Bowel Training

In primitive societies, training a child to defaecate away from the main living area may be not so much for the benefit of the child, but for the benefit of the immediate family group. It is unpleasant living in a compound where there is not an agreed place for defaecation. It is also a health risk. Maybe it is for this reason that humans have a natural revulsion to faeces other than their own and those of their very young.

The associations between bowel training offspring and good parenting

As a society develops, successful bowel training of children becomes associated with being a 'good mother'; it becomes an indication of how caring and proficient a person is as a parent. But of course there were considerable gains for mothers in getting their children clean. In warmer climates, where clothing is at a minimum, or in cultures such as the Rajputs in India where they could cut out the crotch of trousers of untrained children, keeping a child clean was not such a problem. But where it was necessary to swaddle a child, washing the swaddling became a considerable problem. St Bernadino of Sienna (1388–1444) drew attention in one of his sermons to how enormously a woman 'travaileth in washing and cleaning by day and night'. Swaddling clothes were a nightmare to clean and endless washing was part of the medieval routine. Writers recommended 'anointing little limbs with oil of roses to sweeten them' (St Bernadino of Sienna).

The associations with good health

Closely tied in with this was the idea that establishing regular bowel motions was an important factor for the child's good health. From earliest times regularity of bowels and the avoidance of constipation has been associated with good health care practice. The ancient Egyptians dedicated three days in every thirty to the so-called 'Egyptian Days' when they used purges and emetics to clear their systems. Medieval herbals are full of various substances which could be used to purge the system. Purging was second only to bleeding as a cure-all for every complaint. In Victorian times regularity of the bowels was the first rule of health and often the first subject raised by the doctor in presence of sickness. These attitudes may have been reinforced by the general awareness from the 1850s on of public health and the new understanding of the relationship between sanitation (or the lack of it) and disease.

Freud and the effects of bowel training on a child's future mental health

But what made the whole process of training a child more complicated was the advent of Freudian doctrine. Freud taught that neurotic disorders originated in the repression of natural instinctual tendencies like sex and aggressiveness, which being repressed came out in the perveted form of neurotic disorders (Freud 1908). Suddenly toilet training took on a new perspective. How your child was trained could have alarming repercussions on the child's later emotional and psychological health. Coercive bowel training was felt to have serious effects. Children could be left with a fixation at the anal level of development leading to neurotic manifestations in later life. Through Freud's influence, toilet training became a major topic of interest to twentieth century writers on child care. Mothers were subjected to a range of often conflicting advice from articles in magazines, from their own mothers, from child care specialists. Anthony (1957) set out to investigate the alleged causal relationship between bowel training, bowel functioning and presence of subsequent negative attitudes in children. The abnormal training methods of mothers of soiling children then became the main subject for intervention.

But do abnormal training methods lead to bowel dysfunction?

According to Hersov, 'There are difficulties in this hypothesis. Not all children who are coercively trained develop faecal soiling, and not all children who have bowel dysfunction experience abnormal training. Finally primitive children with deviant training according to our standards do not appear prone to bowel dysfunction' (Hersov 1977, p. 617). Present approaches to bowel training have tried to link these various ideas. Hugh Jolly, writing in his *Book of Child Care* (1977), advised a relaxed attitude to bowel training.

> Whatever the age of your baby when you start to pot train him, it is essential to relax about the whole business . . . don't nag him because he does not use the pot . . . nagging could lead to the idea of using his newly acquired skill to annoy or please you; he might deliberately choose to keep it as a weapon . . . a child who senses his mother's excessive concern about his bowel movements is likely to develop the commonest variety of constipation at this age, stool holding. This arises from his reaction of not doing what his mother wants. He refuses to give in to the need to evacuate and holds on instead of letting go. (Jolly 1975, p. 249)

Present day theorists advise mothers to be relaxed about bowel training, but it is hard for them to forget the history. When so much has been invested in successfully bowel training a child, it is not surprising that some parents have found the whole process intensely bewildering and distressing. Nor is it surprising that sometimes things go wrong.

SUMMARY

Bowel control is generally established by the fourth year. Normal bowel function is a complicated process involving both voluntary and involuntary actions. These actions can be influenced by emotional states and diet. In all cultures bowel training is the function of the mother, and most children are successfully bowel trained between two and four years of age irrespective of the training methods used. Present attitudes to bowel training are influenced by the concepts that early and successful bowel training is a sign of good parenting, and has associations with good physical health. Freudian doctrine has suggested that how a child is bowel trained may also be associated with later mental health. Hersov (1977) has indicated that the evidence does not support the hypothesis that abnormal training methods alone lead to bowel dysfunction. Modern theorists advise mothers to take a relaxed attitude to training their children, but when so much is invested in the process, it is not surprising that sometimes things go wrong.

CHAPTER 3   Children who soil

A unique feature of encopresis differentiates it from most other functional disorders; namely, youngsters so afflicted almost never have knowledge of any others. Parents also are likely to be unaware of its existence as a common childhood problem. In many cases they attribute the conditions to laziness or poor hygiene and are reluctant to bring it to the attention of a physician. Personal shame and cultural taboos also may cause a family to delay in seeking help. (Levine 1982)

Most parents of a soiling child have never heard of another with a soiling problem. Since 97% of all children entering primary school at five will have achieved bowel control, it is perhaps understandable that parents are reluctant to admit their child has a difficulty. It is also embarrassing, a sign of failed parenting, and so it remains a family secret. And yet the problem is not that uncommon (Table 2).

Bellman's (1966) figures may well underestimate the disorder. Of the 132 children she found who soiled, in only 15 was there any mention of this in their school record card. One can hypothesise that there were other parents who may have been reluctant to mention the difficulty even in her confidential survey. Indeed, under-recording may be a factor in all studies on the incidence of soiling in children. All the surveys, however, are consistent in finding that boys are nearly twice as likely to soil as girls, and this remains the situation whether the child is four or 12. In the USA the ratio of boys to girls has been placed much higher at 6 to 1 (Levine 1982).

In Table 2 the study by Davie et al was based on the information gathered through the National Child Development Study and referred to all children born in one week in March 1958. Butler's study was the third national cohort study and was based on all children born in England, Wales and Scotland between 5 and 11 April, 1970, while Bellman's study was based on children enrolled in the first class of Stockholm in Sweden on 15 September, 1962. Rutter's study was based on the total population of 10, 11 and 12 year olds living in the Isle of Wight. It is relevant to note that all the figures in Table 2 are based on parents completing or responding to the questionnaires as

Table 2. The extent of the problem

Study	Date	Age of children	Girls	Boys	Total
Davie et al (15 468 children)	1972	'Soiled by day after 4 years of age'	0.6%	2.0%	1.3%
Butler & Golding (13 135 children)	1986	5 years. 'At the present time does the child ever soil or mess in his/her pants?'			
		Occasionally	2.2%	3.9%	3.1%
		At least once a week'	0.8%	1.5%	1.2%
Bellman (8683 children)	1966	7 years. 'Does all or part of the child's bowel movements go into its clothes at present?' (At least once a month for last three months)	0.7%	2.3%	1.5%
Rutter et al (3964 children)	1970	10/11/12 years. 'Soils or loses control of bowels' (during last 12 months).	0.3%	1.3%	0.8%

requested, and it is quite possible to imagine that some parents may have chosen not to admit that their child had a soiling problem, even if they had been traced and had agreed to take part. Given these limitations, the studies have produced some valuable findings.

Associations Found in the Studies

Butler's study also showed that there were no significant regional differences in the prevalence of soiling nor any association with the type of neighbourhood or social class, and the symptom was no more common in children of mothers who worked than in those whose mothers stayed at home. He also noted that the parents of children who soiled were no more likely to smoke than other parents. There was no significant difference between ethnic groups.

Rutter (Rutter et al 1970) found that of the children who were soiling, over half were soiling at least once a week, and he also found a highly significant association between enuresis and encopresis. Bellman (1966) found about half the 'encopretic' boys had presented their symptoms continuously since infancy, while the other half had an interval of bowel control lasting up to one year. Butler & Golding (1986) found a relationship between birth weight and soiling, and demonstrated that the prevalence of soiling was 50% greater if the child had been of low birth weight. The difference was even more pronounced if soiling at least once a week was considered, in which case there was a three-fold difference in prevalence rates.

Butler & Golding also found that soiling was much more common in all situations where there were not two natural parents and the association was most marked in single parent families. This was supported by the author's study where only two-thirds of children taking part were living with their natural parents (Buchanan 1990).

Soilers: Heavy Users of Resources

Studies in specialised settings suggest that not only is soiling quite a common problem but that children presenting with disorders of defaecation are heavy users of resources. Taitz et al (1986) indicate that faecal soiling is a common cause of referral to general paediatric services and accounts for some 25% of the paediatric gastroenterological workload. He also suggests that primary or secondary referral to child psychiatry services is considerable. In the USA a similar picture emerges. In 3% of all children treated in paediatric outpatient clinics chronic constipation usually accompanied by soiling is the presenting problem (Loening-Bauke & Younoszi 1982). In studies of child guidance caseloads, soiling of an unspecified form or frequency occurred in 6% of the caseload in one study (McTaggart & Scott 1959) and in 10% in another (Vaughan 1961). In a pilot study undertaken by the author of Reading's (Berkshire, UK) child and family guidance clinic in 1985, soilers represented 10% of the current caseload.

The Causes of Soiling

The literature suggests that soiling in children is a problem that may arise in several quite different ways, and that the initial assessment is all important. Some symptoms have an origin in a medical disorder, and some in a psychological disturbance, some in environmental factors and many in a combination of causes. Recently it has been suggested that soiling may be an indicator of sexual abuse (Hobbs & Wynne 1986), although the Cleveland Report (1988) and Buchanan (1989) advise extreme caution in such cases. In this chapter the three main causes of soiling will be examined in turn; medical, psychological and environmental. Traditionally, as will be seen in the next chapter, it was felt important for clinicians to make a decision on what had been responsible for the soiling problem in order to decide the best avenue for treatment.

Rutter (1975), in his book *Helping Troubled Children*, provides a useful diagram (Figure 3). This does not include sexual abuse as it predates the current concerns. Factors relating to sexual abuse will be discussed in detail in Chapter 13.

Rutter advises that when presented with a soiling child, the first question which should be asked is whether or not the motions are normal in appearance and consistency. If they are abnormal, there is the issue of why the motions are loose or slimy or whatever is wrong with them. The next question is whether the child has a 'mass' of constipated motions. Evidence of a faecal mass indicates that the child is likely to have a problem known as 'retention with overflow'. The

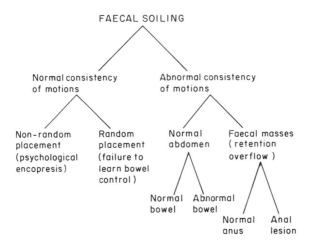

Figure 3. Faecal soiling (from Rutter 1975, *Helping Troubled Children*, reproduced by permission of Penguin Books Ltd)

basic problem is one of constipation which becomes so severe as to lead to a partial blockage of the bowel, which results in some of the motions liquefying and seeping past to produce faecal soiling. The soiling occurs because the child has lost the normal reflex to defaecate through the excessive constipation and subsequent dilation of the bowel. If there is no faecal mass, then the problem is one of diarrhoea with secondary soiling. The diarrhoea may be due to physical disease, in which case there is likely to be evidence from an examination by a physician or from the history or from medical tests. Alternatively it may be due to excessive anxiety in which the nervous effects include alterations in bowel function.

Rutter concludes that if the child's motions are of normal consistency and appearance, there is no reason to suspect bowel disease.

Clayden (1980) gives another useful flow diagram. In this diagram he is considering only children with chronic constipation and soiling (Figure 4). As can be seen from Clayden's flow chart, primary disorders can lead to secondary problems.

Levine (1975) also suggests that the same child can present in quite different ways at different times and sometimes it is not possible to separate out those whose symptoms may be related to a medical disorder from those whose symptoms are related to psychiatric disturbance.

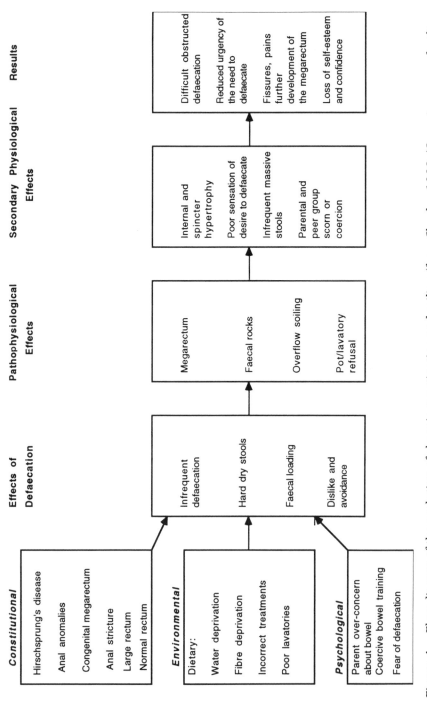

Figure 4. Flow diagam of the evolution of chronic constipation and soiling (from Clayden 1980, 'Organic causes of soiling in childhood', *ACPP Newsletter*, **5**, 1–4; reproduced by permission of the Association of Child Psychology and Psychiatry)

This hypothesis is also supported by the author's research (Buchanan 1990). Indeed when children at referral to a paediatric department for physical causes for soiling were compared with those at referral to a child psychiatric clinic for psychological causes for soiling, there were few significant differences, either on physical presentation of the problem or the presence of emotional disorders. The most significant finding was where the child had first gone for help. If the child had presented at a medical agency (general practitioner, health visitor) he was then referred to the paediatric department of the hospital and generally speaking received physical methods of treatment. If he had presented at an educational agency (school psychological service, head teacher), he was referred to the child psychiatric agency which in the area under study was run by education services, and received psychological help for his problem. The implications of this will be discussed later.

In the following pages there is a brief summary of the main causes of soiling: medical disorders, psychological disturbances and environmental factors. It is, however, one of the main themes of this book that soiling in children is in many cases caused by a combination of factors, and it is important to consider the 'whole child'.

Medical Disorders Associated with Soiling

It is not intended in this brief study to give a comprehensive review of all the medical disorders associated with soiling. However, it is felt important that where a non-medical clinician is involved in the treatment of soiling children, he/she should have an awareness of the more usual organic conditions connected with the disorder.

Constipation/retention with overflow

By far the most common cause of soiling is the condition known as retention with overflow (Figure 5).

As mentioned earlier the basic problem is one of constipation which becomes so severe as to lead to a partial blockage of the bowel. As a result of the blockage some of the motions liquefy and seep past to produce faecal soiling. The rectum is normally an empty tube which

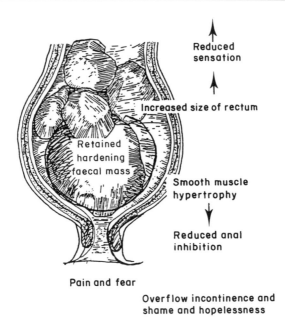

Reduced
sensation

Increased size of rectum

Retained
hardening
faecal mass

Smooth muscle
hypertrophy

Reduced anal
inhibition

Pain and fear

Overflow incontinence and
shame and hopelessness

Figure 5. The rectum loaded with a faecal mass. Illustration by Graham Clayden

gives rise to the sensation of needing to defaecate when faeces enter and stretch its wall. A soiling problem can arise when the urgency signal arising from the rectum being overloaded by faeces malfunctions. This happens when the faeces are held in the rectum instead of being emptied. If the bowel continues to remain unemptied, new waste material arrives in the rectum from above, building up a growing blockage of faeces. The size of this mass can make attempts at emptying difficult and even painful—and eventually the mass of waste matter fills up back along the large intestine distending the abdomen.

It used to be felt that the stretching of the rectum by overloading led to a weakness in the circle of muscles which control the escape of faeces rather like a balloon which has lost its elasticity through being overstretched. It is now known that the reverse is in fact the situation. In recent research Clayden (1988b) has shown that when the bowel is frequently overloaded, the rectal muscles become *overactive* while at the same time the anal muscles *relax* reflexly in response to the rectal activity. This means that as the muscles go on churning to eliminate the blockage, the child has no voluntary control over his soiling. The condition arises where a child for some reason fails over a prolonged period to empty his bowel. Children may avoid defaecation if it is painful, as it can be if there is a small fissure or split of the anus. Complaints of 'anal fissure' are a common finding in children with a soiling problem; 9.3% of parents of Bellman's soilers as opposed to 1.3% of her controls said their child had experienced pain on defaecation and fresh blood had been observed in the faeces (Bellman 1966).

Any condition which causes constipation may result in soiling as a result of overflow. A tendency to constipation is a common finding. This was supported by the author's research, where it was established that 60% of all soilers had a 'present or past history of constipation' (Buchanan 1990). Coekin & Gairdner (1960) in a study of 69 soilers argue that there may be a congenital factor which provides a predisposition to constipation and soiling, and this may be triggered off by apparently trivial incidents.

Although retention with overflow is strictly a medical condition, the reasons for the child 'stool holding' may often have a psychological basis.

Hirschsprung's disease and ultra-short
segment Hirschsprung's disease

The possibility that a child may suffer from undiagnosed Hirschsprung's disease is often considered where a child is soiling. But true Hirschsprung's disease is very rare and only reported in approximately one in 5000 births. In these cases, it may present as a complete obstruction soon after birth when without treatment it can be fatal, or as chronic constipation later. In Nottingham it accounts for about 10% of neonatal intestinal obstruction (Hull & Johnston 1981). Although true Hirschsprung's disease is rare in later childhood, research has suggested that a variety of the disease known as 'ultra-short segment Hirschsprung's' may affect over 9% of children with severe chronic constipation (Clayden 1976), and that soiling may also be associated with this condition. However, these figures relate to children referred to a secondary specialist referral centre, and figures may not be so high in non-specialist centres.

The disease consists essentially 'of hypertrophy and dilation of part or whole of the large bowel, associated with a narrowed terminal

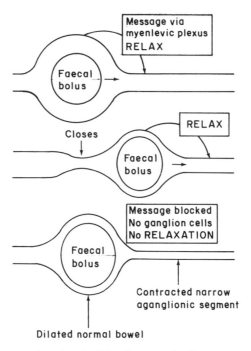

Figure 6. The bowel action in Hirschsprung's disease

segment and giving rise to abdominal distension, extreme constipation and interference with growth and development. The megacolon is secondary to the narrowing of the terminal portion of the gut, where the parasympathetic ganglion cells are deficient and spasticity results from unopposed sympathetic action' (Ellis 1962). Figure 6 graphically illustrates this problem.

Clayden (1976) indicated that Hirschsprung's disease should be considered in any child presenting in early childhood with difficulty with defaecation, and particularly where there was a history of alternating hard stools with diarrhoea, and/or loose stools but difficulty with defaecation, and/or a history of early onset of the bowel problem. Diagnosis is made by rectal biopsy.

Clayden believed, and this is where controversy reigns, that in children presenting with chronic constipation (mostly going back to the first years of life), there was a further group who have Hirschsprung's disease involving only a very narrow segment of the bowel. With some of these children, their problem might erroneously have been attributed to psychological factors, where in fact the psychological problems were secondary to the ultra-short segment Hirschsprung's.

Intestinal obstruction

One of the most dangerous conditions that could be associated with soiling is intestinal obstruction, where the passage of the intestinal contents is interrupted by mechanical factors. This could be caused by a variety of mechanisms, from a foreign body, to a hernia, to a tumour. Obstruction may be acute or chronic, and either partial or complete. The cardinal signs are, 'severe abdominal pain, vomiting, abdominal distension and later ladder-patterning. The faeces are pale and toxic, the clinical picture is sufficiently characteristic to indicate that obstruction is present though not necessarily to establish the cause' (Ellis 1962). Ellis also notes that 'it should be remembered the faeces represent the commonest abdominal "tumour" encountered in childhood, and the nature of the mass is generally obvious from palpation, when it is found it can be indented' (Ellis 1962).

Congenital anomalies, hypothyroidism, gastrointestinal disease

Most of the more serious congenital anomalies would become evident at birth or within the first few weeks of life and as such would not be of concern to children presenting with soiling over the age of four. For example, children born with the anus absent need very special post-operative training and medication.

Tripp & Candy (1985), in their *Manual of Paediatric Gastro-enterology*, indicate that with any child presenting with chronic constipation the clinician should be alert for hypothyroidism, particularly when there is evidence of growth failure.

Certain authors have pointed out that children contracting repeated intestinal disease in their early years may be traumatised to the extent that they subsequently become excessively prone to develop faecal incontinence. However, as can be seen from Table 3, Bellman found that gastrointestinal disease did not occur in her 75 encopretics to a greater extent than in her controls.

Intestinal polyps were held responsible in a case of encopresis described

Table 3.   Encopretics and controls with a history of gastrointestinal diseases

Diagnosis or type of complaint	No. of cases in the encopretic group (75 boys)	No. of cases in the control group (73 boys)
Repeated attacks of diarrhoea	1 (up to 2 yrs)	1 (up to 1 yr)
Hospitalisation for diarrhoea on one occasion	0	2
Occasional prolapse of the rectal mucosa	1	0
Anal fistula	1	0
Haemorrhoids (physician's diagnosis)	0	1
'Stomach cramp'	1	2
Abdominal migraine (physician's diagnosis)	1	0
Threadworm	1	1
Pylorospasm	2	1
Periodic vomiting	0	1
Vomiting in conjunction with colds	2	0
Total	10	9

From Bellman (1966), 'Studies in encopresis', with permission.

by Bennholdt-Thomsen (1954). The symptom remained after surgical removal of the polyps but the author supposed that there may have been other tumours or deformities higher up.

Brain injury/developmental factors

Bellman also examined encopretics and controls to see if there was a relationship between a history of complaints liable to involve injury to the central nervous system and soiling. As can be seen from Table 4 the difference was not statistically significant, but it should be remembered that their study excluded children with an IQ below 50.

Butler & Golding (1986), however, in their study of 13 000 children found an association between low birth weight and soiling. Slow language development and poor coordination has also been noted (Bemporad et al 1971). The author's research supported some of these findings.

Although there were no figures on vision defects, 17% of the soiling children had a birth weight of less than 5.8 lb, 27% had received intensive care treatment after birth and 27% had a history of convulsions. In addition 27% had a history of delayed speech development. The suggestion is that whatever may have been responsible for the other factors may also have had an effect on the child's intestinal tract resulting in a soiling problem.

The excess of boys with a soiling problem also hints at a developmental aetiology in some cases. A certain degree of maturity is necessary for complete control of bowel function and different children may reach this stage at different times. It is probable that children whose general range of development is retarded may also be retarded in this area. If this process is hurried it may bring about some of the psychological problems so well described in the literature.

Soiling and other neurological disorders

Soiling is also associated with other diagnosed neurological disorders such as spina bifida. Dr Clayden discusses issues surrounding this topic in Chapter 11.

Table 4. Encopretics and controls with a history of complaints liable to involve injury to the central nervous system

Complaint	No. of cases in the encopretic group (75 boys)	No. of cases in the control group (73 boys)
Forceps delivery	2	4
Asphyxia at birth	5	2
Replacement transfusion without complications	1	1
Parotitis or other viral meningitis	3	4
Whooping cough before the age of 2 years	3	0
Cerebral concussion	2	2
Total	16	13

From Bellman (1966), 'Studies in encopresis', with permission.

Psychological Factors Associated with Soiling

The association between psychological factors and soiling has a long history. One of the earliest descriptions of a soiling child appears in 1881 and is described by Henoch in Berlin. An eight year old patient improved after only one injection of distilled water close to the anus. Henoch's success led him to believe the symptom was psychogenic and the injection served as a medium for suggestion. He continued to treat further cases with similar injections and as a further suggestive measure gave a couple of 'strong blows' with the hand to the perineal tract. In 1881 he also found it useful to treat the patient with a branding-iron and electricity. After Henoch's publication Fowler (1882), reacting against Henoch's approach, reported two cases treated successfully by reducing the psychic pressure of the environment. Thus a seven year old boy with no previous symptoms started to soil his trousers when his parents raised their demands on his achievements at school. Dismayed by the symptom, the parents beat the child. Fowler prescribed: no beatings, no books, less pressure. The symptom disappeared in three weeks.

The role of coercive toilet training

With the advent of Freud, interest switched to how the child was pot-trained. To the infant child there is nothing dirty, disgusting or nauseating about faeces (Freud 1905, 1917). They are part of the child's body. During the first years of life the child learns to distinguish between what belongs to its body and what does not. He learns from the environment that faeces are something dirty and nasty. In this way psychic dramas of shame and disgust are built up against instinctive drives. As this feeling develops and because the mother requires a certain pattern for the deposit of faeces, the child learns this and refrains from the primitive, convenient method in order to retain his mother's love. Freud felt that an anal fixation was largely determined by how the child experiences pot training. Both rigid, early training and lax or late training may lead to faulty development. Both Pinkerton (1958) and Anthony (1957) developed these ideas. Pinkerton found that in cases of constipation with encopresis there was a high degree of strict training before the child was sufficiently mature, as well as an over-anxious, tense supervision by the mother. Anthony developed the idea of the 'potting couple'. 'The potting situation is full of unspoken language in which a system of minimal cues plays its part . . . the average mother learns this language without much difficulty . . . in the normal situation the mother's prompt response to the child's physiological cues and her own communications during the process gradually make the child aware of his own cues, so that he is able eventually, to take over mother's role in the potting situation and thereby become autonomous' (Anthony 1957). In his study there were two sorts of deviations from normal. 'There were mothers who hopelessly muffed all the cues so that the child's learning of them appeared to be deficient. He was spoken of as passing motions without being aware of it. Then there were the mothers who anxiously misinterpreted every physiological cue of the child, responding to each and every crisis with the production of the pot. In time the child appeared to become hypersensitive to this association and would run frequently to the toilet under the merest pretext, until every disturbing situation had this effect' (Anthony 1957).

Bellman in her analysis of special factors related to pot training showed that the mothers of encopretic children had used coercive methods to a greater extent and had expected that the child control its bowel movements earlier than the average child. The literature places much emphasis on the role of coercive pot training, but Kanner (1953) pointed out that inadequate pot training can also result in soiling. The child has been untrained. In particular pot fear was common among the 'encopretic' boys.

But as we have seen in the cross cultural study in the previous chapter there are difficulties with this hypothesis.

Whether it is coercive pot training, psychopathology in the child or the parents, the difficulty remains whether these are primary or secondary to the symptom or both. For example, many writers report that some soiling children have a tendency to pass abnormally large stools. This in itself could lead to a psychological fear of defaecation and consequent 'stool holding' leading to a retention with overflow problem, but the primary cause of the large stools may have been a physical problem.

The parents of soiling children

In Bellman's study (1966), encopretic children's mothers were shown by a psychiatric assessment to be anxious, less reliable, vague, emotional and in relation to the child, over-protective. When the child had an 'accident' and soiled his clothes the mothers had been prone to react with beating, punishment and anger. The encopretic boys' fathers, on the other hand, were more liable to demand excessive discipline. In the author's study, 64% of the mothers were noted to be 'very tense' but only 17% remained tense after treatment for their child's soiling. The difficulty is in assessing whether the 'tension' predates the soiling problem or develops as a result of it (Buchanan 1990).

Characteristics of the soiling child

Bellman also found that the number of nervous symptoms was greater in the encopretic group. Here too it is of course difficult to determine whether these symptoms were primary or secondary to the encopresis. She found that a larger proportion of the boys were reported to be anxiety prone, lacking in self-assertion and had a low tolerance for demands. In general they seemed to have greater difficulty than her controls in handling aggression. In the author's study 40% of the soiling children scored over 4 on the Rutter 'A' Neurotic scale index, whereas only 20% scored over 4 on the Anti-social scale (Buchanan 1989). Bellman also felt a greater proportion were excessively controlled, and a larger proportion of the encopretic children were mother dependent. The encopretic boys had poorer relationships with friends and this was supported by observations by both parents and teachers. The teachers' assessments showed that encopretic boys were more likely to be very disturbing in school and to have serious problems of adjustment.

Food refusal

In Bellman's study, an interesting finding was that food refusal was also common; 21% of her encopretics had been food refusers at some time (Bellman 1966). Fenichel (1954) also found that many children with encopresis had previously been food refusers. He felt that in many cases the child's contact with his mother had already been disturbed before the onset of the encopresis, and that the child unable to express aggressiveness in the usual way eventually obtained his revenge through the soiling.

> There are difficulties and even dangers in this hypothesis. As we have seen, many soiling children, particularly those with retention problems, cannot control the soiling. Children with a soiling problem are at great risk of physical abuse as we will discuss in Chapter 12. The danger is that if parents believe the child's soiling is an expression of aggression, that it is a deliberate ploy, this is likely to increase the parents' own aggressive responses to the child.

Learned helplessness and depression

The role of depression in soiling children has largely been unexplored. It could be hypothesised that if there is a relationship between depression and constipation, as discussed in Chapter 2, there could also be a relationship between depression in a child (or mother) and soiling.

In 1975 Seligman published his theory of 'learned helplessness' in relation to depression. The patient unable to find a solution for the difficulties learns to become helpless. Maybe the child unable to control his soiling enters a similar state of helplessness with the consequent effect on his bowels. This is also the theory behind the work of Sluckin (1981).

The role of fear

Finally, as already mentioned, there is the phenomenon of involuntary defaecation in the face of fear. Bellman noted a few children in her pilot study who defaecated involuntarily under certain frightening circumstances—a symptom which she felt resembled the behaviour of birds which are scared in flight. It is quite possible that some of the anxious boys described in her study, whose parents reacted violently and aggressively to their child's soiling, might be conditioned rather like a Pavlovian dog to soil involuntarily in anticipation of the anger.

Factors in the Environment

With soiling children, it is difficult to separate environmental factors from physiological factors or psychological ones, because any situation which adds additional stresses on the vulnerable child, can affect the ability of the child to control his defaecation habits.

*High stress environments and social
situations*

Burns (1941, 1958) noted that the evacuation of children from their parents during the Second World War led to increased rates of encopresis and enuresis. Bellman noted that some children age five and over with so-called 'cures' (particularly those who had experienced frightening scenes at home such as living with an unstable, mentally ill or violent father) would relapse during a short visit to the home. Bellman suggested 'such sequences of events strongly indicates a disturbed contact with the home environment'.

> However, more recent research (Levine 1982) and in particular the author's own research suggests that relapses are the 'nature of the problem' and the primary physical cause may be more important than straight psychological explanations. What, however, is fairly explicit is that there is a relationship (but not an exclusive relationship) between high stress levels in the environment and a soiling problem.

What then are the stresses in the environment apart from those already mentioned? Butler's figures (Butler & Golding 1986) found a very positive association between single parents and soiling. It could, of course, be that the child's soiling itself is a factor in the break-down of the parents' marriage.

Alcoholism in a parent is also a very stressful situation for a child. Indeed in Bellman's study eight of the 75 fathers of the 'encopretic' children were declared alcoholics and a ninth was discovered during check-up at the Temperance Board. However, in her control group, there were a similar number.

A number of writers report on the stress generated by separation from mother, particularly before the age of five. Ahnsjo (1959) found an increase in soiling in preschool children admitted to summer classes. Bellman found 27% of her 'encopretics' has been separated from their mothers for at least two months at a stretch before the age of five.

As can be seen from Table 5 the incidence of somatic and mental disease in the biological parents of 'encopretic' children is interesting.

In the author's study, there was a high rate of family social stresses in

Table 5. Somatic and mental diseases in the biological parents of encopretic and control children (significant differences only)

Type of disease	Parent	No. in encopretic group (n74)	No. in control group (n71)	z	Level of significance
Mental requiring hospitalisation	Father	7	1	+ 1.77	10%
	Father or mother	10	2	+ 2.02	5%
Nervous for which a doctor was consulted	Father	17	10	+ 2.02	5%
Somatic	Father	22	13	+ 2.31	5%
Enuresis	Father or mother	17	6	+ 2.29	5%

From Bellman (1966) 'Studies in encopresis', with permission.

all three study groups, and what was interesting was that there were no significant differences between the groups. Overall 39% of the families were experiencing marital stresses, 16% had housing problems, 41% financial difficulites, and in 33% there was evidence of chronic illness (often mental illness) in a parent (Buchanan 1990).

Contributing to the problem: school toilets/
home toilets

Entry into primary school can also be a difficult and stressful time for a child. It is interesting that many studies report that around this age a child who has previously been clean starts to soil. One can hypothesise that there may be other factors apart from the stress of separation from mother and the start of school; one subject that is hardly mentioned in the literature is the children's feelings about and access to the toilet. As mentioned earlier it is important that a child should not unreasonably postpone the urge to defaecate. Sluckin (1981) mentions 'it is very common for encopretic children to dislike using the school lavatory and they frequently complain of poor standards of cleanliness and lack of privacy'. The author's paper (Buchanan 1989b: 'Soiling in school age children') highlighted this point.

Morgan (1981) and Clayden (1980) also mentioned that poor toilets might be one factor in the development of bowel problems. The child's access to a toilet at home and his feelings about it may be important. Bellman found two children in her study who were living in an apartment without a toilet of its own. There were two other children who had been very frightened as young children while sitting on the toilet. The author discovered one family where the alsations were regularly housed in the family toilet and another where the family lived in a caravan with very poor outside facilities. Inadequate toilet facilities at school and home may play a much greater role in at least maintaining an existing soiling problem than is generally realised.

The child's individual response to stressful
events

It is very difficult from these figures to assess the importance of each particular stressful event for each particular child in the genesis of soiling. Experimental studies with careful controls may suggest that living in an 'incomplete' home, or living with a father who is an alcoholic, may not be significant when compared with the control group, but this does not mean to say that none of the children experiencing these stresses were affected to the extent that it was a factor in their soiling.

When all the environmental stresses were grouped together Bellman probably reflects the views of most writers that 'a larger proportion of the encopretic children (than those not suffering from encopresis) had been exposed to potentially traumatic environmental factors' (Bellman 1966, p. 109), and this is generally supported by the author's findings; but what is stressful to one child may not be stressful to another.

Sexual abuse

One potentially traumatic environmental factor not considered by Bellman, and indeed not considered by the literature until very recently (although should we not now reassess some of Freud's work (1905, 1917)?), is the possibility that children presenting with soiling may have been sexually abused. This topic is discussed in detail in Chapter 13 and is only mentioned here in order that it is not forgotten as a possible causal factor.

The role of diet

The literature on the soiling child focuses heavily on medical and psychological causes. Surprisingly little has been written about the role of diet, particularly when constipation appears to be so prevalent. Roger Morgan (1981), writing in *Childhood Incontinence*, mentioned that it was worth reviewing the diet of a child with a soiling problem. A poor diet was unlikely to cause severe soiling, but it could adversely affect bowel regularity and the consistency of the faeces, so that what bowel control did exist came under severe strain. A diet tending to 'loose' faeces could cause problems where regular toileting was not established and there was a degree of non-control. One leading towards constipation could make defaecation difficult and encourage retention. The aim is a reasonably balanced diet with a good proportion of 'roughage'.

Paediatricians have long recognised that an inadequate diet, under-feeding or a poorly balanced diet could be causes of constipation. The stool varies in consistency and frequency depending upon the amount of fibre in the diet and it is of no surprise that stools in the Third World are considerably heavier than in the UK, and constipation and soiling is also much less common there (Clayden 1981). Jolly, in his *Book on Child Care* (1977), mentions that the amount of fluid being lost through vomiting or excessive sweating due to fever could also cause constipation. Ellis (1962), another paediatrician, says 'the most common cause of constipation in infancy is under-feeding with the result that very little residue reaches the lower bowel and the stools which are small are passed perhaps only every second or third day . . . although the nutritive value of the diet is perfect.' A diet high in protein and/or fats also tends to produce hard constipated stools which are difficult to pass.

Davidson et al (1963) highlighted the role of milk as a causal factor in a soiling problem. It was thought that ingestion of large quantities of milk reduced the desire for other foods, which contain more roughage. Because of the low residue and high calcium content, the milk may itself be constipating. In approximately one half of the patients in this series in whom there was a long standing history of constipation prior to the onset of soiling, milk was reduced to the equivalent of one pint daily. As some of the youngsters were allowed to resume the intake of higher amounts of milk, constipation returned with reduction once again when they had less.

Coekin & Gairdner (1960), in their study of faecal incontinence in children, found 27% of those children suffering from colonic inertia had a history of constipation in the first six months of life. It is possible that a number of these could be attributed to poor diet, particularly with the difficulties associated with artificial feeding. The possible role of diet is considered in greater depth in Chapter 10.

Incorrect treatments

A more controversial area yet is the role of incorrect treatments in the genesis of the soiling child. Clinicians a hundred years later will recoil at the thought of Henoch's treatment of a soiling child with branding-iron and electricity. In another hundred years one wonders whether some treatments advocated today will still be acceptable. Clayden (1980) in his flow chart on the evolution of chronic constipation and soiling (see Figure 4) lists 'incorrect treatment' as a possible environmental cause. It may be controversial, but it must be probable that both incorrect medical and psychological treatments, although not initiating the problem will not have helped the soiling child and his family, and may even have exacerbated the situation.

Conclusion

Soiling is a problem which arouses strong emotions in most people. Accordingly family responses are not always a good guide to how the soiling arose. Severe secondary psychological components may arise even when the soiling has a physical basis'. (Rutter 1975)

Rutter in understanding children's problems suggest that 'typical childhood disorders are multifariously determined'. From our preceding discussion this must be particularly true of the soiling child. The doctor may ask 'How did the problem arise?' but in this situation he will find difficulty in separating what was the primary condition and what came as a result of the symptom. Undoubtedly physical, psychological and environmental causes all have their role in the causation of soiling. Some strong themes emerge. Many children have a constitutional bowel weakness, many children also have evidence of psychological problems either within themselves or within their family dynamics; many other children experience environmental stresses which may aggravate or initiate a problem in an already vulnerable child. In particular, sexual abuse has recently been associated with soiling and needs further investigation. There are also other neglected ideas: the role of diet and practical issues like the design of school toilets, as well as a child's fears related to his own facilities at home. There is even the very worrying thought that some treatments may not help but actually make the problem worse.

SUMMARY

Soiling in children is an unspoken problem. Soiling children are heavy users of resources. The more common medical disorders associated with soiling are: constipation with overflow, Hirschsprung's disease and ultra-short segment Hirschsprung's, intestinal obstruction, gastro-intestinal disease, hypothyroidism, soiling following brain injury, developmental delay, congenital anomalies and known neurological disorders such as spina bifida. Psychological factors noted in many soiling children are nervous personalities, food refusal, learned help-lessness and soiling as a response to fear. It has also been noted that parents are often 'very tense'. Environmental factors which may play a part are associations with separation, with disrupted families, and possibly in some cases with sexual abuse. Other factors such as inade-quate school/home toilets, diet (especially a high milk diet) and incor-rect treatments may also have a role in the causation of the disorder.

CHAPTER 4   Classification

There is a need for classification . . . typing a disorder allows one to draw on knowledge available from studies of children with a similar label. This may lead to management or the prediction of outcome. Typology of disorders can help to clarify thinking about the nature of the problems which a child may present . . . (but) there are various problems with existing schemes which make them less than satisfactory (Graham 1986, pp. 2–4)

If the causation of soiling in a child is diverse, then so is the treatment. The traditional medical model is first, after taking a history and examining the symptoms in the patient, to diagnose the disorder and then to prescribe the treatment that is generally accepted to be effective in managing that disorder. In diagnosing, the clinician makes a classification of the disorder, and this classification provides a rough guide to the aetiology, treatment and prognosis. As Philip Graham indicates in the above quotation, classification schemes have important attributes, but they also can have their problems, and this is particularly true in the case of soiling disorders. Classification schemes involve a judgment of the nature of the problem from a number of possible options, and in making this judgment, the clinician effectively decides the treatment route. But quite apart from the fact that in making the judgment the clinician effectively excludes other options, when it comes to soiling problems there is considerable confusion about the meaning of the various labels that have been used in classifying different types of soiling. In this chapter we will examine some of these issues while in the next chapter we will show how treatment approaches have evolved from the classifications.

If one follows Rutter's flow diagram (Figure 3) shown in the previous chapter, there were two major treatment routes depending on the initial classification. These depend, broadly speaking, on whether the child presented with normally or abnormally formed stools at the initial assessment. If the child presented with abnormally formed stools the child was classified as having a physical disorder of defaecation and should be seen by the paediatric department. If, on the other hand, the child presented with normally formed stools the soiling was seen as a symptom of emotional disturbance and he was therefore the responsibility of the psychiatric department. The paediatric treatment route would be concerned about the function of the bowel: the presence or absence of disease, the role of constipation. Treatment would probably involve the use of softeners, laxatives and if necessary enemas and suppositories, and for particularly resistant cases the possibility of surgical treatments. The psychiatric route would seek to treat the discordant family relationships with individual or family psychotherapy, or with behavioural approaches seek to re-educate the child into better bowel habits. The question remained whether children with a soiling problem could be divided into two distinct groups.

Even with the two distinct treatment routes, there were difficulties in that the terminology used to classify a particular type of soiling problem often meant quite different things to different specialists. For this reason the principal terms that have been used are discussed: firstly those terms suggesting a psychiatric problem, and secondly those terms suggesting a paediatric problem.

Classifications which Traditionally Suggested the Soiling was Related to a Psychiatric Problem

Encopresis

Bellman (1966) says 'as a rule encopresis is defined in the literature as repeated involuntary evacuation of faeces in the clothes without there being any gross explanatory cause'. Weissenberg (1926) is generally accredited as having first used the term 'encopresis'. In fact Pototsky (1925) had already written an article in German entitled 'Die Enkopresis'. Weissenberg proposed that the concept of 'encopresis' should be used in much the same way as 'enuresis' had been used to describe a bedwetting problem. Earlier there had been a term 'incontinential alvi', but this had been used to describe all faecal incontinence irrespective of genesis. Kanner in 1953 used a term 'partial encopresis' for those children who partly used the toilet and partly soiled their clothing. Kanner (1953) also used the term 'encopresis with obstipation' for those children where constipation was an important factor. Anthony (1957) demanded 'incontrovertible evidence of the regular passage of formed motions of normal or near normal consistency into the clothes, bedclothes or any receptacle not intended for the purpose' before using the term 'encopretic'. He subdivided his study group into 'continuous encopresis', 'discontinuous encopresis' and 'retention of faeces'. Macgregor (1961) used the term 'encopresis' to describe those children who passed their faeces in unsuitable conditions but using normal physiological mechanisms. 'Not those where rectal musculature was so distended that further filling no longer elicited sensory stimuli or those where there was chronic constipation'.

Various writers have subdivided encopresis into 'primary' or 'secondary'. Bellman talked about 'primary encopresis' to describe those children who had never been clean while 'secondary encopresis' was used to describe those children who had a period of bowel control of at least one year. Barker in *Basic Child Psychiatry* (1983) talks of 'regressive encopresis' where the child is under stress and 'aggressive encopresis' which he feels is usually a manifestation of a disturbed relationship between parents and child. 'Aggressive encopresis' could either be 'retentive' or 'non-retentive'.

Different uses of the term 'encopresis' in the USA and UK

Encopresis in the USA has a much wider meaning than here in the UK. Levine (1975) in the USA uses the term 'encopresis' to describe any child over four years of age who has regularly passed formed, semi-formed or liquid stools into his underwear or pyjamas with no apparent primary organic aetiology. He justifies including constipated faecal soilers because he has found that in some cases children phased in and out of retentive or constipating patterns while continuing to manifest faecal incontinence. Levine's broad definition contrasts with Clayden in the UK who reserves the term 'encopresis' for children passing normally formed stools into socially unacceptable places including clothes.

Faecal soiling

Hersov (1977) uses this term to describe disorders of bowel control occurring in children over a certain age in the absence of physical abnormality or disease, 'where it is known that there is adequate bowel control in the sense that the child can control the physiological process of defaecation but deposits his normal faeces in inappropriate places'. He feels this is different from constipation with overflow, diarrhoea associated with anxiety or where the child is unaware he is soiling due to an inability to control his bowels.

Functional faecal incontinence

This term is used by Berg & Vernon-Jones (1964) to describe a group of children who pass stools into their clothes without there being any satisfactory explanation in the form of organic disease. They include in this group cases both with and without constipation.

Classifications Traditionally Suggesting a Physical Problem

'Overflow incontinence'/'constipation with overflow'/'retention with overflow'

Constipation incontinence is first referred to by Bloch (1932) to describe those cases where large hard lumps of faecal matter build up in the rectum. Thorling in 1923 had proposed the term 'Obstipationsinkontinenz' and Jekelius (1936) the term 'obstipation paradoxa'. Today the condition is called by Rutter 'retention with overflow'. 'Here the basic problem is one of constipation which becomes so severe as to lead to partial blockage of the bowel. As a result of the blockage some of the motions liquefy and seep past to produce faecal soiling, the soiling occurring because the child has lost the normal anal reflex through the excessive constipation and the subsequent dilation of the bowel' (Rutter 1975). Other names for this condition are 'overflow incontinence' and 'constipation with overflow'.

Megacolon and Hirschsprung's disease

Clayden (1981) reviewed the major milestones in the understanding of megacolon. As early as 1691 Frederick Rysch of Amsterdam reported a five year old girl who had died of an abnormally dilated colon. In 1886 Harold Hirschsprung of Copenhagen presented two cases of young children (age 2 months and 11 months) who had died. Autopsy showed a dilated colon but not a dilated rectum. In 1949 Bodian et al reviewed 73 cases of previously diagnosed idiopathic megacolon and limited the use of the term 'Hirschsprung's disease' to those who when examined neurohistorologically after a barium enema were found to have no parasympathetic ganglion cells in their intramural plexus. The others they called 'idiopathic megacolon'. Richmond et al. (1954) separated out a further group from the idiopathic megacolons: those she called the 'psychogenic megacolons' whose conditions appeared to be a result of psychological fear of defaecation.

Ultra-short segment Hirschsprung's disease

Rehbein & Von Zimmerman (1960) first made the suggestion that some children's constipation problems may be related to their having a segment of Hirschsprung's diseased colon, so short as to be virtually unseen on a barium enema. This sparked a debate still unresolved as to how far, if at all, children with very severe constipation (and 'soiling') may have abnormalities of their gastroenterinal tract. In the UK Clayden (1976, 1980) has been notable in this field, but he has developed his own terminology. Because his focus is to treat all children with bowel problems, when he is talking about 'children with constipation', it should be noted that not all of these children have a soiling problem. Clayden uses the term 'constipation' to describe infrequent defaecation leading to pain, distress or overflow incontinence, and 'soiling' to describe 'continuous or intermittent passage of loose stools into the clothing'.

The following definitions (Figure 7) are given in the *Manual of Paediatric Gastro-enterology* (Tripp & Candy 1985), and probably represent the traditionally accepted classification of the problem in the UK.

Recent Research Suggests Soiling Children Cannot be Segregated into those with Psychiatric and those with Physical Problems

Clayden (1976) and Levine (1982), the leading authorities in the UK and the USA, have found that, quite apart from the different definitions

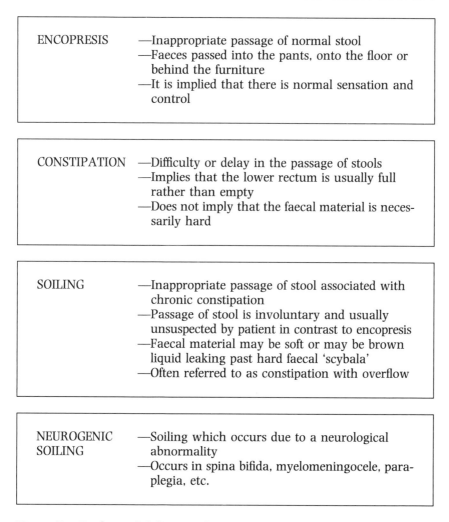

ENCOPRESIS	—Inappropriate passage of normal stool —Faeces passed into the pants, onto the floor or behind the furniture —It is implied that there is normal sensation and control

CONSTIPATION	—Difficulty or delay in the passage of stools —Implies that the lower rectum is usually full rather than empty —Does not imply that the faecal material is necessarily hard

SOILING	—Inappropriate passage of stool associated with chronic constipation —Passage of stool is involuntary and usually unsuspected by patient in contrast to encopresis —Faecal material may be soft or may be brown liquid leaking past hard faecal 'scybala' —Often referred to as constipation with overflow

NEUROGENIC SOILING	—Soiling which occurs due to a neurological abnormality —Occurs in spina bifida, myelomeningocele, paraplegia, etc.

Figure 7. Traditional definitions for encopresis, constipation and soiling as given in the *Manual of Paediatric Gastro-enterology* (Tripp & Candy, 1985). Reproduced by permission of Churchill Livingstone. © Longman Group UK Ltd

given to describe different or overlapping conditions, the children with soiling problems do not nicely segregate out into recognisable groups. Even in the extreme, as Bentley (1964) a leading authority from Scotland said, 'there are difficulties in differentiating idiopathic or psychogenic accumulation of faeces from a typical Hirschsprung's disease with an ultra short distal aganglionic segment, as patients have similar historic symptoms and physical signs and there may be little difference in the appearance of the distended bowel' (Bentley 1964).

Further Drawbacks of Existing Classification Schemes

Philip Graham (1986), in his book *Child Psychiatry: A Developmental Approach*, highlights a further drawback to traditional classification schemes which make them less than satisfactory, and this drawback is particularly pertinent when considering soiling problems. He notes that classification schemes focus the nature of the problem 'within the child' excluding the possibility that there may have been factors 'outside the child', for example disturbances within the family system, or between the child and the wider world, which may have had an important role in the aetiology of the disorder.

Finally there is yet another problem with traditional classification schemes which needs mentioning. As we saw from the last chapter, the possible causative factors in a soiling problem are many, but traditional classification schemes rarely allow for an interaction of factors which, although insignificant on their own, cumulatively produce the disorder. In order to treat a soiling child effectively it may be very important to identify this interaction of factors.

SUMMARY

There is a need to classify different disorders so that knowledge of treatment responses from studies of similar children is available. However, weaknesses of current schemes for classifying soiling children are: the different labels can mean quite different things to different practitioners in different countries; the labels can in themselves become straitjackets excluding the role of other factors in the aetiology of the disorder. Classifications only provide a 'very rough guide to aetiology, treatment and prognosis. They generally need to be amplified by a formulation, giving more extended account of the child's conditions and background features before any action can be taken' (Graham 1986). This is particularly true for soiling children.

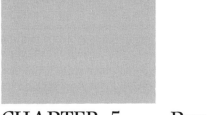

CHAPTER 5   Previous forms of treatment

Authors (of research papers) have naturally focused on the aspects of the problem which interests them most as Surgeons, Psychiatrists, Pharmacologists, Pathologists . . . (Clayden 1976)

As we have seen, the traditional medical model is first to diagnose, and in diagnosing the disorder, to classify, and then prescribe. This may be difficult in a patient who has a number of medical problems requiring a number of different specialists, but is particularly difficult when there is no general agreement about who is the best equipped specialist to deal with one specific problem. In the case of the soiling child, not only are there a number of different specialists, but also a number of different disciplines who feel they alone have the necessary expertise. The situation is further complicated by lack of agreement within each discipline about which is the best method of treatment. In this chapter we will first follow the history of treatment approaches which evolved from the traditional classifications, and secondly we will demonstrate how modern clinicians are moving across the barriers of specialisms and disciplines in an attempt to offer a treatment approach which focuses on the 'whole child'.

Clinicians' efforts at classification underline the great problems they have had in deciding how best to treat a child presenting with a soiling problem. What is notable from research studies is how uncomfortably the bulk of soiling children fit into *either* the paediatric *or* psychiatric mould (except for those children with clear-cut physical problems such as Hirschsprung's disease). The history of treatment approaches reflects the difficulties clinicians have found in classification; it is a history which swings from one speciality/discipline to another as each new finding opens a door to a new understanding and new focus; it is a history which slowly gives birth to the realisation that you cannot treat part of a person, . . . and that the best treatment results are likely to come from approaches which focus on 'the whole child'.

Early Ideas on Treatment: Physical and Emotional

Until 1941, the main treatment for constipation and/or soiling was a physical approach focusing on emptying the bowel. Laxatives, enemas, suppositories or manual evacuation were used. This approach had been recommended as early as 1888 by Wallace (1888) and a similar approach was supported by Frolich (1931) and Hungerland (1936). In 1941 Burns showed evidence of psychopathology in children suffering from encopresis. He felt psychological treatment was desirable for all cases of encopresis, and advocated play therapy and/or conversation therapy. Burns was also a realist. Although he felt psychological treatment was desirable he recognised it could not always be arranged, but that all measures in a sense were psychological—perhaps implying other specialists could undertake limited psychological treatment. He also recommended that any obstipation should be treated, and that by 'removing the symptom this eased the tension from the parents'. Lehman (1944) generally supported these views but felt that medication acted if at all by removing the symptom without resolving psychic conflicts and without improving the child's mental health. He felt play therapy and psychotherapy would have more lasting results. Bodian (1952) had noticed that an initial emptying of the bowel did not necessarily produce lasting results. His solution was a course of enemas over several weeks to allow the bowel to shrink. It was understandable that psychiatrists trained in the analytical tradition might be uneasy about what they saw as physical attacks on the psychological health of children by the paediatric treatment of encopresis. In 1908 Freud had published *Character and Anal Erotism* and again in 1917 *On Transformation of Instincts as Exemplified in Anal Erotism*. In 1957 Anthony, who at that time was Senior Lecturer in Child Psychiatry at the Institute of Psychiatry, undertook an important study to investigate 'the alleged causal relationships between bowel training, bowel functioning and the presence of certain subsequent negative attitudes'. His conclusion was 'with certain reservations, some prejudices at least can be traced back to the primary care of the intestines in childhood'. Anthony described the mother and the child as the 'potting couple'. He felt that if the relationship between the mother and child around the pot was one of coercion then this problem was bound to increase during the child's natural negativistic period between the ages of two and four years. In his study of 76 encopretic children, he found 30 children were 'continuously encopretic', that is they had continuously soiled since birth; another 30 children were 'discontinuous encopretic', and a further 16 children had a mixed classification. For the continuous soilers, Anthony advocated pot training for those who had not had it, and for all others psychotherapy. For the discontinuous group, Anthony advocated psychological treatment even in cases of obstipation.

A year later Pinkerton (1958) reported on a study of 30 children with encopresis and obstipation. He too felt that neither the child nor the parental response stood to benefit from the use of laxatives and enemas, in all but one of the children in his study he felt that negativism expressed by the child towards the symptom had developed during the first three years of life. Pinkerton demonstrated how in psychotherapy the children often confided that they felt highly aggressive towards the person giving the enema, experiencing this as an encroachment. He did, however, suggest that a paediatrician should be present during the first session with the parents, to assure them that there was nothing organically wrong. Twenty-one out of Pinkerton's 30 cases improved on a psychotherapeutic programme where they were encouraged to express their fantasies, and aggression. McTaggart and Scott in 1959 also found psychotherapy helpful. In a study of 12 encopretics, 10 out of 12 improved with psychotherapy. Jolly (Jolly & Levine 1985), an influential paediatrician in the early sixties, supported this psychiatric view 'in the light of deep psychological causes of constipation, it is obvious that an attack on the rectum is not the way to treat the problem. A bucket and spade approach with washouts and laxatives will produce short term success but long term failure. Having practised both methods of treatment for a long time and having now not prescribed laxatives, washouts or enema for many years I am sure psychotherapy is the answer'. Jolly added 'this could be achieved at paediatric level in most cases, though some families will require deeper psychiatric help'. Jolly felt the reason there were more encopretic boys than girls was that boys were more aggressive by nature.

The Development of the Modern Paediatric Approach

In 1960 Coekin and Gairdner published a careful study of 69 cases of faecal incontinence in children. Though recognising that the problem could be emotionally based they felt it was wrong 'to take up so doctrinaire a stand—as to withhold normal treatment from a child with severe faecal impaction, merely because impaction is the end result of an emotional disorder. Such an approach is surely a "reductio ad absurdum" of the policy of symptom tolerance which Winnicott has urged paediatricians to adopt towards the somatic symptoms of emotionally disturbed children.'

In their study 64% of the soiling was judged to be mechanical, that is the result of constipation. They found when the constipation was treated the soiling usually disappeared. They felt if the constipation was not treated this could lead to overflow incontinence. They also felt there was evidence of a congenital disorder. In a further 22% the incontinence was judged to be psychogenic and some of these children needed psychiatric treatment in conjunction with the physical. In only 14% were the factors so interwoven that neither could be ascribed a primary role.

Nixon (1961), in a study of 45 children seen in a paediatric surgical clinic, recommended keeping the rectum empty allowing it to shrink. He advocated a pattern of defaection by clock; manual evacuation of faeces under general anaesthetic; daily rectal wash-outs with up to 20 pints of saline or enemas or suppositories; and a regular bowel action later encouraged by senna or bisacodyl. Selander & Torold (1964) found 61% of their 157 cases had recovered after paediatric care alone. Those not cured were sent on for treatment by child psychiatrists. Davidson et al (1963), in New York, also questioned the strong psychiatric emphasis given to children suffering from encopresis. 'It is unfortunate that the term psychogenic is universally applied in those instances in which faecal retention occurs and Hischsprung's disease is not found.' Experience with a minority of children in his series confirmed the picture of the hopeless nature of the condition and strong psychological needs for retention of symptoms in such patients which the literature has stressed. However, in a majority the mineral oil regimen resulted in early and complete clearing of symptoms, which suggests that one may not generalise regarding the degree of emotional disturbance. He felt 'the overtly disturbed Mother–Child relationship and resistance to toilet training may be the result of symptomatology rather than the other way around'. A three part treatment regimen was used: firstly enemas to clear the initial impaction, and then doses of mineral oil to keep the bowel regular (if there was no clearing of the symptom or where there was associated abdominal pain, after three weeks of mineral oil regimen, immediate investigation for organic disease was undertaken). Secondly, those who had come through phase one, moved on to phase two, which was a toilet training exercise, with a gradual reduction of the mineral oil, and thirdly follow-up for a period of at least one year. At the end of this Davidson showed a success rate of 75% for clinic cases, and for his private patients he felt he had achieved 90%. Ten per cent were rated as failures as they could not be weaned off the laxatives without recurrence of difficulties. Some of these patients were then referred on to psychiatric care. Davidson found that on follow-up two-thirds of the total number were improved sufficiently by the regimen that they had been free of symptom for periods ranging from six months to seven years. The earlier figures of 75% and 90% are therefore a little deceptive.

Treatment for severe or protracted
constipation

Surgeons had known of Hirschsprung's disease since 1886, and in the 1960s started to consider whether in other children not diagnosed as having Hirschsprung's disease there might be a further condition which resulted in severe obstipation and soiling (Bentley et al 1966). In 1960 Rehbein and Von Zimmerman suggested that some patients might have a Hirschsprung's segment so short as not to be identified on barium enema, and in 1964 Bentley in Scotland described treatment of ultra-short segment Hirschsprung's disease by anorectal myectomy. What was interesting about Bentley's study of 22 patients was that his anorectal excisional myotomy operation, intended as a diagnostic operation, proved to be therapeutic as well. Earlier Hurst (1934) had found that chronic accumulation of faeces could be dramatically relieved at least for a short time by stretching the anus under general anaesthetic. Bentley felt that most patients with anal achalasia, especially where the specialist skills necessary for myectomy were not available, could probably be helped by stretching the anus under anaesthetic, and this would relieve symptoms for some considerable time. Bentley also felt that for as many as one-sixth of children with chronic accumulation of faeces in the rectal ampulla the underlying cause was anal achalasia involving a failure of the anus to relax reflexly. This had been shown on anal manometry (a method that uses an inflatable balloon to measure the pressure in the anus). In many cases the cause of the non-relaxation of the anus was ultra-short segment Hirschsprung's disease.

Clayden and Lawson in England developed these ideas in a study in 1976 of 106 children referred for paediatric surgical assessment of severe chronic constipation. At an initial anal manometry 10 (9%) ultra-short segment Hirschsprung's were discovered and 11 with other known conditions, e.g. coeliac disease. The remainder showed evidence of hypertrophy of the internal sphincter on anorectal manometry and had vigorous anal dilatation (to accept four fingers) under general anaesthesia. After this 38% were able to be weaned off all medication, a further anal dilatation and internal sphincterotomy allowed another 10 children to stop laxatives. Clayden undertook a further study after he set up intestinal motility clinics at great Ormond Street and St Thomas's Hospitals. The results also indicated that vigorous anal dilatation was effective in reducing the length of time the child needed stimulant laxatives and also that internal anal sphincterotomy was effective in those relapsing after anal dilatation. It must be noted that only 71% of Clayden's sample presented with soiling (Clayden 1981).

Recently psychologists have experimented using methods involving the direct conditioning of the anal sphincter. Olness et al (1980) used biofeedback techniques with 40 patients aged between four and 15 years with histories of chronic constipation and soiling ranging from three to 15 years. All had received earlier treatment. A balloon was inserted in the anus and pressures in the anus were transmitted to an oscilloscope visible to the children. They were trained to alter their sphincteric responses voluntarily via the visual feedback using anal and buttock muscles. Twenty-four patients acquired normal bowel habits with complete cessation of soiling while 14 continued minor soiling. The treatment was not recommended as an initial therapy of choice for young children, but the studies do suggest that even without the mechanical invaders children may be able to help themselves by becoming more aware of their body signals.

Developments from Small Scale Psychological Studies

While paediatricians and paediatric surgeons and psychologists were wondering how to treat children with severe chronic constipation and soiling, psychologists were also showing good results using a variety of different behavioural methods. Although some studies included children with constipation, in most of these studies cases of severe or protracted constipation would be excluded.

Way back in 1957 Anthony had recommended 'habit training under happier conditions with a warm relaxed person using a consistent regimen' for those children who had never been clean. He found children could be trained in three to five months but tended to relapse when returned to the stresses of their old environment. Neale in 1963, taking four cases of discontinuous soilers, that is children who had been clean at some stage, showed that with the help of Isogel to soften the stool and by rewarding the child for passing faeces in the toilet, with sweets, chocolate bars, peanuts etc., there was rapid relief of symptoms in three out of the four cases. Gelber and Meyer 1965 took a child age 13, continuously encopretic since birth, and rewarded him in a hospital ward for defaecation again with successful results. Edelman (1971) in Florida cured a 12 year old girl with a history of chronic encopresis by periods of isolation as a punishment for faecal soiling and rewarding her by relieving her of dishwashing chores when clean. This approach, however, took 41 weeks.

Pedrini & Pedrini (1971) supervised a reward programme for defaecation for an 11 year old boy in a school setting. Conger (1970), in Canada, rearranged the social consequences so that the soiling behaviour of a nine year old boy was not reinforced by his mother's attentions and the soiling behaviour disappeared with no adverse sequence over a three month period. Sluckin (1975) used a reward programme for defaecation for four boys in the home. Two of these boys had reverted to soiling after successful inpatient treatment. In a further paper in 1981, Sluckin reported similar success using behavioural methods with soiling children. Her conclusion was that 'treatment through training had a better prognosis than treatment of the underlying causes'. The concern, however, in traditional psychiatric circles was that there could be inherent dangers in focusing on and removing the symptom, and that if the child stopped soiling another problem would emerge. Levine et al (1980), in a careful study of 47 children who had been treated for encopresis, 'with an initial catharsis, maintenance laxative therapy, demystification, symptom-related counselling and close follow up', showed that 'paediatric cure of encopresis is unlikely to result in a major deterioration of behaviour. In fact relief of incontinence was associated with a generalised improvement in the traits surveyed.'

Webster (1980) described a team approach for intractable encopresis. Six children were admitted to hospital, a 20-bedded paediatric ward in a nearby general hospital. A hospital-based behaviour modification intervention was established making the child responsible for his own toilet management through a system of rewards and sanctions. This was followed by social work intervention on a broad form, with the family, designed to motivate the parents over a sustained period, and the use of the pastoral care system of the school in monitoring and maintaining appropriate behaviour. Although some of the children relapsed on leaving the hospital, with the support of the social worker, five out of the six became clear of symptoms. The sixth child withdrew from treatment.

Family therapists were also making their contribution to the treatment of selected soiling children. Bulkeley & Sahami (1984) treated long standing encopresis in a 12 year old child with behaviour modification within a framework of family systems theory. Knights (1987) presented a paper at an Association of Child Psychology and Psychiatry meeting demonstrating a paradoxical approach to children presenting with treatment-resistant soiling. Naomi Richman set up one of the few controlled trials of treatment at Great Ormond Street. Although this has not been published she also reported her results at an Association of Child Psychology and Psychiatry meeting in 1983. Families of children referred for treatment for encopresis were randomly allocated to family therapy or behavioural treatment. Of the 28 children who entered the study the improvement rate was 57% (16), but improvement was not related to the type of therapy received. More children (18) received behaviour therapy, partly due to chance factors. but also because it was more difficult to engage families in family therapy (10). Although not statistically significant 61% (11) improved under behaviour therapy as opposed to 50% (5) of the family therapy group. Although both therapies were clearly defined, they did share common elements. As Naomi Richman noted, it was hard for the family therapist not to get involved in setting behavioural tasks; similarly it was hard for the behaviourist not to get involved in family work (Richman 1983).

The Coming of the 'Whole Child' Approach

As early as 1961 Kempton had advocated joint care by paediatrician and child psychiatrist, but over the years other forms of joint care developed. Kempton also noted that it was important to follow up cases as children often dropped out of treatment even though the symptom had not disappeared. Berg & Vernon-Jones (1964) advocated a joint psychological/physical approach encouraging the use of the toilet and prescribing laxatives. They noted that many children were not emotionally disturbed. In a later paper Berg et al (1983), using joint paediatric/psychiatric services, set up a controlled study of 44 children. However, there were no significant differences between those who received medication and those who received no tablets. Overall 67% were free from soiling after one year and there was 'no evidence either during the trial or subsequently, when Senokot was employed to supplement behavioural treatment, that this laxative contributed in any way to relieving the problem.' But this sample may not have included more extreme cases of obstipation.

Taitz et al (1986), in an interesting study of 47 children referred to a paediatric outpatient clinic with defaecation disorders (children with identified bowel disease or who had neurological handicaps were excluded from the study), achieved a success rate of 63% (defined as cured: at least five normal stools each week without soiling, only occasional use of laxatives; or improved at least three stools each week and soiling less than once a week). Children were treated with simple incentive-based behaviour modification with or without psychotherapy involving outpatient visits every four to six weeks. Laxatives and enemas were used where necessary but in general their use was minimised. What was notable in this study was that compliant patients, that is patients who attended regularly and kept the required records, had a higher success rate than non-compliant. Non-compliant patients were more likely to come from very deprived families with many social problems.

Clayden, following his 1976 studies, felt 'that a broad spectrum of treatment is needed for the children with chronic constipation and soiling provided by multi-disciplinary teams, with great care that the particular child has his needs met in the most appropriate way.' Under his inspiration such a team has been set up and is known as an

Table 6. Basic types of childhood soiling and constipation (from Clayden 1981)

Type	Main features	Probable effective treatment
Environmental	Poor appetite Many food fads Low fibre diet High milk intake Relatively low water intake Dry stools Straining Normal anorectal physiology	Increase dietary water and fibre
Reluctant group	Pot refusal Painful defaecation with blood in stool plus fissure Low incidence of soiling Moderate delays between stool No or inappropriate treatment Some enlargement of rectum physiologically	Stool softeners plus senna to re-establish more frequent defaecation
Retaining group	Onset around age 2 years Intermittent soiling (when loaded) Passing massive stools Some pot refusal or 'school loo refusal' Infrequent stools Some speech or learning difficulties Large capacity rectum with late sensation Some excess smooth muscle rhythmical activity	Bulk laxative plus senna plus anal dilatation

Group	Features	Treatment

Megarectum group	Onset early infancy
	Continuous soilers
	Abdominal distension and marked faecal loading on examination
	10 day delays in defaecation
	Family history of constipation
	Low incidence of infantile colic
	(Including anal strictures and Hirschsprung's disease)
	Poor sensation on anorectal manometry
	High rectal volumes required and little inhibition of internal sphincter rhythmical activity
		Bulk laxatives—senna
		Anal dilatation
		    plus internal anal
		    sphincterotomy

'Psychosomatic' group	Very long delays between stools Soiling and encopretic when bowel habit improving Coercive or emotionally distant parents Suppressed anger Tendency to other psychiatric symptoms and sabotaging treatment Relapses with emotional stresses High volume rectal capacity and poor sensation with active rhythmical activity in smooth muscle of internal sphincter	Laxatives (anal dilatation) Social work support Psychotherapy

Table 7. Treatment of soiling children: principal studies

Author and date	No.	Sample definition	Treatment	Improved	Notes
Bellman 1966	75	7 years with soiling problem	No treatment	56%	Follow up 2 years Cure defined as clean 6 months
Anthony 1957	76	Boys and girls visiting CG clinics	Psychotherapy Bowel training for some		(Precise fibures hard to extract from report)
Pinkerton 1958	30	Children with encopresis and obstipation	Psychotherapy	70%	
Coekin & Gairdner 1960	69	All children with faecal incontinence presenting at paediatric clinic (Ex. MH)	*Mechanical soilers:* enema then laxative *Non-mechanical* psychiatric care	64%	This figure includes *all* children in study
Davidson et al 1963	119	Children referred to private or public paediatric gastrointestinal clinic in New York with severe and protracted constipation (Note: 36% no soiling)	1. Enemas if necessary 2. Mineral oil (tests for Hirschsprung's disease if indicated) 3. Long term follow-up	67%	Includes drop-outs and Hirschsprung's

Study	N	Sample	Treatment	Success	Comments
Levine 1975	102	Children with faecal incontinence	1. Demystification 2. Enemas for emptying 3. Laxatives/softeners 4. Bowel training 5. Regular follow-up 6. Recognition encopresis is a chronic disease.	70%	Assessed at end of one year
Clayden & Lawson 1976	106	Long standing chronic constipation and soiling (Note 38% no soiling)	1. Medical management Cologel and Senokot 2. NR: trial of anal dilatation 3. NR: further anal dilatation 4. NR: Partial sphincterotomy	59%	10% had Hirschsprung's ?Whole sample very severe
Berg & Vernon-Jones 1965	44	Children who had soiling as main complaint and complicated faecal incontinence (40% unusually hard motions)	Senokot or placebo plus behaviour modification—bowel training	67%	Controlled study Assessed on previous 4 weeks
N. Richman 1983 (not published)	28	Children referred to psychiatrist for encopresis Those with organic cause suspected were excluded (61% history of constipation)	Behavioural modification or family therapy	57%	Controlled study: BM (may have been treatment overlap) High drop-out from FT

Table 7. Continued

Author and date	No.	Sample definition	Treatment	Improved	Notes
Taitz et al 1986	47	Children referred to paediatric clinic with abnormal bowel function Children with organic bowel disease excluded (8% no soiling)	1. Demystification 2. Enemas if necessary 3. Minimum use of laxatives/softeners 4. Behaviour modification 5. Diet advice	64%	Follow-up 1 year after start of study
Hein & Beerends 1978	23	Referred to paediatric clinic for 'encopresis'. All had symptoms for at least 6 months	1. Counselling, physical and emotional aspects 2. Enemas 3. Diet: Low milk, bananas, apple, high fibre.	61%	This figure excludes drop-outs
Buchanan 1990	30	Children 4–16 with soiling	'Whole child approach' (see Chapter 6)	77%	

CG, Family and child guidance clinics; BM, Behaviour modification programme; FT, Programme based on a family therapy approach.

'intestinal motility clinic'. Table 6 outlines his classification and treatment regimens.

The 'Whole Child' Approach

The 'whole child' approach, which seeks to incorporate treatment of the psychological, physical and social aspects and which has been developed by the author, is outlined in detail in the next chapter. This approach was a natural next step from Clayden's work. It was recognised that most local communities would not have the resources for a multi-disciplinary intestinal motility clinic. In her study (Buchanan 1990), the treatment outcomes of 66 soiling children were compared. Of these, 30 children took part in an experimental 'whole child' approach. The key therapist for this group (Experimental) was a behaviourally trained social worker working under psychiatric supervision, with access to hospital paediatricians. Out of the original 66 soilers, a further 18 were treated by the local paediatric department (Hospital study) and another 18 children were treated by the local child guidance clinic (Clinic study). Although in the short term all groups achieved fairly similar results (Hospital 78%; Clinic 72%; Experimental 77%), over a longer period the Experimental group was significantly more successful. (Hospital 28%; Clinic 28%; Experimental 90%). The Experimental group was also more effective in improving the overall quality of the child's and parents' lives: fewer behavioural problems, fewer school problems, and fewer parental/child relationship problems. Some of the findings from this study and their implications are considered in more detail in Part III.

Table 7 summarises the principal studies. Taitz et al (1986) incorporate a similar summary in their paper although in this case a more comprehensive list has been included. They adjusted some of the published 'improved/cure' figures by including 'drop-outs from treatment' and special categories such as 'mechanical and non mechanical soilers' developed by Berg. This gives a much clearer inter-study comparison. A similar practice has been used here. Where adjustments have been made, these are indicated under the Notes section.

SUMMARY

This chapter traces the developments of treatment programmes used

by the different professional groups at different times. Although classifications tried to make the clear divide between those children with a
physical problem requiring paediatric care and those with a psychiatric problem requiring psychiatric care, when it came to the principal
treatment studies, clinicians found it very difficut to make this divide
except in cases where there were very obvious or severe problems such
as Hirschsprung's disease. One may conclude from this that, in all
probability, the majority of children with a soiling problem fall somewhere along a continuum with varying degrees of physical and emotional problems, which are either primary or secondary to the
problem, and need a treatment programme which reflects this reality.

The second point highlighted by the studies is that, in recent years,
there appears to be a trend for 'packages of treatment', rather than one
preferred treatment to be used. Hein & Beerends (1978), Clayden
(1976), Davidson et al (1963), Levine (1975), Taitz et al (1986) have
all formulated treatment packages with common elements which can
be individually tailored to the child's needs.

Thirdly, the definition of 'cure or improved' in these studies is of
interest. Hidden in the literature is the idea that the soiling problem
does not just one day get cured, but that relapses are common. Finally,
the results from the author's 'whole child' treatment for soiling children indicate that this approach may be more effective than more
traditional approaches.

There is, of course, one major area that has not been touched on in this
literature review, and indeed is barely mentioned before the late
1980s. This is the relationship between soiling and sexual abuse.
Because of the current interest and controversy in this area, this is
considered in depth in Chapter 13.

PART II

The 'whole child' treatment

CHAPTER 6   The 'whole child' approach for soiling children

The cure of many diseases is unknown to the physicians of Hellas (Greece) because they disregard the whole, which ought to be studied also, for the part can never be well unless the whole is well. (Plato, trans. Jowett 1943).

Any attempt to separate the physical and mental health needs of children is doomed to failure . . . in considering the health needs of our children we need to be concerned with the 'whole child and his family'. (Graham 1986, p. 414)

From Plato in ancient Greece to Philip Graham, consultant child psychiatrist at Great Ormond Street Childrens' Hospital in the 1990s, the idea of 'whole person' care is not new, and yet in recent years there has been a multi-disciplinary movement across professional boundaries towards the rediscovery of 'whole person' or 'holistic' care.

But what is 'whole person care'? How does the concept work when it comes to soiling children? What is the ethos of the approach and is there a relationship between 'whole child care' and the present legal developments in children's practice and community care? What are the likely 'whole child' needs of soilers and in order to meet these needs what 'packages of care' should be developed? How do you design a system to respond to those needs and what roles does each professional play in the system? These are some of the questions that we will address in this chapter.

'Whole Person Care'

'Whole person care', 'psychosomatic medicine', 'holistic care'—they all suggest an 'inseparability and interdependence of psychosocial and biological aspects' (Lipowski 1986). 'Whatever label is chosen to describe holistic care and whatever term is used to designate the incorporation of—and benefit from—advances in its scientific foundations, this care remains an enduring feature of much medical practice' (Christie & Mellett 1986).

Both the Greek philosophers Plato and Aristotle recognised the inseparability and mutual dependence of 'psyche' and 'soma'. Lipowski, in his scholarly paper (1986), notes that many medical writers since Greek times have implicitly or explicitly advocated a mind–body approach, but notes that 'western medicine since Hippocrates, with notable exceptions such as Gaub (1747), Rush (1811), Tuke (1884), Osler (1928)' has in the main, tended to adopt a 'staunchly naturalistic and somatic physiological approach' (Lipowski 1986). Christie argues that before the Medical Act of 1858 in London, there were opportunities for 'holistic care' despite the divisions between the physician, surgeon and apothecary: 'Maybe there was little more than that on offer at the time as effective treatment' (Christie & Mellett 1986). But with the coming of the Act, which brought about the registration of all medical practitioners and the supervision of their education, there followed an explosion of scientific knowledge (e.g. Pasteur and micro-organisms, Lister and antisepsis, Jenner and smallpox). This explosion of knowledge necessitated the fragmentation and specialisation of medicine and a mechanistic approach to patients and their care. It was not until 1968 when the Royal Commission on Medical Education (the Todd Report) was published that 'whole person care' gained official recognition. Following a growing awareness, supported by research, the importance of psychological and social factors could not be ignored, and responding to the growth of pressure groups demanding that medicine be 'humanised', the Todd Report advocated greater integration of specialisms, greater consideration of psychosocial factors and a more sensitive awareness that patients were people. Indeed with the ever increasing economic difficulties of the National Health Service, there was a growing awareness that if more notice were taken of psychosocial aspects of disease, it might be possible to change the emphasis from the expensive 'curative' focus to a less costly 'preventative' health service, responsive to community needs. From Plato to the Health and Community Care Act, maybe we have come the full cycle.

Current Influences

The recent legislative changes in the UK, notably the Children Act

1989 and the Health and Community Care Act 1990, were intended to revolutionise the caring and healing professions. The two Acts, with their emphasis on creating a 'service provision' in line with a market economy, demanded a massive change in professional values and attitudes. The Health and Community Care Act was, in part, a recognition, or re-recognition (in Plato's time there was probably little care other than that provided by the family/community) that 'whole person' care means an awareness of the influences of the person's social environment. It recognises the value in preventative and curative terms, both medically and socially (but not one suspects in financial terms as may have been hoped), of fostering these family/community networks. Similarly the Children Act 1989 was, in part, a recognition of the same factors. But more dramatically, both Acts were about breaking away from the expectations created by a 'sick role', a 'victim role', where the client or patient became incapacitated by the very label that came with being a consumer of the service. The Acts were about 'empowering' the clients (parents and children) or patients to make informed choices and take responsibility for the decisions that affected their lives, with the assumption that having chosen a life plan there would also be a commitment to follow it. The Acts were also about choosing care options to be put together into 'packages of care' individually tailored to meet the needs of the person. In the Acts too, there was the implicit assumption that, however good the assessment processes, these could never be complete, as the only person who knew the missing factors and influences that made up the 'whole person' was of course the person himself. That was why, in the final analysis, he had to make the choice of care. The 1990s will demonstrate whether the hopes for a better deal for the consumer invested in the two Acts will be matched by the reality.

The Ethos of the Whole Child Approach for Soiling Children

The ethos of 'whole child approach' for soiling children reflects some of these influences. The approach evolved from the author's early behavioural treatment of soiling children. Although this had some success, factors in the child's family, school or social environment would intrude and sabotage progress. From these early attempts, and from the literature search, evolved the holistic focus. From this work too came the recognition that as far as possible the child needed to be treated/supported in the community whence he came. Removing a child from his community, whether to a hospital or other setting, meant the double stress of leaving his home and then returning. Relapses could be related to this or to the unreliability of behavioural programmes in 'generalising', that is carrying over the learning from one setting to another (e.g. continuing the toileting routine that had been taught in hospital, when back at home). Another important aspect of the 'whole child approach' was 'empowering' the child; breaking into his 'learned helplessness'; taking away the sick role (soiling was a problem to be overcome, not a sickness) and giving the child back the responsibility for his own bowels. Linked with this was an important message that no-one was to blame. Soiling was a common problem with many causes, and the child did not do it deliberately. The child may not be able to prevent his soiling, but he could learn to help himself. The 'whole child' approach was also about knowing how your inside worked—'demystification'—so that you could make informed choices on what you would do. Finally the approach was about creating a service which was responsive to the needs of the child and his family but which also recognised their strengths and was able to put together treatment packages (if necessary multi-disciplinary), individually tailored for the 'whole person'.

Possible Needs of the Soiling Child and his Family

As we have seen from the literature review, broadly speaking soiling children will have three types of needs: physical needs, psychological needs and needs relating to their social circumstances or environment. The task of the assessment process is to identify the unmet needs of the 'whole child' and to create a package to meet these needs. Chapter 7 looks at the assessment process in greater detail. Not all soiling children will need formal psychological help, but most will need positive help in regaining their confidence that they can do something to help themselves. Not all soiling children will need on-going medical help, but all should have an assessment from an experienced medical practitioner to make sure that constipation or other conditions are not part of the problem. They may also need on-going medical reviews.

Similarly, some soiling children may have no problems in their social circumstances, but the chances are that they will need at least some help in this area, if only to cope with other children's reactions to their soiling. It may also be important to assess and encourage modification of his diet; toilet facilities may be at the root of his difficulties; high stress levels in the home could also be a factor. Finally, all soiling children need to know what their problem is and what sort of things they can do to help themselves.

THE PACKAGES OF TREATMENT– THE POSSIBLE INGREDIENTS

Demystification

Levine (1975) was the first to coin the term 'demystification' as an important adjunct to treatment. The idea is very simple. A child, and his family if they are to help him, need to know about the mechanics of his bowel problem. If a child is to be motivated to help himself, he needs to have some clear idea what he is trying to do. It is also something to do with owning the bit of body which is causing a problem, and empowering the child to help himself. If it is the doctor's responsibility to 'get the inside working properly', this means it is his fault when it goes wrong; this also means that in effect the child is 'learned helpless' (Seligman 1975). But if, on another hand, there is the concept that the doctor is only there to assist the child, his family and anyone else involved to overcome his problem there is a feeling of 'empowerment' in the child.

The other important role of 'demystification' is to help the parents and the child understand that the soiling is not deliberate. Until they know the facts, most parents believe that the child can 'if he really wants to' control the soiling. Indeed he may be able to for limited periods by holding on to his stools, and this evidence may further reinforce the parents' belief. This belief that the child can control his soiling can lead to worrying abusive situations.

Linked into the idea of explaining to the child how his bowel works is explaining to the child and his family the likely course of his problem. One of the most common problems in treating soiling children is that they naturally have an expectation that getting better is getting 'clean'. So when they have a short period of being 'clean', which may be related to holding on to stools and avoiding defaecation, there is great despair when the 'overflow soiling' starts. But, as was demonstrated by the author's research (Buchanan 1990), the natural course of the problem is that soiling relapses are a common feature, even after quite extended periods of normal defaecation and no symptoms. Holidays, other illnesses, new stresses, even something as simple as a new toilet in the child's home, can all spark off a new episode of constipation and soiling, which has to be tackled in the same way as the initial episode. It is also probable that any child who has not overcome his disorder by the age of six will have repeated episodes of soiling throughout middle childhood (Buchanan 1990). If at the start of treatment, the child and his parents are not aware of this, the temptation is for the parents to dismiss the agency trying to help the child and start a damaging treatment-trip around the agencies, which further reinforces the child's original failure, and does little to help the delicate relationships between the child and his parents.

Some specialist settings who see soiling children have produced their own 'Demystification' leaflet for the child and his family to take home and study. The leaflet used by St Thomas's Intestinal Motility Clinic in London is reproduced in the Appendix.

Physical Treatment: Medication

All soiling children need a medical examination to determine whether there is any identifiable physical cause for their condition, and/or to determine the extent of any constipation or faecal loading. Depending on this assessment, the physician will decide what type of physical treatment the child needs. This may be one of three main options: medication, suppositories and enemas, and/or inpatient care for further assessment or treatment procedures. This is discussed in detail in the next chapter. However, most children will make no progress in overcoming their soiling problem until the blockage of faecal matter in their bowel is cleared. There has been much controversy about how this is done and how the child's bowel is maintained in good condition.

Basically, there are two types of medication generally prescribed. The laxatives, with their irritant action on the bowel such as Senokot, and the softeners, which add bulk. The main controversy is around the use of the irritants. Berg et al (1983) found no significant difference as regards outcome between those children treated for their soiling problem with Senokot and those treated without, but it has to be remembered that the children in this study had been assessed as 'having uncomplicated faecal incontinence'. As Berg et al said 'none of the cases was so grossly impacted that alternate forms of treatment need be considered'. Even if it were felt desirable to withhold physical treatments, in reality it is very difficult to deny treatment to a child who is suffering considerable distress from severe retention, who may also be sick with a related fever.

However, there other concerns about the use of medication. Smith (1968) has shown that excessive intake of irritant laxative can lead to constipation with 'gross histological damage to the myenteric plexus'. Read & Timms (1986) feel that prolonged intake of irritant laxatives by constipated patients may damage the colon and exacerbate the condition.

There is also the concern about the possible toxic effects of certain products used as laxatives (Clayden 1981).

However, quite apart from the controversies surrounding the use of irritant laxatives, other factors need to be taken into account in prescribing medication.

Non-compliance, not taking the medication as prescribed or even at all, was a not uncommon factor in the author's study (Buchanan 1990). One child was making very limited progress. His parents were of limited ability. It was hard to understand why he was making so little progress until they showed the author the cupboard full of unused medication. When the medication was given daily by the school nurse, he made rapid gains. Other children, not liking the taste of the medication or its effect (stomach cramps), found excuses to avoid taking it, but then did not want to tell the doctor for fear of 'upsetting him' (Buchanan 1990). In Chapter 8 Dr Clayden gives a detailed account of the different laxatives used for soiling children and indicators on when and how they should be used for maximum effectiveness and safety.

Physical Care: Suppositories/ Enemas

The use of suppositories and enemas is another controversial area. Those involved in treating children will be familiar with the distress some children demonstrate when given suppositories or enemas. 'Are you a bomb lady' was the greeting given to the author on meeting a soiling child for the first time. The child was hiding in terror under the table (Buchanan 1990). However, it was not until current concerns about sexual abuse and the child abuse crisis of the Cleveland Inquiry (1988) that medical practitioners began to wonder if what they were doing in the name of treatment might be interpreted by the child as a physical assault. In the author's study one child admitted to pleasurable feelings when 'pushing his faeces back inside him with his fingers'. The child had been treated for many years with suppositories. Another child who had been treated with suppositories drew highly sexualised drawings, which could have been misinterpreted as a possible sign of sexual abuse (Buchanan 1990).

Despite the controversies, in some situations, suppositories or some sort of bowel wash-out may be necessary and to be recommended as the lesser evil.

Physical Treatment: Inpatient Care

Many soiling children who have experienced long term outpatient care without success obtain relief from their symptoms when appropriately managed on an inpatient basis. However, as the author's study demonstrated, inpatient care is not the panacea that it might appear.

In her study, 50% of the children being treated by the local paediatric department were admitted into hospital. Some of these children had extended periods of inpatient care; although the investigations were welcome, the long periods some children spent undergoing training programmes were rarely successful. As soon as the child returned home the problem returned. This may have been related to the difficulties of 'generalisation' (Herbert 1981); that is, the difficulty in transferring a piece of learnt behaviour, in this case how to manage your soiling, from one setting to another. Relapses after discharge from hospital may also have been related to the child going back to the same pressures and stresses—less appropriate diet, smelly loos, emotional difficulties—that he got away from by going into hospital. Long admission to hospital also created secondary problems for the child; he missed vital school, lost peer group friends (Buchanan 1990). The study also showed that where hospital admission was essential, shorter admissions (under one week) were less disruptive for the child and there was no evidence that these were less effective in outcome than longer ones, especially when the admission carried no promise of 'cure', but was to deal with retention problems or to have investigations (Buchanan 1990).

However, parents of soiling children can be quite persuasive that 'something must be done' to solve their child's problem. In some cases it may be more appropriate to admit the soiling child into hospital for further assessment than to leave him to the fury of his parents. In other cases, it may be felt that inpatient treatment is necessary as there is a real possibility that further investigations may lead to more effective resolution of the problem.

Behaviourable Approaches

The findings of the author's study (Buchanan 1990) strongly supported the use of behavioural methods individually tailored to the child's needs in the treatment package for all soiling children. As we will see in Chapter 8, a cognitive behavioural approach is used to break into the child's 'learned helplessness', and a behavioural program is used to help the child develop normal defaecation routines. In some cases, it may be appropriate to use elements from biofeedback, that is helping the child recognise the signs and signals from his body which indicate that a movement is coming.

The coming of behavioural therapy

Learning theory as a therapeutic tool was slow to make its impression in child psychiatry. Although Skinner published his ideas on learning theory in 1938 and indeed papers by Watson and Rayner appeared as early as 1920, it was not until 1962 that Rachman published his seminal paper entitled 'Learning theory and child psychology: Therapeutic possibilities'. Rachman was at this time working in the

Children's Department of the Maudsley Hospital and his paper outlined a myriad of possible conditions for treatment. These included phobias, enuresis, tics, stuttering, anxiety states, anorexia, temper tantrums, severe retardation, autism, remedial reading, eating habits, aggressive behaviour and speech delay. Yule (1984), when reviewing Rachman's paper in 1984 in the context of the then current knowledge and treatment techniques, felt the paper showed remarkable foresight but noted an important omission, the treatment of encopresis.

Clinicians using behaviour therapy see 'child behaviour problems as exaggerations, deficits, or handicapping combinations of behaviours common to all children . . . and that maladaptive behaviours can most effectively be changed by the therapeutic application of principles of learning' (Herbert 1981). Herbert also says that there are two basic learning tasks that are commonly encountered in child therapy; firstly the acquisition (i.e. learning) of a desired behaviour in which the individual is deficient (e.g. compliance, self-control, bladder and bowel control) and secondly the renunciation of undesired responses in the child's behaviour repertoire. Learning occurs within a social setting: rewards, punishments and other events are handed out by people within the child's world. Unfortunately according to behaviour therapists the very process which helps the child adjust to life can under certain circumstances contribute to maladjustment. Behaviour therapists are not interested in the child's unconscious thoughts nor in wider theories as to what may have caused the problem. What they do is manipulate the environments so that the desired behaviour is more rewarding to the child than the undesired.

Cognitive behaviour therapy was a necessary extension of the behavioural approach. As any clinician from Freud onwards knew, not all behaviour is rational. The cognitive behaviourists explained this phenomenon by saying there can be 'irrational' thoughts or 'cognitions' which may interfere with the direct stimulus/response formula. In treatment it is therefore important to help the person recognise these 'cognitions' as 'irrational thoughts' and replace them with rational ones (Beck 1970). Seligman's concept of 'learned helplessness' is a development from this thinking (Seligman 1975). Those with an 'early experience' in psychodynamic therapies might wonder about the origins of these irrational thoughts, and question whether the behavioural and psychodynamic approaches are so irreconcilable.

Initially some behaviourists saw learning theory as the main pychotherapeutic approach for child behaviour disorders, and this resulted in an unhappy divide between those clinicians who supported a psychodynamic approach (i.e. who believed in the power of the unconscious) and those clinicians who felt learning theory was all explanatory. Today, as Rutter (1986) says in his article 'Child Psychiatry: Looking 30 years ahead', 'theories about learning have made and will continue to make important contributions. What is really encouraging, is the increasing number of therapists from all major disciplines, who have turned their back on this inter-sectarian warfare and applied their energies to the development of the most effective psychological techniques, whatever the nature of their origins'.

Behavioural treatments and soiling

The first behavioural treatments for soiling came soon after Rachman's paper in 1962. As we have seen in Chapter 5, Neale first published the results of his treatment of four soilers in 1963. He rewarded a child who passed faeces in the toilet with sweets, chocolate bars and peanuts. Edelman (1971), Pedrini & Pedrini (1970), Sluckin (1975), Webster & Gore (1980) among others followed with similar therapies; that is behavioural programmes that rewarded the child for successful defaecation.

It was Sluckin (1981) who first recognised that Seligman's concept of 'learned helplessness' was an important factor in a soiling problem. The soiling child could not win. If the child hung on to his stools to prevent himself soiling, he would eventually become so constipated that he soiled from 'overflow'. Sluckin recognised that it was important to break into this vicious circle of 'learned helplessness', and help the child discover that by regular defaecation he could achieve some control over his soiling.

More recently some clinicians are showing positive results from 'biofeedback' techniques (Olness et al 1980, Kaplan 1985). Biofeedback has been used as an aid to treatment in a number of medical conditions. Essentially it involves teaching the patient to recognise and respond rationally to what their body is telling them. Olness in his study using a rectal biofeedback approach proposed that a characteristic of his approach was that the child achieved a sense of self-mastery and such feelings may have positive carry-over effects (Olness et al 1980). Kaplan's (1985) treatment package included training the child in 'self-mastery' without using the rectal biofeedback instrumentation. He instructed his children to 'teach their bum to talk to them', and showed them how they could help themselves by 'listening better'. The author's study supported these views. Study children were instructed from the start of treatment that it was 'their' problem and that they would have to 'train their tummy'. Linked into this was the instruction that they should listen to their 'tummy' and 'go like a rocket if they felt any need to go'. In the study some children reported that the signs of 'wanting to go' came not from their anus (after years of constipation, they had little sensation there of wanting to go) but high up in their abdomen. Indeed one child who was not included in the study, who suffered from rectal atresia, was successfully trained by learning to respond to bodily signals of colonic movements in his abdomen.

Formal/Informal Involvement of Family

'Whole child care' involves not only an awareness of all the different parts that make up the person, but also an awareness of his family and an awareness of the dynamics within the family which may be related to his presenting problem. This is another essential element in the package of treatment. How far the therapist needs to become involved in the family dynamics will of course depend on each case and will be examined in the next chapter.

The days when the child psychiatrist saw the child and the social worker saw the family to prepare a social report are probably past. The idea that the child psychiatrist should see the whole family at therapy sessions emerged from the USA over thirty years ago. It was a recognition that what goes on between people is as important as what goes on inside an individual. It was also a recognition that the most important and influential people to a child are his family, and as such they had to be 'partners' to any therapy. It could be said that the Children Act 1989 has put a legislative stamp to this principle.

However, the methods used to involve families in their child's therapy, particularly when it comes to a soiling problem, are debatable. In the author's study, 71% of the children's families, whether they were being treated by hospital paediatricians, psychiatrists or social workers, were involved by clinicians in one way or another in treatment.

'Involvement of the family' was a very broad category and included those cases who received formal family therapy at a child guidance clinic as well as those cases where the paediatricians involved other members of the family at hospital appointments, or where the social worker discussed the situation with the family at home. Paediatricians often spent a great deal of time with parents, easing tensions, trying to help them view their child more positively, talking to brothers and sisters. It would be inaccurate to say paediatricians did no family therapy in its broadest sense, when there was ample evidence that some were heavily involved with the child, his parents and siblings, particularly if a child was admitted to hospital. There was also evidence that the paediatricians were acutely aware of the 'systems' within the families and quite skilful at bringing about change in them (Buchanan 1990).

Formal family therapy, in the child psychiatric sense, follows a wide range of schools and models. It is difficult to compare family therapy because family therapy may be quite a different animal from area to area, practitioner to practitioner. Naomi Richman's unpublished study quoted in the Association of Child Psychology and Psychiatry's Newsletter (1983) showed no significant differences between family therapy and behavioural therapy, but results may have been invalidated because the two therapies shared common elements. It may be that family therapy which incorporates a 'task' of persuading children to defaecate regularly, takes the pressures off the child, helps him to view the soiling as his problem, and helps his parents and brothers and sisters support him in his task, is not that far removed from the informal family work done by the paediatrician. The main difference would probably be the locus of the treatment. Formal family therapy would be more likely in a clinic where non-attendance and drop-out from therapy is more likely (Naomi Richman 1983). In real terms this could mean that the child would not receive this treatment package.

In the author's study of soiling children treated in a child guidance setting, it was evident that some parents who had been involved in psychodynamically orientated family therapies without access to paediatric help were particularly angry about the therapy they received, especially when they later found their child had untreated retention problems. They could not understand why the focus was on their problems; 'What right had they to dig up all the family skeletons?' They complained that the therapy made them feel guilty, and the end result was all the family felt angry with the soiling child who was making them all go through such a painful form of therapy. Most of these families dropped out of treatment.

In the author's prospective 'whole child' treatment study, a decision was made to involve families informally. As the treatment took place in the home it was possible to time some visits so that other family members were at home. During these visits, it was possible to assess the dynamics of the situation and make simple interventions. This informal type of family therapy appeared to be more acceptable to the family. There were failures. In one family, the father's drinking was a problem—but this was not amenable to help, and the therapist just had to accept this, and work within this framework.

Other therapists may disagree with this approach. All that can be said is that in the author's study drop-out was minimal during treatment (Buchanan 1990).

Interventions in the Child's Environment

How far the clinician needs to intervene in the child's wider world will of course vary from child to child. But it is important to remember that the child's problem may be related to something as simple as a difficulty in finding an appropriate toilet in which to defaecate. From Burns (1941)—the increase in soiling amongst evacuee children; Ahnsjo (1959)—increase in soiling in preschool children admitted to summer classes; through to Sluckin (1975) and Clayden (1980)— poor school toilets as a cause of soiling; there has been an awareness that environmental factors in the child's wider world might have a role in a soiling problem. The current concern about sexual abuse (Cleveland Report 1988, Hobbs & Wynne 1986) is a sharp reminder that the child's wider environment should be considered in the treatment and management of a soiling child.

Diet is another factor which can usefully be considered. The importance of diet has been mentioned in various studies (Davidson et al 1963, Coekin & Gairdner 1960, Hein & Beerends 1978, Taitz et al 1986). This is also considered in depth later in the book.

The child spends 15 000 hours in secondary school alone (Rutter et al

1979) and this time may be as important as the time spent with his family. In the author's 'whole child' treatment study, improvements were made when severe stress levels a child was experiencing in school were reduced (Buchanan 1990). However, in approaching the school, care needs to be exercised that the child is happy about any such contact.

To be Kept on the Agenda: the Possibility of Sexual Abuse

A notable gap in examining the possible ingredients of packages is an awareness that some of the children may have been sexually abused, but regrettably it needs to be on the agenda. Chapter 13 examines this concern in some detail. The final completed package for a potentially sexually abused child may be different from that for a child who has not been sexually abused, but many of the essential ingredients will be the same.

SUMMARY

This approach links in to current thinking about 'whole person care'. The therapeutic ethos is one of no blame, empowering the child to take responsibility for his own bowels, and educating him about his problem. As far as possible the child is supported in the community. Packages of care are created to meet the strengths and needs of each child and his family. The focus of treatment is on the physical, psychological and social needs of the 'whole child' in his environment.

CHAPTER 7   The assessment process*

In paediatric practice it is not possible to make a full diagnosis or to draw up an appropriate care programme without some knowledge of the child, his age, size, abilities and personality. Furthermore, a child is part of a family; to understand him one must know something of his family, particularly his parents, their life styles, their family life, their capacity to look after children and in particular their relationships to our patient and attitudes towards his illness. Families live in communities and as the child grows older and becomes more independent he relates more directly to the community, in particular his school and his peers . . . the mode of presentation, the symptoms and even the signs of disease, may be influenced by the nature of the child, his family and their surroundings and experiences. (Hull & Johnston 1981)

This then is the assessment task—the linking of the physical signs and symptoms with the history of the problem and a wider assessment of the 'whole child's' world.

Assessment is not a once and for all process. Children change from day to day; they develop in vastly different ways; they have infections, accidents, emotional crises; their families have good times and bad; their school can be happy places for them or sad; all these events affect the child, and more important still they affect the child's bowel, a 'veritable mirror' of his physical and emotional well-being. Assessment is therefore an on-going interactive process.

After the initial investigations, what the child presents in the context of physical, emotional and social symptoms and how he responds to any treatment will of course dictate what else needs to be known, and what further investigations may be necessary in order to tailor together, or re-tailor an individual treatment package. Assessment like treatment is therefore an on-going personal affair, and you cannot hope or indeed would not want to discover all on the first acquaintance.

---

*The section on *Medical Assessment* in this chapter is by Dr Graham Clayden.

Finding the Strengths/Stating Needs Positively

Assessment is also about discovering not only what has gone wrong and why, but discovering, despite the difficulties, what has gone well and why. Any treatment programme is likely to be more successful if it builds on the successes of the past. This is especially important in planning a behavioural programme. In recent years there has been a movement amongst those involved in assessing people with disabilities and the elderly to focus more on what the person can do, or has achieved, likes to do, and those around who may be able to help; that is a focus on the persons 'strengths'. Although pathology is identified, as far as possible it is stated positively as a 'needs'. 'Mrs X needs help with her walking . . . Mrs X needs medication to ensure her bowels work regularly' (Barrowclough and Fleming 1986).

This is a useful model to use with the soiling child and his family. For if the child is to feel 'empowered' and the family are to be supported, it is important to acknowledge their previous successes—their 'strengths'. It is also more positive and 'empowering', and easier to see the way forward if problems are restated as 'needs' 'John *needs* help with his toilet routine . . . John *needs* help to overcome the ribbing he gets from his brothers and sisters . . . John *needs* medication to clear the blockage in his bowel', rather than 'John will not use the toilet . . . John cannot cope with teasing . . .'

What the Child Wants/What the Parents Want

Finally assessment is about discovering what the child and his family *want* to do about the problem, and which aspects of the problems are of most concern to them. Although in a few cases the risk of physical abuse may make the situation potentially worrying, and in most cases the child will suffer emotionally, soiling is rarely life-threatening. It has to be remembered that some children and their families may prefer to put up with the consequences of the soiling rather than undergo some treatment options. Also families may have very different priorities about which aspect of the problem they want help with. For some, the actual soiling itself may not be as stressful as problems the child experiences in school. For others, it is not so much the fact of the soiling, but the smell of defaecation and the process of cleaning the child up which is the last straw. What treatment children and families become involved in and what aspects they wish to have help with is their choice and unless there are other overriding concerns such as physical or sexual abuse, this is their right. It is useful to remember that the very fact of exercising this right can often bring with it a commitment to make the treatment work. In this chapter we will consider this assessment task starting from the initial medical, psychological and social information gathering. Figure 8 illustrates the process.

The Importance of Initial Planning

Before the child arrives for the first assessment appointment, parents and children need to get to the starting gate. How children get to the starting gate and what happens when they open that gate can crucially influence later assessment and treatment. The day to day management of this is described by Dr Clayden in Chapter 9, while possible systems to meet the needs of soiling children are considered in depth in the Afterword.

Multi-disciplinary Assessment

In a multi-disciplinary team, each party to the initial assessment process has a written agenda of information they need about the child or his family in order to move forward. Who collects the information, when and from whom, is a matter of negotiation between the team. It may be felt easier for the medical specialist to collect basic social information at the initial interview; it may be felt better, to avoid frequent clinic attendances, for the paramedical support to assess possible on-going constipation or responses to medication in the home. The task is about setting up working relations which are responsive to the needs of soiling children. In being responsive to these needs, teams may develop assessment and treatment procedures which transcend traditional professional barriers. What is important is that who does what, and when, is decided before the child and his family ever come through the door for the initial assessment.

As assessment is not a static process, it is important that there is an

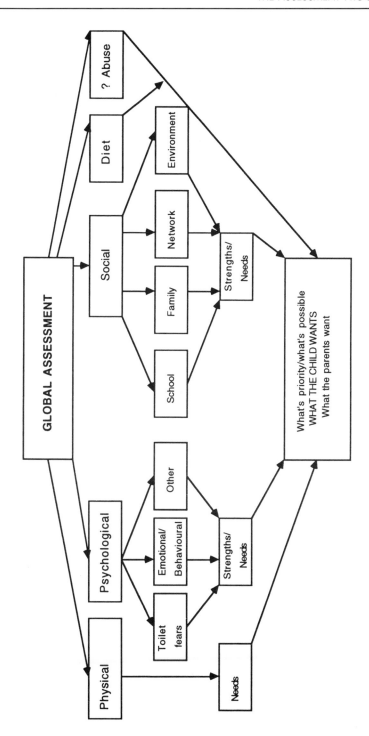

Figure 8.   The 'whole child' assessment process

agreed and effective method of communicating new information about the child or his family between the professionals involved.

The Initial Interview—Setting the Ethos

Although assessment processes are separated here from treatment processes, as any clinician knows this is a totally artificial divide. Therapeutic processes should begin the moment the child steps through the door. The first interview must express an ethos of confidence, hope, no-blame. This message is a therapeutic imperative and can come as much from the way the receptionist greets the family and the surroundings as from the meeting with the clinician. Equally important is to give the child a very strong positive message that there is something he can do to help himself and that in the long term the responsibility for getting his bowel straight is his (but he will be helped), and whatever his mother says you know he wants to get clean.

MEDICAL ASSESSMENT

For many children and their families who are plagued by the problem of faecal incontinence, there is a high level of confusion about the physical aspects. This is due to a combination of inconsistent, conflicting and contrary opinions offered by a variety of professionals over time. This is exacerbated by the difficulty the parents and children have in chatting about the problem with friends and peers. This is a recipe for the development of damaging fantasies and unjust allocation of blame or guilt. The medical assessment is carried out with these problems in mind. In addition to obtaining a clear understanding of the pathophysiology of the child's bowel and sensory system to enable the planning of rational treatment, an honest and coherent model of the physical and psychological factor mix can be drawn up. This should be shared with the family even from the first stage in its development. In this way resistance to acknowledging the psychological or over-reliance on an *exclusively* physical, psychological or social interpretation can be reduced.

The main questions underlying the medical assessment can be summarised as:

- to what degree is faecal incontinence related to a *global delay* in achieving other developmental milestones?
- Is there evidence of a *neurological deficit in the anorectal area?*
- Is the *incontinence secondary to faecal retention* in the rectum?
- Has the child *another illness* interfering with the pattern of defaecation?
- What is the *interaction* between the *physical, psychological* and *social factors* in the causation and persistence of the soiling?

As in most medical assessments questions are explored in the standard method of obtaining a *history*, performing a *physical examination* and carrying out the minimum of laboratory or radiological *tests*. About the only advantage to the patient of having limited time and financial resources within the Health Service is the way this inevitably focuses the mind of the doctor on the most relevant areas. The ideal of asking every possible question, examining every inch of the body and leaving no possible diagnosis neglected by throwing a fistful of investigation requests forms at the child has long since been tempered by the resource restraints as much as by a more humane approach to the vulnerable child. However, this makes the doctor's job more rigorous and inevitably leads to delays in making the diagnosis of rare illnesses or illnesses presenting in an atypical fashion. This delay is usually more detrimental to future confidence of the family in the doctor than to the child's future health. This conflict between doing what is possible and doing what is wise has added to the age-old cry of the physician of knowing what is needed but being unable to supply it. These generalised challenges to the doctor are highlighted in the assessment of the soiling child where the family may be much more reluctant to accept a conclusion that the psychological aspects play a dominant role. Their wish for more and more physically based examinations and investigations may eclipse the more valuable psychosocial assessment. However, it is a wisdom to listen carefully to the opinion of parents on the health of the child as they know the child better than any professional. They have seen changes develop over time and have a clearer view of what is typical or normal for their particular family. As in all medical assessments great emphasis is put on the history as given by the child and family although this is always balanced against the reliability and consistency of these witnesses of the child's health.

Evidence of Soiling as Part of Global Delay

Here the symptoms reflect a continuum of the normal encopresis of infancy and the toddler years. The stools are of normal consistency and are deposited in the nappy or pants at about the frequency of normal defaecation (between three times per day to about every three days). Other aspects of developmental delay are usually present, namely delay in walking, speech and sophistication of play. Other problems such as urinary incontinence and convulsions may be present. Clinical examination may show features of particular illnesses (e.g. tuberous sclerosis) or syndromes (e.g. chromosomal disorders) associated with developmental delay. Usually the causes of the delay will have been sought for when the other delayed milestones were investigated as these are usually detected as part of child health surveillance in the community.

Soiling as a Result of Local Neurological Problems

It is unlikely that a child with a major spinal problem (e.g. spina bifida) will have been missed until the age that their faecal incontinence presents as a problem. Specific problems of children with these disabilities are considered in Chapter 11. However, there are subtle spinal abnormalities (e.g. partial sacral agenesis) which may go unnoticed. Any child who has a combination of urinary incontinence and faecal incontinence, especially with problems related to their walking, should have their lower spine checked. Sometimes a birthmark or large mole over the lower spine gives a clue to the deficient nerves below. The anal appearance may indicate that the anus relaxes very frequently or appears only partially closed (the normal anorectal reflex is exaggerated or unopposed in children with neurogenic rectum). In some children where the anus appears to relax very rapidly, confusion with the signs of sexual abuse can be avoided if an x-ray of the lower spine is performed.

Faecal Incontinence Secondary to Rectal Faecal Retention (Constipation)

Overflow soiling is common and leads to a great deal of confusion in both professionals and families. Unless the involuntary nature of the overflow soiling is accepted and its relationship with the often deliberate withholding of stools understood, rational management is impossible. As explained in Chapter 3, the overflow soiling results from the retained stool in the lower bowel provoking a rectal contraction which reflexly relaxes the anal sphincter, thus allowing an escape of a small amount of often soft or loose stool. The rectum contracts regularly (about every 90 seconds) and so the soiling is virtually continuous. Even if the child were to perceive the rectal contraction (which would be unlikely as it is a continual input to the brain and likely to be screened from consciousness automatically) the inability of the external anal sphincter to be deliberately contracted for more than about 30 seconds in children would make continence impossible. This swinging of the emphasis of the demands on the child from the unfair 'stop soiling' to the reasonable 'try to pass a stool on the lavatory' will only be accepted by families if the degree of faecal retention is believable. Details from the histories will provide an understanding of how and why the child began to withhold stools and how the pattern of soiling is different from that in children with more psychogenic encopresis.

If the difficulty with defaecation started around birth then a *structural* abnormality should be sought. If around weaning then *dietary* factors are usually involved. If around pot training then a mixture of *temperamental* factors in the child and parents and physical factors related to the *capacity* of the rectum is likely. Later onset constipation may be related to a major illness or family disruption which interfered with toileting regularity or food and fluid intake. At all ages any condition that produces anal discomfort or *pain* will lead a child to avoid defaecation and pain provided they have a rectum of sufficient capacity to permit the delay (otherwise they defaecate just after struggling from the pot or as they finally relax in bed or bath!). This is why it is so important to obtain details on early defaecation habits and any pointer to anal discomfort. Figure 9 illustrates the effect of the child's age on these bowel problems.

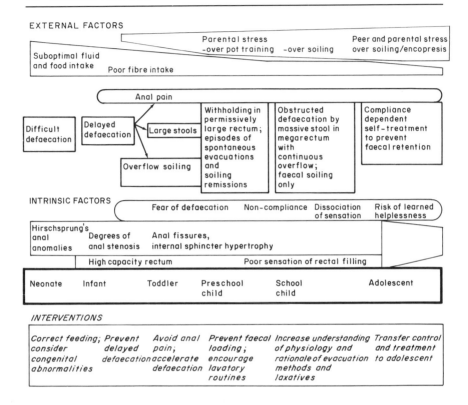

EXTERNAL FACTORS

| Suboptimal fluid and food intake | Poor fibre intake | Parental stress -over pot training | -over soiling | Peer and parental stress over soiling/encopresis |

Anal pain				
Difficult defaecation	Delayed defaecation	Large stools / Overflow soiling	Withholding in permissively large rectum; episodes of spontaneous evacuations and soiling remissions	Obstructed defaecation by massive stool in megarectum with continuous overflow; faecal soiling only	Compliance dependent self-treatment to prevent faecal retention

INTRINSIC FACTORS

| Fear of defaecation | Non-compliance | Dissociation of sensation | Risk of learned helplessness |

| Hirschsprung's anal anomalies | Degrees of anal stenosis | Anal fissures, internal sphincter hypertrophy | | |

| High capacity rectum | Poor sensation of rectal filling |

| Neonate | Infant | Toddler | Preschool child | School child | Adolescent |

INTERVENTIONS

| *Correct feeding; consider congenital abnormalities* | *Prevent delayed defaecation* | *Avoid anal pain; accelerate defaecation* | *Prevent faecal loading; encourage lavatory routines* | *Increase understanding of physiology and rationale of evacuation methods and laxatives* | *Transfer control and treatment to adolescent* |

Figure 9. The evolution and interaction of factors in chronic constipation in childhood. Reproduced from Clayden (1992) Personal practice: management of chronic constipation in children. *Arch. Dis. Child.* by permission of the British Medical Association

Once the role of anal pain in the initiation and persistence of the constipation is acknowledged any blame directed at the overflow soiling can be modified. Once the fear of anal pain is acknowledged, even the annoyance at the child's withholding behaviour can be seen as an understandable phenomenon rather than a deliberate anti-social act. This reorientation from the negative guilt/blame axis to one of sympathy and even admiration for the child's bravery in the face of pain may lift a huge shadow from the self-esteem of the child.

Physical examination does not always demonstrate an abdomen filled with rocky stools; sometimes the faecal retention is soft and many children have been treated for diarrhoea when the degree of retention has been missed. This is where a plain abdominal x-ray will be helpful

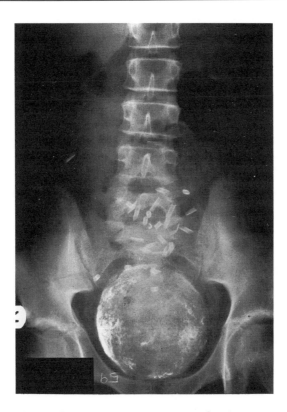

Figure 10. Abdominal x-ray in constipation. This x-ray was part of an intestinal transit study. The small radio-opaque markers are seen above the rectal faecal ball, which is outlined with barium given three months previously

in showing the rugby ball shaped rectum distended with mottled stool. This x-ray may be very convincing to sceptical parents as well as giving the child a clearer insight into the bowel problem.

The physical examination is also important to exclude other anal anomalies which might have led to the original constipation. Inspection of the anus may show that the opening is misplaced or very narrow. Often the anus appears partially relaxed or it may even reflexly dilate during the period of examination. If viewed carefully stool is usually seen high in the anal canal through this relaxed sphincter. However, if there are anal fissures and old skin tags present the appearances may be easily mistaken for those of sexual abuse. Only by reviewing all the physical signs present can a judgment be made on how seriously to take these signs. It is very unwise to jump to a conclusion of sexual abuse on the sign of reflex anal dilatation alone (Clayden 1988a, Cleveland Report 1988) but it must always be borne in mind that the original constipation may have been secondary to the anal pain of buggery.

There is debate about whether a digital per rectal (PR) examination is helpful in assessing the degree of constipation in soiling children. In children beyond infancy it may be very distressing especially when the constipation is likely to be related to anal pain. Little can be learned from a writhing child who is clenching every muscle to protect him/ herself. Abdominal inspection and palpation should make the PR unnecessary although it may be helpful in babies where the diagnosis of anal stenosis is common.

Other investigations beyond a plain abdominal x-ray are usually unnecessary unless the megarectum is very large or there is poor response to carefully timed laxative treatment. Tests such as rectal biopsy, barium enema x-ray and anorectal balloon manometry are mainly used to exclude Hirschsprung's disease, but in these cases the constipation is very severe from infancy, with poor thriving, vomiting and relatively little soiling (because the nerves mediating the anorectal reflex are absent). Anorectal manometry may be helpful in the older child to demonstrate to both child and family the degree of megarectum and the extraordinary high capacity of the rectum, as well as to provide a sensory biofeedback (see Chapter 8). Persistent constipation may result from the whole colon having poor motility and a clue for this may be obtained by giving the child radio-opaque markers to swallow and checking on an x-ray how far they have been moved by the bowel over a standard period of time. One unexpected benefit from this test has been the discovery that some older children or their parents greatly exaggerate the delay of defaecation—sometimes as a result of true Munchausen by proxy and sometimes because the symptom is too valuable for the child or family to give up. Usually the marker studies demonstrate the poor propulsion of the loaded bowel where only the loose stools can proceed to the rectum where they leak out to produce the soiling.

Soiling Associated with Other Illnesses

Another essential role of the medical assessment is the exclusion of illnesses which lead to faecal incontinence by the effect they have on the quality and frequency of the stool. If the history yields evidence of an increased frequency of defaecation especially if the stools are loose, still the most likely explanation is overflow faecal incontinence secondary to constipation ('spurious diarrhoea'). Conditions associated with poor weight gain and loose stools such as food intolerance (especially to cow's milk protein), coeliac disease (intolerance to gliadin in wheat), chronic inflammatory bowel disease (Crohn's disease or ulcerative colitis) and cystic fibrosis may lead to episodes of faecal soiling. Here the loose quality of the stool will help to distinguish these diagnoses from the more psychogenic encopresis (where by definition the stool is of a normal character). The intermittent nature of the soiling will distinguish it from chronic overflow faecal incontinence, although it should be remembered that when a massive stool is passed by a child with megarectum and severe faecal retention there is often a temporary remission in the soiling until the rectal faecal mass reforms.

The Interaction of the Factors in Faecal Incontinence

The individual child's problem is usually a complex weave of factors. Many interact and are more than additive in their distressing effect. Figure 11 shows a typical weave of factors.

It should be possible to draw up such a plan for any child with faecal incontinence although it will be necessary to emphasise certain pathways and exclude others depending on the individual's characteristics. A number of older children have successfully managed to overcome the worst of their tendency to faecal retention but still have rather poor sensation of the urgency to defaecate and are prone to encopretic accidents. This is compounded by their emotional response to this embarrassing trait—usually one of dissociation and denial. During the medical assessment it may appear very clearly that they are embarrassed about the subject and use every means possible to change the direction of the consultation. Often a careful explanation of the physiology of defaecation and how their past history of defaecation difficulty

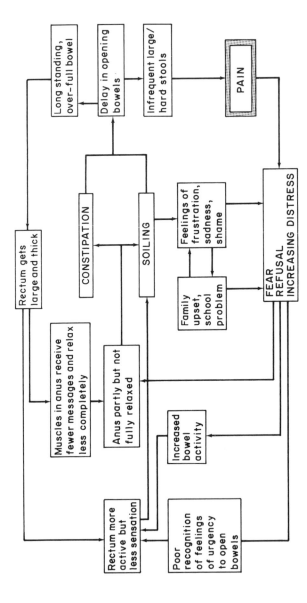

Figure 11. The interaction of factors in faecal constipation and soiling (Reproduced from Clayden & Agnarsson (1991), *Constipation in Childhood*, by permission of Oxford University Press)

still persists as a partly temporary *sensory* problem and partly *psychological hangup* is received with relief. In a similar way with encopretic children who have never been constipated, a clear explanation of the likely inattention to the rectal sensation gives them a model on which to concentrate. Sometimes anorectal manometry is helpful when these older children appear to have very little sensation. In some of the encopretic children poor rectal sensation is discovered even in the absence of evidence of megarectum or neurological deficit. Great care must be taken to ensure that children being assessed with encopresis do not perceive any examinations and investigations as a form of punishment for their incontinence for which they feel so guilty.

It can be debated whether all children with encopresis as their major symptom, as part of their psychiatric illness or psychological response to social disruption, might have a physiological predisposition. This might be an increased sensitivity of the colon to emotion or a relatively poor rectal filling and anal canal opening sensory mechanism. Part of the medical assessment is to explore whether there is any evidence for this. Most children with uncomplicated (normal stool and frequency) encopresis have such clear psychosocial reasons (chaotic training, major family disruption at pot training etc.) that it is not surprising to find no other pointers to bowel problems. However, during the medical assessment many other indicators of a chaotic, unstimulating or unfulfilling home environment (poor general hygiene, delayed speech, obesity, hyperactivity or apathy) may be discovered.

By the end of the medical assessment, the doctor should have a clear idea of how best to time and aim treatment. The child and family will rapidly lose trust and interest if the doctor does not start some potentially helpful treatment. This should be combined with a sharing with the family of the plan of factor interaction so that the treatment being started can be seen as a logical step, but only one on the way to involving other agencies if more help is necessary than the medical treatment alone. It is essential to introduce the idea of combined, parallel or collaborative work with other agencies at the onset of the treatment regime or the family may interpret suggestions to involve other colleagues later as evidence of yet another failure or rejection.

PSYCHOLOGICAL ASSESSMENT

Psychological and social assessment is not something apart from the medical assessment—in telling the doctor how the soiling problem started, the mother and child will reveal much of what they feel about the problem.

As with the physical assessment, time and resources impose limits on the range of the psychosocial assessment. The skill is finding out enough of the right kind of information.

Some possible areas for psychological investigation are:

- *Feelings and issues surrounding the soiling problem.* What does the problem mean to the child . . . how does it interfere with his lifestyle?
- *Feelings about the toilet.* What was his toilet training history? Will the child use the toilet? Has the child had any pain when defaecating in the past? Is he worried it will hurt? How does he cope with this?
- *Feelings around previous treatment.* What has been the previous treatment? What were his feelings about this?
- *Clues from the when and where of soiling.* When does he soil, where . . . does this suggest any clues as to why?
- *Behavioural/emotional other problems.* What other problems are there? bedwetting, tantrums, sleep, eating, stealing etc., emotional adjustment.
- *Interrelationship with other problems.* Are the problems interrelated?
- *Motivation.* Role of soiling in his life plan, ambitions.
- *Finding the psychological strengths.* What the child has achieved despite problems, what the child *likes* to do, what the child is good at; those who are around to help.

Feelings and Issues Surrounding the Soiling Problem

Whoever takes the initial history from the parents and child will soon have a pretty good idea where they are at 'psychologically' with the soiling problem. At one end of the scale will be the very caring mother of an 11 year old boy who maybe has mild learning difficulties and attends a special school, but who really cannot understand why the school are so worried. More usually, there is a situation of a very fraught mother with her four year old son with a huge constipated belly who 'must get him clean before he goes to school . . . they have tried everything . . . he now won't go near the toilet . . . he stands and screams . . . and then as soon as he is away from the toilet he deliberately soils his pants'. Or more poignantly the nine year old boy or girl with wasted legs and arms, large abdomen, dark circles under the eyes who looks at you with an air of total detachment, as the parent tells you how awful he or she is.

One of the first areas to consider is how the child feels about the facilities he uses.

Feelings about the Toilet

'I did not mind the toilet in the old house . . . but in this house, it has never felt quite right . . . it's cold and frightening.'

'I always wanted to do a pooh at school . . . that's the way my inside worked . . . but there was no privacy in the school toilets . . . the locks did not work . . . and they were very smelly . . . and I was frightened the other kids would see me.'

'There is this monster which comes right out of the hole and grabs you.'

Some children have strong often quite illogical fears about their toilet facilities. If a therapist visits the home, it is possible to ask the child to show you his home toilet and to get him to tell you what is special about it. Deep-rooted fears about using school toilets are very common. Indeed some children manage to survive without ever using them. There may also be negative feelings about their previous treatment experiences.

Feelings around Previous Treatment

'Jenny hid under the stairs as I arrived . . . I could just catch a look of real terror in her face . . . 'Yes I told her you had come about her soiling,' said her mother . . . 'she thinks you are a bomb lady . . . when she went to hospital before they used to give her "bombs" to make her go.'

'He won't talk to you . . . he just fed to the teeth with the whole D . . . N thing. He had three periods in hospital of several months each . . . and every sort of investigation . . . he just wants to be left alone.'

'He hated the Senokot . . . it gave him such tummy cramps' . . . or 'He never took the medicine . . . he did not like the taste . . . but we did not like to tell the doctor.'

'We tried all that gold star stuff . . . it did not work.'

If previous treatment failures are not to be replicated, it is important to know the previous history. Parents and children are usually willing to tell you about their previous experiences. Further information can be gained by asking when and where the child soils.

Clues from the When and Where of Soiling

'Timmy always soiled on the way home . . . his mother then assumed it was deliberate and was furious with him . . . which made him more nervous and more likely to soil. In fact the real problem was that he hated the school toilets and used to avoid using them . . . however as soon as he got on his bike to would lose control and mess.'

'Josie never soiled in the day . . . nor did she soil when she stayed with her grandmother, nor did she soil when she stayed with a friend . . . indeed the soiling only started when Mother's boyfriend moved in. He had recently been released from prison after serving a sentence for a sexual offence.'

These quotations illustrate that the when and where of soiling can indicate quite different psychological causes for the problem which might suggest quite different treatment routes. As is suggested in the above, whens and wheres can also be the key to identifying possible sexual abuse. This is of course something that will also be on the doctor's physical assessment agenda. Behavioural and emotional problems may also reveal important clues for treatment priorities.

Behavioural/Emotional and Other Problems

'When he is all bunged up, he is a real bastard and has terrible tantrums . . . you can always tell when his inside is not working . . .'

'We can cope with the soiling, but it is the tantrums that tears us apart.'

'He has always been a quiet boy . . . this soiling has made him even more withdrawn.'

'We have these awful battles over eating . . . I am worried people will think I am starving him.'

'He has always had this jealousy of his sister and they fight like cats and dogs.'

Here again it is important to be aware of other problems. Questionnaires such as the Rutter 'A' or the Pre-School Behaviour Check List (Rutter 1965) are a simple way to elicit the whole spectrum of possible problems. Some of these problems may be quite unrelated to the soiling and need help in their own right. Others, however, such as the tantrums, generalised 'miserable' behaviour and eating problems can be directly related to an overloaded bowel. Behaviour can improve miraculously as the condition of the child's bowel improves. Behaviour problems, however, can rarely be separated from other events in a child's life.

Interrelationship with Other Problems

'While I was trying to train him, his grandfather died and I was very depressed and that may have affected him.'

'We were in the army and never stopped moving in those early years . . . none of us felt settled . . . we are not sure now whether we will be staying here.'

'It started after John, the lodger, left the family for his homosexual lover.'

A soiling problem may be interrelated with other problems. You can often get a clue about these issues by asking the parent what started the problem. Their interpretation is rarely the whole picture, but is usually an important factor. For example, soiling in a child is common after a family bereavement. This can affect the child in two ways: either directly, through their own grief for someone they were fond of, or indirectly, living with a parent who is depressed and grieving. Again possible sexual abuse can be suggested by the timing of other events. Finally the most important part of the psychological assessment is to consider the child's motivation.

Motivation

Opening a channel of communication with a child is an essential part of assessment. One way of doing this is to take along some felt pens and then invite instructions from the child on how to draw key people in his life. As you draw, with your eyes firmly focused on your task, the child's instructions usually give a vivid snapshot of the world as he sees it.

The most crucial aspect of assessment is the child's present attitude to his problem. Does he want to do anything about his soiling? Are he and his family quite happy about the situation and have they only come to see you to please the school authorities? Is the child so alienated by previous treatment that he is quite unwilling to talk about his soiling? It is very easy for a therapist to say that he/she cannot help a child or his family because they are not motivated. It is the task of assessment to find out *why* the child (and his family) are not motivated. Very few if any children want to soil themselves deliberately despite what they and their parents may say. The task of assessment is to get inside the child's 'mocassins' to try and see how the outside world appears to him; then to find a way to change his perception of the world, so that he feels he can do something to help himself. With an older child it may also be important to help the child look beyond the immediate issues. What is his driving ambition, what are his life plans, and where does soiling fit into all these? With one very alienated 14 year old soiler, it was the possible advent of women in his life which was the motivator for change. As in this case the best motivator is using the child's strengths (in this case what he *wanted* to do was make himself presentable enough to win a girlfriend) in order to meet his needs.

Finding the Psychological Strengths

> Parents come to you with the agony of the problem, and very often their first agenda is to enlist your support on how awful things are for them. Having listened, you may have to explain that in order to help them and their child, you need to know what their child has achieved, what he likes to do, and what he is good at, because anything you do is likely to be more successful if it builds on his existing strengths. The beginning of a successful treatment programme can often be achieved by relaying back to the child this parental list of his positives.

Apart from breaking into the child's 'learned helplessness' and enlisting his motivation to work on his problem, it is important to assess the child's strengths in order to focus any future behavioural programme accurately.

This is an outline of factors which may be relevant in the psychological assessment. Some of these factors may be inseparably linked with issues in the child's social environment.

SOCIAL ASSESSMENT

Below is a list of items which it may be relevant to cover in a social assessment. Parents are very sensitive to any suggestion of blame and indeed it is important to enlist their cooperation by creating a no-blame ethos. Parents also have a right for their privacy to be respected as far as possible. However, children do not live in a social vacuum, and in the on-going assessment it may well be necessary to discover more about their social circumstances in order to find clues as to how they may be helped.

- *Family relationships.* Level of tension in mother, family motivation, mental illness in parent, family stresses, relationship between parents.
- *Sibling relationships.* Teasing from brothers and sisters, relationships between siblings.
- *Factors relating to school.* Progress; teasing; reluctance to go to school; periods off school.
- *Social relationships.* How does the child get on with other children, best friends, worst friends.

- *Wider network.* Supportive grannies, aunties, friends etc.
- *Risk of physical abuse.* What indicators are there that the child may be at risk?
- *Sexual abuse.* Could this be a factor?
- *Social needs.* Money/benefits, transport, housing.
- *Diet.* Likes, dislikes, excesses.
- *Toilets.* Access to both at home and at school.
- *Practical needs.* Washing machines, drying facilities.
- *Clean-up routine.* Who does it and how.
- *Social strengths.* What the family have achieved in the past, despite difficulties, what the family likes doing. What they are good at; any special skills they may have; any supportive people around, any special resources.

Family Relationships

'Johnnie's soiling dominated all our lives . . . when he was doing OK, all the family were doing OK. When he was messing we were all at each other's throats.'

High levels of tension, particularly in mothers of soiling children, are very common. In the long term any social assessment needs to sort out whether poor family relationships are secondary or primary to the child's soiling. If they are secondary these will improve as the child becomes clean. Initially it is better to assume that they are secondary. As the family become better known, it may become apparent that other family problems such as alcoholism, mental illness or learning difficulties in a parent are part of the jigsaw. As we will see in the next chapter, clinicians have to be realistic about what can be changed and what is unlikely to change. Difficulties with sibling relationships may also be relevant.

Sibling Relationships

'Tim would never have anything to do with Tom . . . He smelt . . . he was desperately ashamed of him . . . indeed to prove he was not his brother, he would lead the bullying gangs at school.'

In most families brothers and sisters are supportive of each other at least against the outside world. Siblings, however, can be very reject-ing of a soiling brother or sister, and blame them for their smelliness. A simple word from a clinician that the brother or sister has a genuine problem with his/her inside and has no control over his/her soiling can change sibling attitudes dramatically. Very occasionally there are difficult sibling relationships which pre-date the soiling. In stepfamilies, for instance, existing siblings may be very rejecting of the new member, which may be a factor in a child's soiling problem. But problems may not be in the home.

Factors Relating to School

'Tim would cower under the table when it was time to go to school. It was understandable that he had a hard time there because he was a bit poohey. But in the end it was more than that. He had missed an important period in school when he had been to hospital and somehow he never caught up. It was not that he was unintelligent, but his lack of confidence got in the way of progress.'

School is a major part of any child's life. There may be no relationship between a soiling problem and school, but if a child soils in school there is likely to be some teasing. Some children and parents go to enormous lengths to avoid the school learning about their problem and this has to be respected. However, in some cases, as illustrated above, the problems the child has in his school work may interact with the bowel problem. If teachers are concerned about the soiling, it is usually better to encourage the school to have a meeting to look at the overall picture. Long periods off school for whatever reason can crucially interrupt a child's learning and affect future progress. Just as school can be a positive or negative influence, so can the child's relationships within his social network.

Social Relationships/Wider Network

'Gerry hated his special school and had no friends there. But at home he was popular with the neighbourhood lads and was respected as a skilled BMX biker.'

'Gran was much more patient with Sally than Mum was. When Sally went to Gran in the long summer holidays for two weeks, her soiling improved dramatically.'

In long term cases, clues to a way forward can be suggested by finding out more about the child's social life outside the school, as the first case illustrates. This boy only became motivated to take control of his soiling problem when he left the hated special school and went to college. In long term cases, clues for ways to break patterns can also be found by discovering the family's wider network. In Sally's case regular weekend stays with Granny kept the soiling problem within manageable limits, and may have prevented the child experiencing possible physical abuse. Unfortunately an alertness to this possibility has always to be on the agenda.

Physical Abuse and Sexual Abuse

> 'Last night Bobby really got to me . . . he just stood in front of me and soiled. I am sure it was deliberate . . . I just flipped . . . if my husband had not pulled me off him, I really would have done him an injury.'

Although in the author's study, two-thirds of the mothers were recognised as being very tense, there was only professional concern that the child may be at risk in any way in a third of the families (Buchanan 1990). However, this is still a substantial proportion. Risk factors in physical and sexual abuse are examined in detail in Chapter 13. Generally speaking the risk of physical abuse is higher if there has already been an injury; if the parent feels the soiling is deliberate and if there are other stresses. It is important to assess the risk of possible physical abuse at the initial interview and act accordingly to protect the child. With many families the risk will be less by the very fact they have been supported and given hope at this initial interview.

> 'Tim started soiling when he went to the unit by taxi. He later disclosed that the taxi man used to play around with him. In the end it was discovered that it was much more than this. It was no wonder he was soiled when he arrived at school.'

The clinician needs to be alert for signs for possible sexual abuse. The above situation only came to light by accident when another child complained about the same taxi driver. It has also to be remembered that because some indicators can be acquired quite innocently there is a danger of misdiagnosis (Buchanan 1989). With possible sexual abuse, there is rarely the same urgency as with physical abuse. In my experience disclosures are rare. More usually a gradual suspicion builds up that sexual abuse may be a factor. These children can often quite legitimately be admitted into hospital for further investigations for their soiling. It needs to be remembered that a note 'querying sexual abuse' on a child's record can dominate any future investigations.

Finally, when there are so many other issues, it is easy to become out of touch with the practical issues.

Social Needs

'They kept making us go up to the clinic and discuss our family problems. All I really wanted was a washing machine for washing his messed gear.'

'Once we moved out of the caravan into a proper house, Jamie got a lot better.'

'I didn't attend the appointments at the hospital because it was just too difficult. I think they thought I was a bad mother, but have you ever tried taking three children under five on a two hour journey with three bus changes there and back?'

'Once I got the special allowance to pay for the washing I felt a lot better about things.'

The above quotes speak for themselves. it is easy in assessment to overlook the obvious. Parents will often tell us but we need to listen. A child's diet is another area which needs investigation.

Diet

'We made this jam out of prunes and Senokot. He never looked back after that.'

'He just drinks and drinks gallons of milk. I wonder if this has anything to do with it?'

'They said he just had to have a spoonful of bran at every meal. I tried to get it down him . . . but now he won't eat anything.'

'The spoon stand up in his cup because he has so much sugar in it . . . and he eats sweets until they come out of his ears.'

In the author's study, all children were given a record sheet to complete on what they ate for one week. This provided a useful assessment tool, and is to be recommended. Not only could it be seen which foods the child ate to excess, but it also gave the clinician a clue about high fibre foods that were acceptable to the child. Forcing children to eat what they did not like could have serious results. Some children had developed eating problems where parents had been too enthusiastic in persuading the child to eat extra fibre.

Another obvious factor which can easily be overlooked in assessment is the child's access to toilets.

Toilets

'There were ten of us in the family. Although there were two toilets only one really worked. That meant that poor Johnny was always at the end of the queue in the morning . . . because of the rush he never got a chance to go.'

'Jeff's problem seemed to start when his dad was altering the bathroom and we had a portaloo for several months.'

'The school was purpose-built. Although it had five facilities for one hundred boys only one was a sit-down.'

'No-one in school was allowed out of class to go to the toilet. What they did not know was that Kevin could not wait. When he wanted to go, he had to get up there and then.'

We have already discussed the psychological fears that children may have concerning their facilities. More directly it needs to be checked that the child does in fact *have* ready access to a toilet, and in school is allowed to absent himself without too much explanation.

Practical Needs/Clean-up Routines

Cleaning up a soiled child is a miserable business. It is valuable to know what facilities parents have for washing/drying. Whether they need extra money to buy new bedding or clothing for the child. It is also useful to enquire who does the cleaning up. Even quite young children can be trained to clean themselves. This can considerably relieve the pressures on the child.

It is easy in assessment to become swamped by the concerns. A positive effort has to be made to establish the strengths.

Strengths in the Social Circumstances

'Tim used to go to the cubs every week. But when it came to camp his mother felt he could not go because of his problem. But Tim wanted to go very badly . . . so it was left to him to work it out . . . and he did. Although he soiled every night no one knew not even the boys in his tent.'

Strengths are not only what the child likes to do, wants to do, and is capable of achieving, but also those people or events which can help. In this case membership of the cubs proved a very positive experience, and the cub master, even though he never knew it, did much to improve this child's confidence and indirectly his soiling problem.

Finally it is important not to forget the child and his family.

What the Child Wants—What the Parents Want

The final objective of an assessment is to find out what the child and parents want. Very few if any children want to mess themselves. They want to be clean but may not be willing to pay the price in effort and stress that it will take to become clean. Many pretend that they are not bothered by it, as a defence because they have effectively learnt there is not much they can do. Some long term soilers would rather put up with the inconvenience of the mess (the smell of their own defaecation is less offensive to them than to others) than cope with the stresses involved in further treatment procedures.

All parents want their child to stop soiling. For them, there are generally no halfway measures. It has to be total cure.

Unfortunately, the reality is that whatever treatment is involved, around a third of all soilers referred will continue to have soiling episodes throughout middle childhood. The starting point is therefore an ethos of hope, tempered by the reality that setbacks are the nature of the beast. This message has to come at the initial interview. Thereafter the assessment process is a process of negotiation to discover from both the parents and child what small steps would to their way of thinking constitute progress. Sometimes a mother will say that if the child puts his dirty pants in the set place, that would make a difference

. . . Or a child will say he will try a toilet routine as long as he does not have to eat spoonfuls of the hated bran. The steps need to be achievable. Sometimes, if there are strong feelings around the soiling, parents and children may need to focus their first achievement steps on matters right away from the defaecation issues, . . . such as the child getting his clothes ready for school each morning.

Something to Go Away and Do

After the initial interview parents and child should go away with a resolve that they want to start doing something. The clinician needs information about how often the child soils and how often he uses the toilet, before he can move forward; he may also want information about what the child is eating. But it is very important not to lose the family's initial momentum. Before the next interview the family need to have achieved something which takes them one small step forward to 'cure'. We will look at some of the possible steps in the next chapter.

CHAPTER 8   Principles and process of treatment*

Following an assessment the clinician is in a position to formulate the problem. A formulation should consist of the main presenting features, a diagnosis, and indication of the probable causes, an opinion concerning desirable management, and a view on outcome. (Graham 1986, p. 17).

In order to make plans to help . . . we need to know just what a person can do, and what sort of things are a problem to them. This is called making an assessment of the person's strengths and needs. . . . If we carefully complete a strengths–needs list . . . we will have almost all the information necessary to write a goal-plan for the person concerned. (Barrowclough and Fleming 1986)

In an early study on child abuse by the author (Oliver & Buchanan 1979), an account was made of the number of medical and social 'assessments' undertaken on a group of abused children, and compared with the rate of child abuse incidents over the same period. The study demonstrated that the rate of child abuse incidents did not decrease, and it was felt this may have been because the assessments were seen as an end in themselves; no plan to remedy the issues followed.

Medicine has a clearly defined route from assessment to treatment, but this route is harder to follow when moving away from the 'disease' model into disorders which have more of a social bias. Social work and the allied professions have in recent years been forced to become much clearer about what their objectives are in making social interventions, and are now developing expertise in this field. As Philip Graham notes (1986) 'Professionals however broad and comprehensive their own approach, need to be aware of what other groups of professionals have to offer . . . one agreed principle of therapy . . . is that it is desirable for all doctors working with children to have ready access to colleagues with skills in psychology and social work.'

---

*The section on *The Medical Priorities for Treatment* in this chapter is by Dr Graham Clayden.

In this chapter we move from assessment into making treatment plans for soiling children. We will first consider the principles which underlie the treatment approach, before moving on to consider the treatment process. As in the last chapter, the medical sections of the treatment approach have been written by Dr Graham Clayden. Finally we will see how the principles and process of treatment work in practice. The focus of this chapter is on the initial treatment approach following assessment for the new referral with a soiling problem. With careful treatment the author's research demonstrated that over 70% of soiling children could in a reasonably short space of time make a good response. Chapter 9 will focus on the overall 'management' of the disorder.

Principles of Treatment (the Ethos)

The early medical practitioners knew that all treatment was in effect psychological and that confidence in the practitioner and his medications, be they only placebos, had considerable curative qualities. The author's research (Buchanan 1990) has shown that with soiling children, the therapist needs to present a strong message of professional competence to 'empower' the child and his family to break out of their cycle of learned helplessness. 'Empowering' means involving children in the decisions that affect their lives, and involving the parents in supporting these decisions. This process would have started at the initial assessment interview, as we have already mentioned, but needs to be carried forward by all those involved in the therapeutic process. As we saw in Chapter 6 the other important attributes in the ethos of the approach were:

- No blame. Soiling is a common problem with many causes.
- Empowering the child: giving back to the child the responsibility for his own bowels.
- Educating him about his problem . . . breaking into learned helplessness.
- An approach that focuses on *positives* as well as *needs*.
- An approach with builds into treatment the expectation that relapses are common.

The Treatment Process

The process of treatment (Figure 12) follows from Figure 8, the assess-

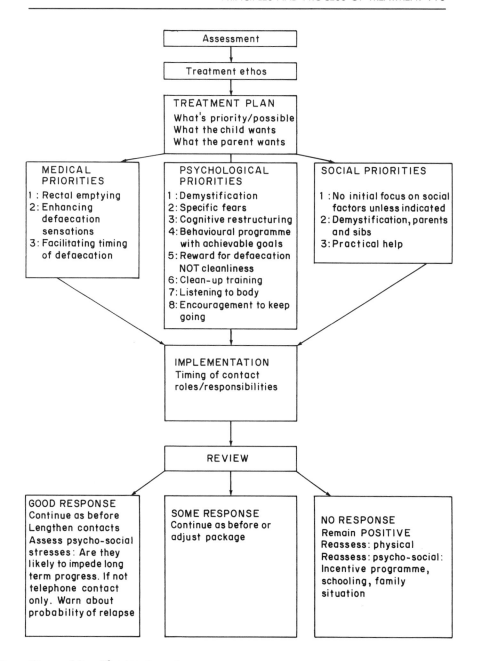

Figure 12. The treatment process

ment process, in the previous chapter. The practical aspects of implementing treatment are detailed in the following sections.

THE MEDICAL PRIORITIES FOR TREATMENT

These can be summarised as:

- Maximising the completeness of rectal emptying.
- Enhancing the sensations related to defaecation and continence.
- Facilitating the timing of defaecation.

It is obvious that the emphasis will vary according to the results of the medical assessment. There may also be a change of emphasis according to the response to treatment or the lack of it. Similarly as can be seen from Figure 9 in the previous chapter, the age of the child will affect the decisions related to treatment.

The medical treatment is ideally carried out in collaboration with those helping the child from the psychological and social direction. However, medical treatment is often started by the family on advice from neighbours, pharmacists, community nurses and doctors before a full assessment shows a better understanding of the relative roles of the physical, social and psychological factors. This may be beneficial in preventing the development of major physiological or anatomical problems, but it may lead to a loss of confidence in medication if this had been used in ineffective doses or at the wrong stage. This loss of confidence can lead to failure of compliance and ultimately to pressure to escalate medical and surgical treatment.

Rectal Emptying

Ensuring *effective rectal emptying* can be achieved by the wise use of laxatives when there is evidence that a child's soiling is secondary to faecal retention. It is important to use the laxatives in the correct order or they will fail at best or aggravate all the symptoms at worst. A simple algorithm will illustrate the factors which influence the order of the laxatives.

The order of laxatives

If there is evidence of faecal retention in the rectum then:

- use stool softener (docusate, e.g. Dioctyl paediatric syrup).

If the stool is soft but still retained in the rectum then:

- use sodium picosulphate (Laxoberal or Picolax) orally to flush out the lower bowel.

If no stools are palpable per abdomen then:

- use regular senna (Senokot syrup or senna tablets) daily in a single dose. To avoid the stools from drying up use lactulose or methyl cellulose.

If there is a tendency for constipation to recur in spite of regular senna, then:

- repeat the picosulphate weekly (at weekends as the accelerated stools may be even more difficult to control than the child's usual stools).

If the docusate softening and picosulphate evacuation methods are insufficient to shift the megastool: a decision whether to use enemas (with or without sedation, e.g. temazepam) or to request a manual evacuation of the retained stool under anaesthetic will need to be made. This will depend on the severity of the faecal loading and the ability of the child to understand the use of enemas and preferably to cooperate and help in its administration.

The use of regular laxatives for many months following an evacuation of a large retained faecal mass is essential if a disappointing relapse is to be avoided.

It may be helpful to give some details on the mode of action of some of the treatment methods mentioned above.

Docusate acts like a detergent by reducing the surface tension and so allows the stool to absorb water and gradually become eroded. It acts rather like the bile salts which the body makes naturally (and which lead to diarrhoea if present in excess). It is surprising to note that the ancient Arabic physicians thought that the lower bowel sensed the need to defaecate by bowel 'tasting' the presence of bile in the stool locally (Cameron-Gruner 1930).

Sodium picosulphate acts as an osmotic load on the bowel. This leads to excess fluid flushing through the intestine which hopefully sweeps the softened but retained stool ahead of it. Stronger osmotic cathartics such as polyethylene glycol 3350 or 4000 (Golytely or Klean-prep) work this way but require the child to drink such large volumes of fluid that unless given by nasogastric tube, it is unlikely that the younger child will take in sufficient fluid. It can then be argued whether an enema is less stressful than the passing of a nasogastric tube. If both are equally devastating for the child then the kinder option is an evacuation manually under anaesthetic, even though this adds the small but important risk of the anaesthetic.

Senna is a mixture of chemicals derived from the plant senna. The flowers and pods of this plant have been used for centuries. Again the intuition of the ancients is remarkable as the shape of the flowers and pods is very similar to that of the megarectum! Senna has had some bad press because of the abuse by some elderly patients who have used it to thrash their tiring bowels into unnatural activity on the grounds that it is essential to continue a regular daily bowel action throughout life. In these patients, and in some younger ones trying to lose weight by excessive purgation, changes in the nerves of the bowel have been discovered. This has not been seen in children who have been taking senna to ensure a normal bowel action.

Lactulose acts partly as an osmotic laxative and partly by producing fibre. Some of the bacteria of the gut thrive in the presence of lactulose and they add to the fibre content of the stools thus keeping them soft.

Methyl cellulose works in a similar way by holding water in the stool, preventing the drying effect of the colon and allowing a larger stool to enter the rectum.

The following is a typical treatment history in a child with overflow faecal soiling secondary to gross rectal faecal loading.

Jimmy presents with a long history of continuous soiling in his pants. His parents cannot remember him ever going longer than a day with clean pants since being out of nappies. On examination he has faecal lumps palpable to just above his umbilicus and obvious soiling around a normal looking anus. An abdominal x-ray confirms the loading. He is given *docusate* three times a day for two weeks which helps with the colicky pains he had been having, as he had previously been on syrup of figs as suggested by his maternal grandmother. The soiling is worse rather than better although the family had been warned of this effect and so had taken precautions (provided small pads and checked that he could change frequently in the staff lavatory at school). He had a dose of *picosulphate* on the Saturday of the second week of *docusate* and a repeat dose in six hours as nothing appeared to happen. At about 6 p.m. rushing from the football results and just reaching the lavatory, he passed such a large stool that the plumbers had to be called in. He and his parents were amazed by the lack of soiling on the Sunday and decided that he was cured and did not take the *senna* and *methyl cellulose* recommended. Five days of clean pants did not disguise the fact that he had not passed a stool since the preceding Saturday and he suggested that he should take another dose of *picosulphate*. Fortunately this worked and he managed to pass the six day accumulation and then go about alternate days when on a large nightly dose of senna and twice daily dose of *methyl cellulose*. He progressed very well with some soiling if there was a delay in defaecation (usually when he had forgotten to take his *senna*). Unfortunately his dog was run over and he had a major relapse. The parents tried the same regime but it failed to move the ever increasing mass. An *evacuation under anaesthetic* was recommended as the doctors felt that the mass was too large to pass without such pain that it would greatly add to the distress he was already in about his dog. He re-established back onto *senna, methyl cellulose* and a weekend dose of *picosulphate*. Over the next year he had to reduce the dose of *senna* as he was finding the urgency of defaecation too inconvenient. After 14 months he had weaned off *senna* but still took *methyl cellulose* ('to be on the safe side' he and his mother said). His only minor relapse in the following year had been precipitated by a build up of stools caused by unwisely using a cough linctus which contained a codeine mixture, which is notorious for leading to constipation.

Sometimes the frequency of relapses in faecal retention indicates that the rectum is so large and overactive that an anal dilatation under the same anaesthetic as an evacuation is performed. This can be helpful in reducing the excessive activity of the anal sphincter and the necessity of a high rectal volume being required before the stool can descend.

Enhancing the Sensations Related to Defaecation and Continence

If the child has little evidence of faecal retention as a cause for the soiling, expecially if the type of incontinence has the character of encopresis (normal stools in abnormal places), medication has little to offer. The exception is when the child has poor sensation of rectal filling. This may be a late effect of constipation and megarectum where the child has successfully overcome the retention but is still left with the inefficient sensation or partially blocked perception. Sometimes by increasing the size of the stool, sufficient sensation is achieved to improve continence. Methyl cellulose may be helpful in this way. If medication has little to offer there may be more help from technology in the form of biofeedback. If a child has confusion about what sensations to react to, or if he/she is uncertain whether there is effective sensation, anorectal manometry may be helpful. Here a small balloon is inserted into the rectum and the child watches the pressure changes as displayed on the computer screen. He/she then tries to connect the sensations and these changes. This can only have value if the child fully understands and cooperates with the manoeuvre, and it is therefore rarely used in the younger child, and especially not in those with a lasting fear of anal procedures or where it is uncertain whether the child understands what is expected.

Facilitating the Timing of Defaecation

Sometimes it is possible with a judicious use of senna to provoke the passage of a stool at a time convenient for the child. Probably the best time is about 4.30 p.m. when the child can relax after school and after having had a snack to provoke a useful gastrocolic-colorectal-rectoanal reflex. Many attempts to get the timing right must be expected, but some children have found this helpful. It probably works best in those who have or who have had some degree of faecal retention, but this is sometimes difficult to assess. The families must be warned that their early experiments with dosage may lead to sudden and dramatic explosions and so they should always try a low dose initially and avoid important social events.

PSYCHOLOGICAL PRIORITIES IN TREATMENT

The psychological priority is to motivate the child to understand his problem and take control of it. In order to take control of his problem the child will need to establish regular habits, and to recognise and respond promptly to any bodily signals of impending defaecation. Evidence suggests that once a child discovers it is possible (that is, when the physical condition of his bowels is managed effectively), most children will eventually become clean through regular toileting and prompt response to any defaecation 'urges'. In teaching children it is important they are *not to be rewarded for being clean*. This will only result in the child retaining stools and building up further retention. A second aim of psychological treatment is to ensure that while the child is still soiling, he maintains a reasonable level of self-esteem.

Getting Started: Using a Behavioural Approach

If after the initial assessment, a behavioral approach is indicated, it is important to get started without delay. The timing of follow-up appointments, and where these are to take place, will also have to be decided. With young children, follow-up appointments for the behavioural programme need to be *at least* every two weeks in the initial stages, and preferably after school.

Managing Specific Fears

During assessment any fears a child may have about his previous treatment and/or fears about toilet facilities would have been elicited. If, for example, a child was very distressed by previous suppository treatment, this should not be the treatment of choice the second time around. Similarly if a child resented previous programmes using star charts, a different behavioural approach would be indicated on referral to a new agency.

Where a child has specific fears about using a toilet, behavioural principles can be applied. For example, with younger children of pot-refusal age, there are now a range of musical pots, or toilet seats which can be 'rewarding' to use. With young children with chronic pot-refusal, the first stage may have to be rewarding actual defaecation in nappies. The purpose of such a programme needs to be explained very carefully to mothers, who may have inadvertently reinforced the retention behaviour by over-chastisement for soiling.

With older children who have toilet phobias, adaptations may be made to the lighting, the warmth, the locks or whatever it is in the toilet which makes it frightening or unacceptable to the child.

Setting up Behavioural Programmes

In setting up programmes, the first step is to discover when, where and how often the child defaecates. With all soiling children it is counter-productive to set up a programme to establish regular toileting before constipation is under control. Parents may be very forceful to get things started, but these pressures need to be resisted, because it is crucially important that the child can achieve some success in the early stages of a behavioural programme, however limited and this is unlikely to happen without careful assessment. Assessment of the child's *strengths*, that is what he likes to do, what he is good at, what he has achieved in the past, and those people he likes to have around to help him, all help in planning. The programme needs to be 'owned' by the child. This means he needs to have a part in setting it up, deciding priorities, drawing or colouring the document. Programmes also need to be levelled at the right developmental stage. Preschool children, for example, have little concept of the value of stars, as in star charts, so sweets or even 'smiley faces', i.e. circle stickers with a drawn smiling face perhaps representing mother, are much more meaningful to them. With a child who has learning difficulties, care has to be taken to focus the programme at the right developmental level, as well as at a level that is age appropriate, whereas with children who are negative about their toileting, or who have failed a previous programme focused on toileting, it is better to focus on other achievements in their lives. In these cases it will be necessary to explain to parents that success in either areas will contribute to solving bowel problems. Some primary school age children enjoy keeping a record of their school achievements and setting themselves challenges for the next month. In time further challenges can be added; for example, things they would like to achieve in the home and finally things they would like to achieve with their soiling problems. The children usually like to display these charts in their rooms. With younger children, a 'getting ready for school in the morning' plan can help them learn that they do have some control over their lives and that their mother will be less rushed and stressed if they do their part. These 'contracts' can be drawn with simple pictures for the pre-reader.

Children with extensive behavioural and emotional problems benefit from careful assessment. Whether these problems are primary or secondary to the soiling may not be apparent until the family are seen together.

It is known that many emotional and behavioural problems alleviate once the soiling disappears (Buchanan 1990), and in the early stages of treatment it may be better to assume that they are part of the soiling problem. But where there is a sleep problem in a preschool child, it makes sense to focus on this, on the grounds that a tired child is likely to be a difficult child and a tired mother is likely to be less patient with that child.

If the child already uses the toilet for defaecation and there are no particular fears, it may be possible to focus directly on a toileting routine. But defaecation targets must be set well below what the child can already achieve. For instance, if the child achieves on average four defaecations in the toilet per week, the first programme would focus on one. As the child makes progress, the targets can gradually be increased, but care must be taken to be alert to other events in the child's life. For instance, during holidays away from home, during Christmas, or during periods of illness, the child may be less responsive. When setting up programmes it helps to link these to the child's special interests. A football chart, adapted for sticking favourite football stars in place, may be a motivating influence on a child who is keen on football. Creativity will be rewarded. Star charts are effective, but a chart more linked to the child's interest is likely to be more effective. Children easily tire of charts so regular changes need to be made. One of the most effective charts used by the author was an Advent calendar type picture of a Snoopy dog, which the child gradually opened as he established a bowel routine. The parents of this child had promised the young person a dog. He had had numerous periods of being clean and then relapsing. The Snoopy dog finally achieved its goal over a six month period.

Behavioural programmes can be reinforced by running a 'covert' club of soiling children. With children's permission first names are passed around to soiling children by the therapist who donates sticker prizes for the children who do best, and gives out 'winner of the month' club cards. Another technique that has been used is awarding children 'Grade' certificates. With one group of children the author outlined the grades young children had to go through before overcoming their disorder. Included in these grades were relapses, so that children felt they were not making good progress until they had had at least one relapse. In monitoring all behavioural programmes, the therapist's

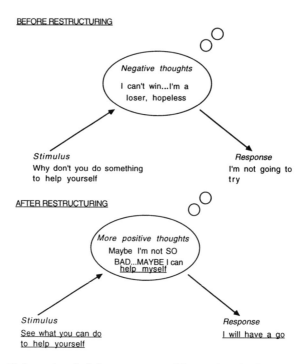

Figure 13. Unlearning helplessness: cognitive restructuring

own enthusiasm and encouragement is an important part of treatment.

Cognitive Restructuring

One of the first tasks for the therapist is to help the child view himself more positively. 'Cognitive restructuring' is the technical name for the method used. Cognitive behavioural approaches, as we saw in Chapter 6, were developed by Beck (1970) and others to break into a person's irrational thoughts and 'learned helplessness' (Seligman 1975). Figure 13 demonstrates the process.

The task of the therapist is to help the child replace the negative thoughts, which block the normal response to the stimulus, with more positive ones. This can be done either informally or formally. Most therapists informally help a child think more positively about himself, not only through what they say to a child, for example remarking on something he does well, but also by how they show him respect and seek his opinions.

Formal cognitive restructuring can be done in a number of ways. A behavioural programme where the child is certain to achieve a positive result not only achieves its behavioural objectives but also helps the child's self-esteem. With older children it is possible to undertake formal programmes which help the young person to look at his thought processes and replace the irrational thoughts with more rational ones (Beck 1970). This approach, in the author's clinical practice, was effective with a young person who having overcome his soiling problem became depressed in adolescence about other issues. In order to change the negative thoughts that a child may be thinking about himself, it is necessary to find out what these are. With younger children drawing can be an effective medium. With older children there are now a number of checklists to which children can reply with a tick to a number of statements, such as 'I get on very well with my parents' or 'My parents are never happy with me' (Porteus Problem Checklist).

Following up the Behavioural Programme

With behavioural programmes, if they do not work, it is not the therapy that is wrong, but the programme. Having said that, every care needs be taken to ensure that the child does make progress in the first stages, for it is considerably easier to follow on from a success than a failure.

In therapy, it may be important for the therapist to 'reframe' a child's early responses. For example, a child who has for the first time achieved a bowel motion in the toilet may be reported by his mother as having completely failed because he only managed to do what he was supposed to do, once. If the therapist 'reframes' this to 'good progress, at this stage of treatment', as indeed it would be, the child may feel more encouraged to continue.

The response to the initial programme is a good indicator of future progress. If there is a response no matter how small it is worth while continuing in the same vein. If, however, the programme has not gone well changes need to be made. Parents may have failed to keep the chart. In this case it is a good idea to give the responsibility to the child, while asking the parent to check that it is correct. Sometimes parents have slipped in a few black 'stars' for soiling days, or removed stickers from the chart. In front of the child it is helpful to tell the parents that removing rewards or black 'stars' are not allowed. Later, in privacy, you may have to explain the theory behind this. Some young children may not have responded because they prefer a challenge, rather than a reward: 'Do you think you are clever enough?' In this case any task given is well within the child's ability. Siblings can be used to inspire competition. In these cases each sibling is given a task, which can be different for each child. It may be that there are other issues that sabotage a programme. In the author's study one child went off to a childminder every day, who used to fill in the chart whether or not the task had been undertaken. In another case, a child conscientiously rewarded himself for a daily defaecation, but it was not until some weeks later, when he had to be admitted to hospital for a wash-out, that it was learned that his reported success was far removed from his actual performance.

Teaching a Child to Respond to his Bodily Signals

As mentioned in Chapter 5, some clinicians are using biofeedback techniques to establish regular toilet habits (Olness et al. 1980). Many children with soiling problems have little warning of impending defaecation. That is, they have little warning from the rectum or anus, but in the author's study some children learned to recognise other warning signs—very often in the form of pain in the upper abdomen, which would indicate that a motion was on its way. All children were from the start of therapy instucted to 'listen' to their bodies, and never delay going to the toilet. 'Go like a rocket' accompanied by a suitable drawing of 'Superman' was the usual instruction on their programmes. Younger children would be asked to demonstrate how they would respond in such circumstances, and would take pleasure in imitating a Superman rushing sound.

Training in Cleaning Up

In the author's study, early in therapy, all children were given practical training in clean-up techniques. Children were also advised to take a 'survival' pack to school, involving 'wet wipes' for the clean-up and a spare pair of pants and plastic bag for the soiled ones. This practical help did much to take the pressure off the child from parents who found it disgusting to deal with the daily soiled linen, as well as giving the therapist credibility with the parents.

Parental Cooperation

In setting up any programmes with children, it is important that parents are metaphorically taken with you. The author's research demonstrated that where parents did not understand the purpose of the programme or for one reason or another did not wish it to succeed, they could be very effective at sabotaging any progress. Sometimes parents have their own complex reasons for wanting a child to fail, or for wanting the therapist to fail. It may be there is a need to 'scapegoat' the child. If this is a major problem a focus on these relationship difficulties may be more effective than any behavioural programme.

Keeping Going

Once the child has made some progress in regular toileting, the first difficult phase has been overcome. The next stage is to keep going. As a general rule, the longer a child has been soiling and the more constipated the child was at the start of the treatment, the longer it will take to become totally clean and to stay clean. There is a temptation to assume once the child has had two clean weeks or even two months, that the problem has been overcome for ever. This, as the author's research demonstrated (Buchanan 1990), is rarely so. Both the parents and child need to be reminded of this. The task of the therapist is to keep the child sufficiently interested so that he consciously maintains his routine over at least a six month period. At this stage telephone contact can be a useful means of following up between visits, as long as the therapist can also talk to the child. In the longer term, the child will need training in the future management of his condition, and advice on how to respond to relapses.

SOCIAL PRIORITIES FOR
TREATMENT

In the initial stages of treatment, there would usually be no specific focus on social issues. If at a later stage, it becomes apparent that the child is unlikely to improve without measures to alleviate some of the stresses surrounding him, parents need to understand why this is necessary.

However, at the initial appointment, parents have often reached such a state of desperation that they express considerable frustration or even anger with their soiling child. This can be helped by 'demystification', that is understanding the mechanics of their child's problem. They may need help in coming to terms with the idea that their anger is likely to impede progress. Similarly, siblings can be unexpectedly cruel to each other. They too can benefit from 'demystification' about their sibling's difficulty.

Schooling may also be a problem for the child. In these cases the therapist needs to discuss with the child and family whether contact with the school is likely to be productive.

Where there are practical needs within the family, it may be appropriate to try and meet these. For example, charities can be very generous in donating washing machines, particularly where a child has a disability.

In treating all soiling children, therapists need to be alert that some parents are so stressed by the soiling that children can be at risk of physical abuse. The possibility of sexual abuse has also to be borne in mind. These issues are dealt with in Chapter 13.

CHAPTER 9   Management*

Management: Skilfully handling (Shorter Oxford Dictionary)

In medicine the term 'management' means more than that. Following a diagnosis, 'management' of a condition is the administrative route map that the clinician follows in logical sequence, through the maze of possible further investigations and treatments. Each new direction depends on the findings of the previous journey. Management of a condition takes on a special relevance where it is known that more than one treatment approach may be necessary, or that the disorder is long term or even lifelong. In these cases good management plans incorporate not only investigations and treatments but plans to limit further damage, distress, suffering, not just in physical health, but in the quality of the 'whole person's' life. When it comes to soiling children, although we know that two-thirds will respond quite positively to initial treatment approaches, we also know that for up to one-third, a number of different treatment approaches may have to be tried. Effectively for these children, this means the soiling disorder will continue throughout middle childhood with short periods of respite, bringing with it a host of associated problems (Buchanan 1990). For this group of children good management plans for the disorder are especially important.

In this chapter we will look at the overall management of soiling in children: the management of the child's physical problems, psychological and social needs, taking into account the whole child's environment. In the final section we will look at some case histories known to the author. With these case histories, details have of course been changed to preserve anonymity.

---

*The section on *Physical Management* in this chapter is by Dr Graham Clayden.

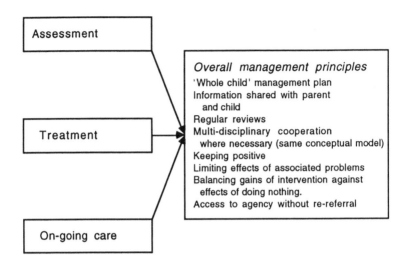

Figure 14. Management of soiling in children

Management of Soiling in Children

Figure 14 outlines priorities for the management plan. Although in this chapter there are separate sections highlighting aspects of physical, psychological and social management, it is important that there is an overall 'whole child' management plan. Where several professionals or disciplines are involved in a treatment plan, it makes sense that the doctor responsible for the physical management of the disorder coordinates management, and that all the professionals share the same conceptual mode of the child's problem.

As Graham Clayden mentions in the next section it is valuable to involve the child and his family in the management plan.

PHYSICAL MANAGEMENT

The physical management is best described as the deliberate adjusting of the interplay of the various factors which operate in a child's bowel problem. An important element in this is the recognition that this is an on-going process where evidence of effectiveness of treatment and reassessment of the diagnosis (or physical factor analysis) is continually performed. The management plan includes the schedule of treatments, the methods for documenting that treatments have been given

Dear Mrs

This is the reasoning behind some of the plans for . . . . . . 's further management. I think we will be able to help . . . . . . most effectively if we can all share a model of the interaction of the various factors involved in her condition. The following is my understanding of where we are and I would be grateful to receive suggestions on modifying this if it does not ring true to you or . . . . . . 's other professionals.

FACTORS	EFFECTS	MANAGEMENT PLAN
large capacity rectum	episodes of faecal loading and overflow incontinence	assess severity with anorectal manometry. Define effective evacuation regime
difficulty in defaecation rectum very full	irregularity in defaecation plus long duration of trying to go	anal dilatation (under anaesthetic) plus senna plus sufficient time to try in privacy
poor sensation of urgency from rectum	inefficiency of relying on normal call to stool	regular visits to loo at set times
absence of sensation of leaking	continuous soiling plus smell risk	regular checks and fresh overflow clothes
embarrassment and helplessness (of soiling)	avoidance behaviour, distractibility	involving . . . . . . in her own management and charting

Yours sincerely,

Figure 15. Letter to a parent

and the results of such treatments. It also includes a scheme of investigations with their appropriate indications. A list of future options and the indications for them is also valuable provided it can be modified in the light of progress and of the results of tests. When the interaction of various factors is complex it is worth listing the problems separately with their associated actions (treatments or tests). This can then be used as part of the interdisciplinary communication as well as being a loose contract with the child and family. Figure 15 is an example.

We have found that the majority of children and parents complete detailed diary forms (Figure 16) very effectively.

They use the sheets as reminders to give medication as well as a rapid method of feeding back the results of treatment to their doctors. In a sample of 96 families the diary sheets were analysed and the following results are shown in Table 8.

CHILDREN'S INTESTINAL MOTILITY CLINIC

Name   Sheet No.   CBNo

DATE																				
DAY	Mo	Tu	We	Th	Fr	Sa	Su	Mo	Tu	We	Th	Fr	Sa	Su	Mo	Tu	We	Th	Fr	Sa	Su
BOWELS OPEN																					
SOILING																					
OTHER																					
SENNA (SENOKOT) ml 25 20 / 1 tablet 15 / =5 mls 10 / 1 teaspn 5 / =5 mls																					
METHYL CELLULOSE (COLOGEL)																					
LACTULOSE (DUPHALAC)																					
DOCUSATE (DIOCTYL)																					
PICSULPHATE (enema, etc)																					
COMMENTS																					

Figure 16. Diary sheets

Table 8. Description of diary sheet completion by parents

Description	Frequency
Very neat with description of both stool and health	3
Complete with description of both stool and health	16
Describes stool or degree of difficulty	16
Describes health but not stool	22
Accurately completed but no extra comments	32
Incomplete with some sections missing	3
Very inaccurate and untidy	4

Part of the management is the plan of follow-up visits. Where possible outpatient visits are kept to a minimum and are used to assess any change in the child which can only be detected on examination. This minimal use of outpatient clinics is not only less expensive and, in terms of travelling and missed work, less disruptive for the family but allows a larger number of children to be seen in specialist centres when necessary. This means that specialist centres must keep in regular touch with referring doctors and with local multi-disciplinary teams. This puts a major emphasis on the need for good communication, which is often very difficult with secretarial shortages and delays. However, computer databases, telephone discussions and parent-held records improve share-care. The main problem in using the minimum outpatient visits is the risk that the child and family do not get to know their doctors very well and may feel very isolated at times of need. This can be offset by allocating a reasonably long period of time at their first visit and having a follow-up visit (to check progress and the results of any tests) within a few weeks. Invitations to telephone between visits can reduce the sense of isolation provided the doctor is honest about the likely timing of the reply and the likely use of answerphones. The telephone calls can be very helpful in advising modifications of medication or in setting certain deadlines for progress before starting the next stage of treatment. The centralised doctor should be careful to avoid promising an ever available service which is likely to disappoint the family when found to be slow to respond or undermine local facilities if it responds too quickly to issues beyond the bowel problem. An aid to telephone communication is a photograph of the child and family and the ability to refer to and add to the medical records during every call. (Computerised records are making this increasingly efficient.) The availability of nurse specialists who work closely with the paediatri-

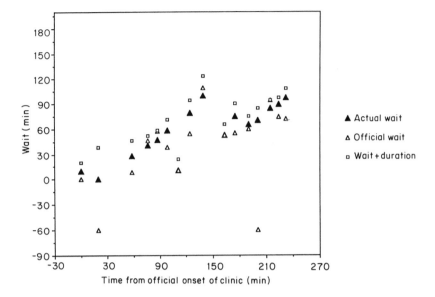

Figure 17. Waiting in children's Intestinal Motility Clinic: timing of appointments—consultation duration against clinic duration

cian greatly improves the level of advice and support. They are usually much more likely to explain the plan to the child and family at the correct pace and be available to answer questions than even the most willing clinician because of the throughput of patients in the out-patient setting. It is helpful to audit the timing of appointments and Figure 17 is an example of this.

Idealised Management Plan

The following is an idealised management plan from the paediatrician's perspective.

- Receive, read and assess referral letter.
- Allocate first visit appointment if suitable.
- Take full relevant history, examination ± x-ray.
- Explain likely interaction of the various factors and how treatments are likely to modify this.
- Provide back-up literature.
- Request that the family completes the diary sheets for progress.

- Plan further follow-up or next stage investigations.
- Offer telephone contact during gap between appointments.
- Produce letters containing conclusion and management plans to referring doctor, GP (if not referring doctor), community child health, other agencies involved with child (with parents permission—preferably using them as go-between and providing them with copy of letter).
- See child and family again in about one month.
- Review diary sheets and receive their comments and queries and feed back any test results.
- Repeat or modify management plan with child and family.
- If planning admission, define exactly why and any technical problems such as bed shortage, late cancellations, short notice which are likely to occur.
- Complete an activity plan for that admission to which all hospital staff will have access.
- Arrange for them to visit the ward prior to admission.
- Arrange post-admission visit and then outpatient visits of increasingly long intervals but maintaining telephone contact.

Although many of these stages appear self-evident many parents have suffered a great deal of anxiety or anger if they are not followed and arrangements have been confused. Throughout these visits opportunities to meet other members of the team are maximised to reinforce the importance to the family of the multi-disciplinary approach. In this way they will not be surprised that at any particular time the surgeon, the psychologist, the psychiatrist, the nurse or the social worker may be joining the paediatrician in the management.

It is very difficult to give a prognosis in any of the conditions which children have in which soiling is a major problem. If there is a significant degree of faecal retention then Figure 18, showing how long children have been on senna, gives parents an idea of the chronicity.

PSYCHOLOGICAL MANAGEMENT

Psychological management is not something apart from the physical management. In 'whole child' treatment of soiling children, the psychological management is incorporated in the overall plan. The prin-

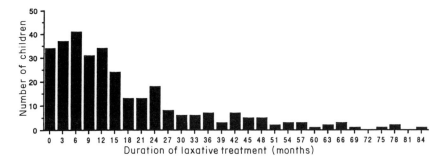

Figure 18. Duration of laxative treatment in constipated children

cipal aim of psychological management in the disorder is to help the child establish a positive self-image. Here it is important to remember that psychological treatments if badly managed can be as damaging as anything that may happen to him in his wider world. If, for example, it has been decided to use a behavioural programme, a decision may have to be taken that it is best to drop the behavioural programme because it is no longer a positive influence or to take a different tack. Behavioural programmes can be very effective early in treatment, and some children are able to maintain charting and monitoring of their bowel disorder over quite long periods as long as they are given sufficient encouragement. But with some long term soilers the behavioural programmes can in themselves become another stick to beat the child. The therapist needs to recognise when this point is reached. It is here where 'whole child' reviews are helpful, and where overall management plans can be made. It may be felt best, while a new approach is taken on his physical problems, to focus on teaching the child psychological coping strategies. Or it may be felt better to delay a new physical treatment while a new effort is made to alleviate psychosocial stresses. Reviews are also helpful to recognise subtle changes in the child or his environment which may indicate he is ready to take a more positive approach to his problem.

Clinicians need to be alert that they do not become so locked in the history of the past that they fail to see the glimmer of change in the child, his physical condition, attitude or social circumstances which may indicate the time is right to take a new step.

SOCIAL MANAGEMENT

When a soiler makes a poor or even slow response to treatment, it may be necessary to reassess the situation of the 'whole child'. As the child and his family become better known, social difficulties which are inhibiting the child's progress may become apparent. With skill it may be possible to alleviate some of these problems. The therapist may be able to improve family relationships; liaise, with parental permission, with the school and even the school psychologist to assess the child's educational situation; arrange an appointment with the hospital dietitian to consider the child's special dietary requirements; help the child join a community after-school club, so that he does not have to wait outside his home until his mother returns. There is no list of treatment options when it comes to social issues. The therapist has to be resourceful and creative, making sure that children and families understand the reasoning behind what is suggested.

Physical and Sexual Abuse

More practically the therapist may have to be alert to signs that carers are not becoming so desperate about the problem that the child may be at risk of physical abuse. In this case prevention is preferable to cure. In tense possibly abusive situations it is often possible to arrange that parents have short breaks from children, that children attend a nursery school, or, for example, that Johnny goes to stay with Granny for a weekend.

In rare cases, a better knowledge of the child and his home may indicate that sexual abuse should be considered. A disclosure from a child means that action has to be taken, but rarely is it necessary to act in a hurry; rarely, for instance, is the child in a life-threatening situation. Initially, where the situation is, as in most cases of child sexual abuse, only a suspicion, it may be possible to have the child admitted into hospital for further investigations of his/her soiling. Chapter 13 gives more information on how to handle this difficult area.

MANAGEMENT IN PRACTICE

Figures 19–22 are a selection of case studies. They have been chosen

A six year old boy referred by the health visitor, presenting with soiling at night. Parents report no other problems.

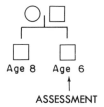

Age 8   Age 6

ASSESSMENT

Physical assessment
Soiling problem: Since birth/never clean. Soiled in bed every night: motions hard but no distension or faecal rocks. No soiling at school. No wetting problem.
Early history: No perinatal problems. Milestones normal. Previous history of painful motions.
Presenting: Well grown child. Height/weight within normal limits. Evidence of mild retention. Family diet apparently good but child eats little fibre.
Psychological assessment
Ability—average/above average.
Emotional adjustment: Rutter 'A' score—15 (Neurotic—4, Anti-social—0). Toilet phobia.
Social assessment
Family: Professional family. No obvious family problems. Good relationship with child and sib. Good sibling relationship. Family, however, very distressed by problem and concerned child may have some abnormality.
Schooling: No problems.
Environmental: Toilet may be a frightening place. Child diet could be improved with fibre that he enjoys.
Social: No obvious problems. Material standards good.

STRENGTHS/NEEDS
Child anxious about his condition and reluctant to use toilet facilities in daytime. But child wants to go and stay with cousin and feels he will not be able to do this because of his soiling. Parents anxious but supportive.

STRENGTHS	NEEDS
Child well motivated	Child needs help to reduce anxiety
Parents supportive	Parents need similar help
Child has goal to work for	May need medication, but diet advice may soften stools

continued on next page

Figure 19. Case study: Joseph.

continued

TREATMENT

Demystification advice for child and parents. After which parents chose to decline laxatives, although they may have been indicated. Cognitive restructuring broke into the child's learned helplessness. Music, lights on in toilet and a new small persons' toilet seat helped with the toilet phobia. An exciting behavioural programme was used to establish toilet routine, with the long term reward of going to stay with cousin.

OUTCOME

This case responded immediately to a behavioural programme and there were no further episodes of soiling. It involved one assessment visit, one visit to home and one telephone contact. No further intervention was necessary. On first and second follow-up, progress was maintained. On follow-up for research purposes mother said 'I can't imagine why there was a problem in the first place.'

Figure 19. (*concluded*)

to represent the range of responses and the different approaches used in treatment. The first case (Figure 19) is typical of many cases that may come forward to treatment. It is a young boy who responded quickly to a behavioural programme.

This was a relatively straightforward case which responded well to a behavioural programme. But it could be hypothesised that without intervention the child might have gone on to develop a long term soiling problem. The author's research has suggested that speedy and efficient intervention at this age has a good prognosis (Buchanan 1990). The next case (Figure 20), we will call Jamie. Jamie despite eight years' previous treatment responded well to a behavioural programme and a little help in his social circumstances.

The prognosis for this boy may not have looked good. But he particularly enjoyed the behavioural programme. He took great pleasure in drawing and keeping his charts over an 18 month period, which he would send to the therapist. In fact he never soiled after 10 months. Obtaining a separate bed and rehousing in this case appeared to be crucial.

The case study in Figure 21 illustrates how a child's inner strengths, if given the opportunity, can overcome major disadvantages. An important aspect of the case was 'allowing' the child despite his social

Boy age 10, referred by the paediatric department, presenting with recurrent soiling, severe abdominal pains and a very distressed mother.

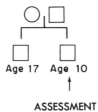

Age 17   Age 10

ASSESSMENT

Physical assessment
Soiling: Discontinuously, some clean periods. On referral, soiling daily. Severe constipation/abdominal distension/abdominal pain. On-going paediatric care. Eight years previous outpatient treatment with laxatives and softeners, suppositories and wash-outs. No wetting.
Early history: No perinatal problems. Milestones normal. Height—75th, Weight—25th percentiles.
Presenting: Sickly looking child. Very thin for height. History of poor/faddy eater.
Psychological assessment
Ability—average/above average.
Emotional adjustment: Rutter score—15 (Neurotic—4, Anti-social—0).
Fears: Unwilling to use school toilets.
A 'perfectionist' personality.
Social assessment
Family: Natural parents. Apparently stable marriage. Older brother had finished schooling. Now working. He shared bed with child.
Schooling: Some teasing. But child making good academic progress, despite days off school for medical treatment.
Social: Parents lived in caravan on a caravan estate. Very poor toilet facilities.

STRENGTHS/NEEDS
This boy was more able than either his parents or his brother. He was doing quite well at school but still underachieving because he was regularly sent home from school with abdominal pain. Only occasional soiling in school. His parents had not told the original clinician that they lived in a caravan. Child was very involved in his mother's anxieties about him.

continued on next page

Figure . 20. Case study: Jamie

continued

STRENGTHS	NEEDS
A perfectionist personality	Understanding of problem
Good ability/drawing skills	Chance to establish bowel routine
Caring family	Regular medication to keep stools soft
Would like help with housing	Advice regarding diet
	Less time off school
	Coping strategies for teasing at school
	May benefit from separate bed
	Family need help with housing
	Mother needs help to contain anxieties

TREATMENT

Demystification for child and mother to ease anxieties. Behavioural programme designed and drawn by child to establish regular defaecation. Close liaison with clinician supervising physical care to enable better management of abdominal pain and less time off school. Coping strategies to handle teasing. Liaison with Housing Department. Bed for child.

OUTCOME

This boy became completely clean in under 12 months. During this time he gained 10 lb in weight. He had a short relapse on entry into secondary school, which was dealt with very quickly. On research follow-up two years later, he was making extremely good progress both at school and physically. His social confidence further improved on rehousing. The child was very pleased with the new toilet in his new home. However, he still refused to use school toilets.

Figure 20. (*concluded*)

problems to help himself. Often when therapists see children with major social disadvantages their very sympathy for the child further deskills them. When this child understood that he could avoid the distress and pain of severe retention, and the consequent unpleasant wash-outs, by taking his medication regularly and establishing toilet routine, he took this opportunity to take control. With a reduction of his personal stresses and a change of school, he was able to cope with his home situation.

Figure 22 illustrates the complex interrelationship of factors seen in some soiling situations. Assessment in these multi-problem families is an on-going process. Factors bearing on the problem have to

Boy age nine referred by the paediatric department with a history of continuous soiling, severe abdominal pain, reluctance to go to school and concern about his progress in school.

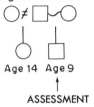

Age 14   Age 9

ASSESSMENT

Physical assessment
Soiling: Since birth. Some clean periods. Soiled several times a day. Severe constipation/abdominal distension/severe abdominal pain. Four years previous treatment. Paediatric inpatient/outpatient care. No wetting problem. History of non-compliance.
Early history: No perinatal problems, but 'late talker and slow to acquire basic skills'. Previous inpatient treatment for wash-outs and habit training. Outpatient laxatives and softeners.
Presenting: Height/weight within lower level normal limits. History poor eater/faddy.
Psychological assessment
Ability—low average but performing well below ability level (IQ 85/90 WISC-R).
Emotional adjustment: (Rutter score—12, Neurotic—4, Anti-social—1).
School phobia: related to teasing and poor progress, also home stress.
Treatment stress: Child very anxious about wash-outs and invasive methods of treatment.
Social assessment
Family: Parents unmarried but living together since birth of child. Older half sister suffering major emotional disturbance. Violence in the home at times. Poor marital relationships. Father: drinking problem, but some affection when sober. Mother depressed. Overprotective relationship with son.
Schooling: Teasing from peers. Behind in basic academic skills. A stressful situation for child. Reluctance to go to school despite warm/caring primary school.
Social: Material conditions poor; although father worked minimal housekeeping money given.

STRENGTHS/NEEDS

In assessment it become apparent that the child viewed his soiling problem as the fault of the paediatrician who could not cure him. Initially his strengths were only guesses.

continued on next page

Figure 21. Case study: Tommy

continued

STRENGTHS	NEEDS
?Hidden psychological strengths in child	To take responsibility for bowel problem
?Higher ability than estimated . . . read books	To understand problem and purpose of medication . . . help for
Caring mother	physical problems
Father who stayed with family	To have supervision in
Child prefers non-invasive	taking medication
treatments	Opportunity to establish toilet routine
	Regular physical reviews
	Assessment of school problems
	Help with family—sibling/father
	Practical resources for family

TREATMENT

Treatment priorities were worked out, focusing first on the physical needs of the child, and secondly on the school problems with the help of the educational psychologist (this child chose to go for a temporary period to a school for slow learners which greatly improved his confidence). A management plan was also agreed to deal with any crises. During home visiting by therapist, medication was supervised, which enabled more conservative management of his retention problems. After demystification, child took responsibility for his bowels. Sister went to boarding school. Mother's depression lifted. Father's drinking problems remained but housekeeping money was more reliable. Washing allowance was obtained for mother.

OUTCOME

Despite what might have appeared a poor prognosis at the start, this child made a good response and in under 12 months was completely clean, doing well at school and ready to transfer to normal secondary school.

Figure 21. (*concluded*)

be broken down into manageable pieces and intervention focused where it has the best chance of success. Because of the 'clustering' of factors associated with soiling—recurrent urinary infections, behavioural problems, poor parental relationships—the possibility of sexual abuse was considered. But investigations did not have

An 11 year old girl originally referred by her primary school, at age 10, with continuous soiling, also day and night wetting and very withdrawn behaviour.

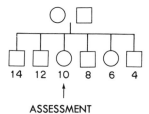

ASSESSMENT

Physical assessment
Soiling: Since birth. Soils several times a day. Severe constipation/abdominal distension/pain. Previous paediatric care. Now refusing hospital treatment. 'Did not like enemas/suppositories.'
Wetting problem: Day and night. History of recurrent urinary infections. Unreliable at taking prescribed medication.
Early history: Low birth weight. Below 2.5 kg. Intensive care after birth. Milestones normal.
Presenting: Thin poor-grown child. Height/weight—below 10th percentile. Poor eater.
Psychological assessment
Ability—low average.
Emotional adjustment: Rutter score—17 (Neurotic—5, Anti-social—0).
Very withdrawn behaviour: Hiding in corners at home. Severe secondary school phobia.
Social assessment
Family: United parents—but long history of marital problems and violence. Father generally unemployed. Some positives in family relationships but girl 'scapegoated' in family.
Schooling: Girl 'just about' survived in primary school, helped by remission in soiling. Unable to cope with secondary school. Severe school phobia.
Social circumstances: Material conditions very poor. Depressing environment. Father occasionally worked with disastrous results as social security benefits were reduced. During the holidays children were very poorly fed.

STRENGTHS/NEEDS
Here again it was hard to establish strengths. But despite the problems, the child made it clear that she wanted to remain at home. The possibility of sexual abuse was suggested.

continued on next page

Figure 22. Case study: Jenny

continued

STRENGTHS	NEEDS
Child wants to remain at home	Knowledge of condition
	Non-hospital physical care
Mother caring but stressed	Help for urinary problems/ assessment of
Father responds to positive approach	possible infection
	Assessment of school situation
Child prefers non-invasive medication for retention	Family need help with resources, holidays etc.
	Free school dinners for child

TREATMENT

This was another case where treatment priorities had to be carefully worked out. The possibility of sexual abuse was raised, but on limited evidence (child's behaviour, repeated urinary infections, father's role in family, reluctance to take child to hospital). First steps were demystification. Arranged that the child saw her local doctor, who checked urinary infection and prescribed for urinary problems and bowel retention. Home visiting therapist set up behavioural programme to improve child's confidence (not focused on toileting as this was felt to be too negative). Diet was helped with free school dinners and holiday clubs. Home teaching was provided through school psychological service gradually moving child into a unit out of the home. Positive relationship was established with father by home therapist who relieved mother of the care of some of the boys. Family provided with washing machine by a charity. Eventually child spent short period in child psychiatric unit, assessing her school phobia, soiling and also considering the possibility of sexual abuse.

OUTCOME

By the age of 13 this child had overcome her soiling but was still inclined to retention problems and urinary infections. Her confidence increased. She was gradually fed back into mainstream schooling after her period at the adolescent unit. Investigations for sexual abuse were negative or unconfirmed.

Figure 22. (*concluded*)

to take priority over other matters. In all probability if sexual abuse was a factor it had taken place over a period and therefore a few more weeks were unlikely to make much difference when balanced against the need for careful planning. As it happened the results were negative/inconclusive. As we have seen, many children with long term soiling problems can develop possible symptoms of sexual abuse and the danger of misdiagnosis is great. The fact that other approaches work may suggest that sexual abuse had not been a factor. In this case the father responded very positively to support from the worker and took a much greater part in family life. With hindsight because this child was unwilling to visit the hospital, her physical problems were never completely assessed. It is just possible that this child may have had ultra-short segment Hirschsprung's disease, but social problems can have the effect of clouding the issues.

PART III   Associated problems

Soiling is a problem which arouses strong emotions in most people. Accordingly family responses are not always a good guide to how the soiling arose. Severe secondary psychological components may arise even when the soiling has a physical basis. (Rutter 1975)

This section brings together some of the published research with the author's own findings from her doctoral thesis on the treatment and management of soiling children. One of the aims of research is that it might suggest new ideas and indicate new avenues for exploration, and that these thoughts will be assimilated in the annals of knowledge and maybe somewhere, sometime, someone will open a page, to find something that will start them on a journey to the unknown. The following chapters are therefore dedicated to these voyagers. To stimulate this future research, some of the topics covered in these chapters may be controversial. The first chapter raises some questions about the range of physical problems associated with soiling. In Chapter 11 Dr Graham Clayden contributes an important chapter on neurological disorders and faecal incontinence, and in Chapter 12 the author returns with a chapter on social and emotional problems associated with soiling and another chapter, originally written just after the Cleveland child abuse crisis in England, which discusses the vexed question of soiling and sexual abuse. The final chapter in this section considers the future of the soiling child, with a particular focus on the 'relapse' factor.

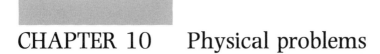

CHAPTER 10   Physical problems

The prevalence of soiling was 50% greater if the child had been of low birth weight. Children who were soiling were significantly more likely than expected to complain of stomach aches, have a squint, vision problem or speech disorder. (Butler & Golding 1986)

In a number of medical/emotional conditions in childhood there is a continuing debate about which condition is primary and which condition is secondary to the problem. The above quote from Butler's study (Butler & Golding 1986) is interesting. In this study, he did not separate those children who were felt to have a physical disorder from those children who were felt to have a psychological disorder. He was looking at *all* children who 'at the present time soil or mess' in their pants. Those children, who were only five years old, may not be representative of all children who soil. Nevertheless, the hypothesis presented in this chapter is:

> Soiling children as a whole represent quite an abnormal population when compared to children in the total population, and for many of these children there may be a physical cause which gives them a vulnerability to a future soiling problem. This vulnerability may be sparked off by psychological and/or environmental factors.

In presenting some of the arguments we will consider three areas. Firstly the role of constipation in the development of the soiling problem; secondly the link highlighted by Butler between the range of medical and developmental concerns; thirdly the more tentative link between diet, allergy and atopic conditions (asthma, eczema, hayfever etc.). Finally although this is not the focus of this chapter we must keep on the agenda the possibility that some children could have been a victim in sexual abuse, and in extreme cases this could have a physical effect as well as emotional.

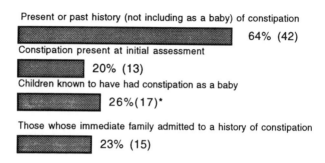

Present or past history (not including as a baby) of constipation

64% (42)

Constipation present at initial assessment

20% (13)

Children known to have had constipation as a baby

26%(17)*

Those whose immediate family admitted to a history of constipation

23% (15)

*All but 3% had a later history of constipation.

Figure 23. Sixty-six children with a soiling problem (Buchanan 1990)

The Role of Constipation

In the author's study, 64% of the total 66 children had a 'present or past history of constipation' (Figure 23; Buchanan 1990). But what is constipation?

'Constipation is a symptom rather than a disease, and because any symptom is the subjective interpretation of a real or imaginary somatic disturbance, it is difficult to define.' (Read & Timms 1986)

It is also difficult to diagnose when a child has a soiling problem. 'Vague historical documentation, along with a normal abdominal and rectal examination, may prompt the clinician to describe a child as having "encopresis without constipation".' (Levine 1982)

How valid then is the very vague category 'present or past history of severe constipation' used in the author's studies?

> Patients may complain of constipation if their stools are too hard, or too small, if they have to strain to defecate, if they only defecate infrequently, if defecation is painful, or if they have a sense of incomplete evacuation, necessitating unproductive returns to the toilet. Some patients may even interpret a feeling of distension or lower abdominal cramping or excessive flatulence as constipation (Read & Timms, 1986)

This in Read & Timms' (1986) experience is an adult definition of 'constipation'. When a mother says 'yes my child has been constipated', is that what she means? If so, she is saying that her child has experienced the type of constipation that is associated with soiling.

> Virtually all children with encopresis retain stools at least intermittently.

This proclivity may be subtle and clinically elusive. It is common for children to gradually develop "occult" constipation or stool retention that may be asymptomatic or manifest itself as recurrent abdominal pain. Some such youngsters may, in fact, defecate every day but produce bowel movements that are incomplete. Their stool retention may not be severe enough to alter physical findings. Some children have predominantly rectal constipation so that palpation of the abdomen reveals little. A rectal examination in such cases also may be difficult to interpret. (Levine 1982)

Given the above it would appear important with soiling children that very special consideration should be given to diagnosing possible constipation.

However, in only 13 of the children in the author's study (20% of the total group of 66), was constipation 'present' or recognised at the initial medical assessment (Buchanan 1990). It does seem unfortunate for all the other children who may have had constipation alleviated that morning, before coming to see the doctor, that they were labelled: 'encopresis without constipation', indirectly inferring theirs was a psychological problem. It is equally unfortunate for the parents, who on top of the shame of the soiling, may be made to feel that they are in some way to blame.

Another significant factor was that 23% (15) of the child's immediate family admitted to a history of constipation (Buchanan 1990). In my clinical experience this figure is too low. Parents did not readily admit to this problem. It might be argued that these children could be a product of their environment in that these households might create such a state of anxiety surrounding the state of their bowels, that this anxiety becomes a self-fulfilling prophecy for their children. Anthony (1957) talked about the 'potting couple'. It is easy to imagine a mother who has for years suffered with her own bowels being especially anxious about her child.

The link with a family history of constipation might also suggest an inherited condition which may predispose a child to a later soiling problem. Twenty-six per cent (17) children were known to have a history of constipation as a baby (Buchanan 1990). Again, this figure is likely to be too low. With the space of time, many parents do not remember the condition of their baby's bowels. Levine (1982) feels that 'children whose past history suggests significant bowel dysfunction during infancy and the toddler years may be revealing a constitutional or congenital predisposition to encopresis.' A condition of 'early colonic inertia' has been described as an endogenous tendency toward immature or generally inefficient function. It is felt the disorder is common, and some authorities including Levine (1982) feel it may result from genetic factors.

The role of constipation in the causation of a soiling problem has been discussed at length here because its importance may have been underestimated in the past; as a result many soiling children assumed to have a purely psychological problem are treated as such. 'It should never be assumed that all children with bowel incontinence are emotionally disturbed' (Levine 1982), and need to be seen by a psychiatrist. 'It is inappropriate and unfair to prejudge a child with this problem' (Levine 1982).

An alternative explanation, which may be attractive to psychiatric lobbies, is that although the child suffers from constipation, it is the emotional problems that have brought about the constipation, and because the emotional problems are therefore primary they need a primary therapeutic focus. It is, however, very difficult to know what condition is primary and what is secondary. A child who is constipated could suffer psychological distress either specifically in that the passing of oversize motions is so painful that the child develops emotional problems which permeate to other spheres of his life; or more generally in that the stress of living with a totally unsocial disorder, which causes great distress to those around, which also causes the child considerable upset, mainfests itself in behavioural difficulties. What we do know is that once the constipation is effectively managed and the child's soiling decreases, many of the emotional and behavioural problems improve to an extent that they do not need treatment in their own right (Levine et al 1980). This was also the author's experience in her study. Given this it seems important that whatever the role of constipation is, efforts should be made with every child who has a soiling problem to ensure that any constipation is effectively diagnosed and treated, and if the child does not improve, he should be re-examined at regular intervals.

However, it has also to be remembered that the solution for the constipation can itself cause problems. The methods used to cure the constipation such as indiscriminate use of suppositories, bowel washouts and the like may in themselves be responsible for further psychological damage to the child. But that is the focus of Chapter 12.

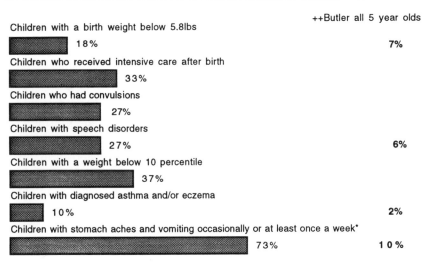

*Classification from Rutter "A" categorisation (Rutter 1965)

++Butler (1986) used Rutter "A" classifications in his study

Figure 24. Medical and developmental concerns in 30 soiling children (Buchanan 1990)

The Link between Soiling and Medical and Developmental Disorders

Figure 24 is also taken from the author's study and is used to open the discussion on the possible link between soiling and medical and developmental disorders.

The quote at the beginning of this chapter (Butler & Golding 1986) noted that the prevalence of soiling was 50% greater if the child had been of low birth weight, and children were significantly more likely to complain of stomach aches, have a squint, vision problem or speech disorder.

The author's findings supported this view although there were no figures on vision defects. As we can see from Figure 24, 27% of the children had a history of convulsions and a further 37% had a weight below the 10th percentile. Children with a soiling problem were indeed an abnormal population when compared with children in general. Following on logically from this finding, one needs to ask a further question. Is it not possible that whatever caused the squints, vision problems, speech disorders or convulsions may also have had an effect on the child's gut leading to a retention/constipation problem?

Of course it could be argued that these low birth weight babies with speech defects, squints or sight problems had 'bonded' less easily to their mother. Maybe they had spent long periods in intensive care, or being 'delicate babies' were separated longer from their mothers at some other crucial stage, and maybe it was this lack of 'bonding' which caused relationship difficulties with their mothers and later emotional problems and finally soiling. However, recent research has placed a less dramatic interpretation on the role of 'bonding' and 'attachment' behaviour in infants (Sluckin et al 1983). It could also be argued that the later poor weight and height percentiles seen in some soiling children may be related to an emotionally based failure to thrive (Hobbs 1989, personal communication). But in this case it could equally be concluded there was a more straightforward explanation, and this is that some children are so overloaded from faeces retention that they have no wish to eat. Indeed in the author's experience once the child was 'unloaded', the appetite returned.

An alternative explanation, suggested to the author by a paediatric nurse, is that some babies who have been in intensive care may soil because of the hourly rectal temperature-taking they endure when on the ward. It is hard to know what credence to place on these ideas. What we do know is that Read in his research on adults with bowel problems said 'it is probable that most patients with chronic idiopathic constipation have a predisposing disturbance in the motor or adaptive functions of the colon or mechanism of defecation' (Read 1986).

What we also know is that other researchers who are looking into abnormalities of the bowel associated with faecal incontinence (Leoning-Bauke & Younoszi 1982, Clayden 1986, Molnar et al 1983, Meunier 1984) have come up with some positive findings. These studies are mostly concerned with chronic cases, but when one remembers that over a quarter of the study children suffered from constipation as a baby, it could be hypothesised that some of these children may have had a minor abnormality which left them vulnerable to a later soiling problem, and that later relationship difficulties were secondary to the physical problem.

If indeed some of these children do suffer minor bowel abnormalities what can be done about it? Clayden & Lawson (1976) have pioneered some of the more radical surgical interventions, but such techniques would only be used as 'end of the road measures'. However, there are simple non-invasive techniques which can be helpful. Even in severe cases there is a role for the behavioural approach, working conjointly with other measures. Much of the behavioural work is about increasing a child's motivation to overcome what appears in his mind to be an insuperable problem, and it is always surprising, given adequate motivation, what difficulties a child can overcome. A behavioural approach is unlikely to harm a child and may bring about dramatic improvements, eliminating the need for more radical surgery.

The Possible Link between Diet, Allergy, Atopic Conditions and Soiling

Those working with disturbed children will know that in recent years there has been considerable interest in the role of diet. What children eat or don't eat can make them hyperactive, have learning difficulties (Feingold 1976, Conners 1980, Egger et al 1985, Schauss 1981), and cause behaviour problems and even delinquency (Egger et al 1985). Pollutants in the child's environment, leading to a zinc deficiency, can also have similar effects, particularly lead and cadmium (Bryce-Smith 1977). Again a sense of balance is required in interpreting the findings from these studies.

Two studies are of special interest: that by Buisseret (1978) 'Common manifestations of cow's milk allergy in children' and that by Egger et al (1985) 'Controlled trial of oligoantigenic treatment in hyperkinetic syndrome'. The relationship between cow's milk, constipation and soiling has been noted by Coekin & Gairdner (1960), Davidson et al (1963) and Levine (1982). What is interesting about Buisseret's paper is that he says 'Abdominal pain was a major symptom and in this series constipation was more common than diarrhoea'. As we have seen, in the author's study (Buchanan 1990) 73% of soiling children suffered abdominal pain compared with 10% of Butler's 'all' children (Butler & Golding 1986). This could raise the question, were some of these children reacting to some sort of milk allergy? Anecdotally, there is a case quoted in the author's study of a mother who discovered her child became constipated and soiled following any product from the cow, milk, beef, or cheese. The mother coped with this difficulty by going to the chemist and buying a product designed to combat cow's milk intolerance. This child rapidly overcame her soiling problem (Buchanan 1990).

The Egger study (1985) from the Hospital for Sick Children, Great Ormond Street, is especially interesting because it was a carefully controlled double-blind trial of diet management in hyperkinetic children, which shows there was some improvement in the children following diet management. Although constipation was not mentioned as a clinical feature, headaches, abdominal discomfort, excess of boys over girls, and, of course, behavioural problems as in soiling children were all common findings. Cow's milk was one of the most common allergens, but there were over 40 other substances. The suggestion from this study is that, if there is a link between diet, allergy and soiling, more than just milk may have to be considered. These thoughts are all very hypothetical. Levine (1982) notes 'dietary indiscretions, such as excessive ingestion of milk or chocolates, tend to exacerbate the (soiling) problem. Children with attention deficits or hyperactivity are particularly prone to develop encopresis.' Further research may shed more light on this. Children in the author's studies also suffered from more atopic type conditions, such as asthma and eczema, than children in the general population. As we can see from Figure 24, the figures were small and may well be due to some hidden variable (Buchanan 1990). What was interesting was the observation (unfortunately no figures were kept) on the number of mothers who suffered from migraines. Many of these mothers told the author that they found their migraines could be controlled by 'being careful with their diet'. What we do know is that 37% of the children in studies suffered from headaches compared with 6% in the child population of Butler's study (Butler & Golding 1985). The question is could there be a link?

The other aspect of the problem is the more general relationship between an inadequate diet or an unbalanced diet and constipation. Figure 25, taken from the author's study, raises questions about the possible link between a child's diet choice and soiling.

All the children in the author's prospective study of soiling children, and where possible also their nearest-in-age sibling, were asked to keep a diet sheet for two weeks. It was anticipated that these diet sheets might show an interesting relationship between what the child ate and the child's constipation problem. Indeed in cases such as in Figure 25

Mon	Tues	Wed	Thurs	Fri	Sat	Sun
NON-SOILER: age 10						
Salad, cheese, bread roll, black-currant drink	Salad, cheese, bread roll, apple drink	Two fish fingers, chips, beans, black-currant drink, biscuit	Salad, cheese, bread roll, biscuit, apple drink	Salad, cheese, bread roll, biscuit, apple drink	French bread, cheese, crisps, salad, apple	Chicken, butter beans, cabbage, stuffing, roast potatoes, currant crumble
SOILING BROTHER: age 8						
Beef-burger in roll, drink, crisps	Sausage roll, chips, 2 Yoyos, drink	Sausage roll, Wagon-wheel, crisps, orange drink	Beef-burger in roll, mini-potatoes, biscuits, drink	Beef-burger in roll, rice crispy cake, drink	French bread, cheese, crisps, salad, apple	Chicken, butter beans, cabbage, stuffing, roast potatoes, crumble

Figure 25. One week's midday meals for two brothers using the same school canteen. The children selected their own midday meal (Buchanan 1990)

there did appear to be some relationship. These two brothers went to the same primary school where they were able to choose what they ate for their midday meal in the school canteen system. Now if we are to believe Barker (1982) (see Chapter 3), these children's in-built mechanisms which regulate our food choice and lead individuals to select a varied and balanced diet, should have been in operation. However, beefburgers and chips or sausages and chips every day does not sound like a varied and balanced diet. Cabanac (1971) found that non-nutritive sweeteners such as cyclamate could produce the same reaction as a nutritive sweetener and disturb a child's natural instinct to 'choose the right foods'. With many schools adopting canteen type systems, and with many of the foods given for dinner containing artificial flavourings and colourings, there just could be a relationship between the diet choice and soiling.

However, as any experienced dietitian will know, finding out what anyone *really* eats is notoriously difficult, and overall it was not possible to draw any clear conclusions from the diet sheets. What was interesting and dramatically illustrated from the diet sheets was the

Mon	Tues	Wed	Thurs	Fri	Sat	Sun
Breakfast None	Toast, chocolate drink	Toast, chocolate drink	Toast, chocolate drink	Toast, chocolate drink	None	Toast, oats
Midday School meal	School meal	School meal	School meal	School meal	Shepherds pie, beans, gravy	Lamb, roast potatoes, beans
After school Toast, water biscuits	Toast, chocolate drink	Wotsits, Wagon-wheels	Ice lolly, Dr Who stick	Sweets, cheese	Crisps, roll, sandwich	Cheese sandwich, Coke
Evening Nothing	Nothing	Doughnut	Nothing	Nothing	Biscuit, cheese roll	Drink
Snacks/drinks None/water	None/water	None/water	None/water	None/water	None/Coke	Water

Figure 26. Diet of 10 year old soiling girl, from a family of eight, father unemployed (from Buchanan 1990)

difference in diets seen in children in different occupational groups. The variety of foods offered to children in the higher occupational groups contrasted vividly with the very limited diet in the poorer families, and yet in both types of families there were thriving brothers and sisters eating the same food. However, in the extreme, especially where a child was already vulnerable through other factors, the paucity of a diet may have been important, as Figure 26 illustrates.

This diet sheet came from a child whose father was unemployed and there were six children in the family. The child's soiling and severe constipation improved during the term when she had free school dinners, but always deteriorated during the holidays. She was underweight (below the 10th percentile). Although shortage of food may not have been entirely responsible for her problem, in this extreme case, it may have been a factor.

The current concern about the safety of certain foods (eggs, chicken and certain cheeses) illustrates how little we know about the food we eat. At present the conclusion seems to be that for most of us, we can eat what we like without ill effect, but for some vulnerable groups the effects of some foods can be serious. Who would have thought a few years ago that a mother could bring about a miscarriage by eating unpasteurised cheese? It is not that long ago that it was discovered that gluten products were death to a coeliac child. Could it be that for some soiling children there is an additional relationship between what they eat and their problem, but at this stage we do not know what?

SUMMARY

In this chapter we have raised some questions and even possibly without knowing it, some red herrings. What can be said with some certainty is that because human gastroenterology is so complex and because the physical and emotional aspects of its functioning are so interlinked, there is unlikely to be a single cause or a single treatment solution. Indeed for many children we may never know which is the chicken and which is the egg.

CHAPTER 11 Neurological disorders and faecal incontinence

by Graham Clayden

Introduction

The neurological conditions which have afflicted children have shown a changing pattern over this century. The scourge of poliomyelitis has been eradicated virtually from the developed world by effective immunisation starting in infancy. The wards of paralysed children and 'iron lungs' of the 1950s have disappeared. The rapid development of paediatric surgery and paediatric anaesthetics in the 1960s allowed a large number of children born with spina bifida to survive infancy. However, these children were often left with neurological deficits in their lower limbs and major effects on both bladder and bowel control (Scobie et al 1970, Arhan et al 1984). A reduction in the incidence of babies born with spina bifida has been seen throughout the 1980s partly due to improved vitamin and folate acid intake of mothers but mainly due to screening by maternal blood, amniotic fluid and detailed fetal ultra-sound examination and subsequent termination of the pregnancy. The recent change in the abortion laws has virtually abolished the age limit in gestation when a pregnancy with a fetus with severe malformations can be legally terminated. This reduction in numbers of children with spina bifida should mean that there are more resources available for those who have been missed at screening or who have not been terminated for religious reasons. This is not obviously the case and the knowledge that they are suffering from a handicap which is usually the indication for termination of pregnancy may add to the distress that these children suffer especially as adolescents where the soiling also is particularly unbearable. Children with cerebral palsy (spastic children) have problems coordinating their muscles during defaecation and so may present with constipation and often overflow faecal incontinence (Clayden & Agnarsson 1991, pp. 45–47). The overall incidence of cerebral palsy has improved but this is masked to some extent by a change in the severity pattern. Improved obstetrics and neonatal resuscitation have reduced the incidence of cerebral diplegia where the lower limbs are more affected than the arms. However, the extension of intensive care to smaller and smaller extremely preterm babies (especially below 25 weeks of gestation) appears to be associated with a high incidence of more severe cerebral palsy often associated with other brain problems (deafness, partial sight, mental retardation and epilepsy). Rarer spinal diseases such as spinal tumours in children remain at the same incidence but although improved surgery and radiotherapy greatly improve their survival, some have irreparable damage to some of their spinal nerves, producing problems identical to spina bifida.

Basic Management

The basic management of the bowel problem in a child with any of these neurological problems is identical to that of the ordinary child. Assessment will require a full history of the type of faecal incontinence and especially whether there is associated constipation. The reaction of the child and family to the incontinence with an estimate of the levels of guilt, blame, despair or dissociation is as essential. Examination and special investigations should confirm the main areas of pathophysiology and indicate the most appropriate treatment regime. Children with complex disabilities usually have a wide supporting team of professionals particularly in physiotherapy, special teaching and occupational therapy. It is very important that the usual bowel team integrates and communicates well with them to avoid contradictory advice and professionally 'stepping on toes'.

Any neurological condition which is associated with learning difficulties or major developmental delay is likely to delay the acquisition by the child of the normal milestones of bowel control. A useful check is to ask whether a child with the mental age of the child in question would be expected to have achieved continence. The rest of this section will therefore be concentrated on the two major problem areas for continence: *spina bifida* (including other spinal lesions having a similar neurological effect) and *cerebral palsy*.

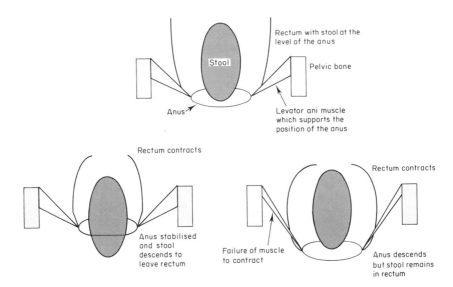

Figure 27. Schematic diagram of relative movement of stool in health (lower left) and in children with spina bifida (lower right)

Spina Bifida

When a baby is born with spina bifida, the nerves coming from the lower spine and a portion of the spinal cord are exposed. The normal folding of the tissues in the embryo, which give rise to the spinal cord, failed to occur and the skin, vertebrae and meninges were interrupted in their covering of these delicate structures. So the nerves to the legs and bowel and bladder are often severely affected.

During defaecation the anus is held in a stable position by the contraction of a broad diaphragm of muscles acting as a floor to the pelvis (levator ani muscles). Without this stabilisation the stool has great difficulty in passing through the anus. It is similar to a person trying to leave a room through a rather stiff door which is fixed to an elastic wall. The more he pushes the further the door and the wall move away from him. Parents may report a similar finding in the baby with spina bifida; they see the stool in the partially relaxed anus being pushed down but the anus is moved down as well because of the paralysis of the supporting muscles (Figure 27).

This may lead to constipation and, over time, the development of a megarectum with associated overflow loose stools. This problem is compounded by the effect of the absence of the spinal nerves on the relaxation response of the automatic internal anal sphincter to rectal contractions. As described in Chapter 3 the internal anal sphincter relaxes each time the rectum is distended (usually by a stool entering from the colon above). In the child with loss of the appropriate spinal nerves, this reflex is exaggerated. This means that there is a sudden and often complete inhibition of the anal canal pressure by relatively small volumes in the rectum. As the children also have a paralysis of the external sphincter, they can do nothing to oppose this relaxation and any stool in the rectum will come out. If this fundamental factor is acknowledged it clearly indicates that any retained stool in the rectum is likely to be expelled at any time the rectum contracts. So the essential of management is to ensure that the rectum is empty. This can be achieved by very regular training from quite an early age. Parents may be able to make the most of the gastrocolic reflex which occurs after eating and which activates the large bowel. This then fills the rectum which then automatically inhibits the anus and the stool is evacuated. Provided the stool is of a soft enough consistency and the anus can be stabilised by carefully holding the child a pattern can be developed. This may require very strict adherence to the timing of meals and pot/loo visits (Clayden & Agnarsson 1991, p. 56).

The importance of the avoidance of faecal retention in the rectum is clear. Any retained stools will provoke random and frequent rectal contractions with their automatic relaxation effect on the anal sphincter leading to soiling. If the after-meal loo visits are insufficient to maintain continence then careful use of senna may allow the stool to move at an appropriate time of the day (usually about 24 hours after it is taken). Making the stool a little larger but softer with methyl cellulose liquid is often helpful. But for many of the children the only certain way of being sure that the stool is safely out of the rectum is by the use of manual evacuations, enemas or suppositories (Clayden & Agnarsson 1991, pp. 51–56). If you have been reading the other sections of this book you may think we have lapsed into inconsistency, remembering the warnings about unpleasant anal procedures. However, children with neurogenic rectum have, in addition to the muscle paralysis and exaggerated rectoanal relaxation, a sensory deficit. This naturally adds to the difficulty of achieving continence but it does mean they suffer no pain or discomfort from the anal faecal evacuation procedures. However, it is embarrassing for the older child

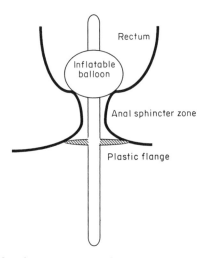

Figure 28. Example of continence catheter in place

to be helped in this way and they are difficult to perform without help. Another problem is that in some children with very rapid rectoanal relaxation (Agnarsson et al 1989) the rectal fluid used for enemas or wash-outs immediately flows out before it has had a chance to provoke the required faecal evacuation. There have been some useful developments to help in these circumstances. Tubes which temporarily block the anus can be helpful; the stoma wash-out tube has a wide conical end which can be held firmly against the relaxed anus and removed when all the rectal fluid has been run. On removal of the cone, the fluid plus the faecal contents are propelled out by the rectal contractions through the completely inhibited anal sphincter. Another device is a balloon catheter with an external flange to prevent too high insertion which again temporarily blocks the anus until rectal filling is complete when it can be rapidly deflated and withdrawn (Figure 28) (Shandling & Gilmour 1987).

Once the rectum is empty the internal anal sphincter regains its normal smooth muscle tone and prevents any further leaking until the rectum fills from above (hopefully not until the next day). This sounds difficult and it is, although some families and some individual teenagers manage extremely well if they have well ordered colons to deal with. Many children have more chaotic colonic activity or such a degree of megarectum that the once a day wash-out system is never effective. A number of children have experienced the association with emotional changes and the degree of chaos in the colonic filling of the rectum in similar ways to that seen in the more psychogenic encopresis. This psychological link should never be ignored just because the child has such an obvious cause for the faecal incontinence in the neurological problem. If the child with spina bifida has even a slight degree of sensation, biofeedback using a rectal balloon and a computer to provide a screen display can be used to help them be more accurate in perceiving the sensation and timing their use of the lavatory (Whitehead et al 1981, 1986, Loening-Baucke et al 1988).

New developments in surgery may play an important role in children where these other methods have not been successful. It is possible to bring the appendix to the surface and to use it as an entry point for a small tube to be passed to wash out the whole colon. This allows the older child to perform the wash-out using both hands and watching what is going on. It can be performed on the lavatory making the whole procedure less messy and less embarrassing than the rectal wash-outs. However, it does mean surgery and some children may find the idea of a hole in their abdominal wall rather daunting. The hole is capped with plastic and it should not leak stool on to the surface (one way only). This is a promising idea but full evaluation of its safety and effectiveness is awaited. Another development which has been used in adults with spinal injuries resulting in neurogenic rectum is the creation of a new external anal sphincter (Williams et al 1990) from a muscle pulled from the leg and swung around the rectum. This is then stimulated electrically to maintain its squeeze but can be turned off using a surface magnet when defaecation is desired. This offers hope and control but probably could only be used when the child has reached full size as modifications with growth would be very difficult.

The final surgical solution if all else fails is to open a colostomy. This is extreme but it may be very liberating for an active but wheelchair bound young athlete who is plagued by sudden soiling episodes. It should also be remembered that the anus is difficult to reach when trying to balance on a lavatory in spite of many postural muscles being paralysed and where it is impossible to stick on a bag to receive any loose stools. Figure 29 illustrates the main factors involved in faecal incontinence in neurogenic bowel disorders.

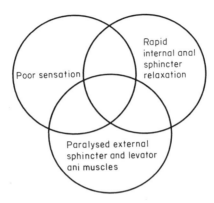

Figure 29.   Factors involved in faecal incontinence in neurogenic bowel

Cerebral Palsy and Faecal Incontinence

Cerebral palsy affects the nervous system which is concerned with the central control of motor (movement) functions of the body. This is mainly to do with the voluntary muscles and their control. Most children have cerebral palsy as a result of a development problem of the brain, damage from lack of oxygen or sugar around birth or from infections such as meningitis. The loss of the control of some of the voluntary muscles of the body leads to problems with posture, walking and coordination of muscles involved in speech, swallowing and often defaecation.

The degree of cerebral palsy varies in its pattern of limb involvement and whether the muscle tone is high (spastic) or low (hypotonic). Children with spasticity find it particularly difficult to relax sufficiently to allow defaecation to be performed properly. This may lead to faecal retention especially if the swallowing or feeding difficulty leads to a dietary constipation also. Children with this faecal retention may go on to produce a megarectum with associated overflow loose soiling.

Children can be helped by dietary care and the sensible use of stool softeners. It is important that children with cerebral palsy are helped to develop effective defaecatory patterns. They should have the lavatory adapted to cope with their postural problems or muscle weaknesses. Vigilance to avoid faecal retention must be used as for ordinary children. There is no sensory abnormality in these children and so the same respect for the avoidance of anal discomfort or pain is essential. Any discomfort during defaecation is likely to provoke a sudden spasm of the spastic muscle groups which if they involve the external anal sphincter or the levator ani will obstruct easy defaecation. When the child has multiple other neurological problems caused at the same time as the cerebral palsy, such as deafness, balance problems, severe learning difficulties or epilepsy, defaecation may be particularly difficult. As already mentioned learning difficulties will inevitably delay the acquisition of continence. Children with epilepsy appear to have more fits if they become constipated. If a child has a convulsion it is likely he will become faecally incontinent during the fit. This adds to the stigma and embarrassment of the convulsion.

Many children can be helped by the usual programme of:

- reasonable fibre and fluid intake,
- regular pot/lavatory visits,
- incentives for defaecation,
- stool softeners,
- laxatives where necessary to time the stool or to avoid retention and overflow,
- care to avoid anal discomfort (especially by avoiding anal treatments).

Sometimes anal dilatation or faecal evacuation under a general anaesthetic is necessary but the added risk of anaesthetics to children with cerebral palsy and the problem of chest infections must be carefully considered.

SUMMARY

Children born with spina bifida and surviving due to advances in paediatric surgery are often left with neurological deficits to their lower limbs with major effects on both bladder and bowel control. These children suffer especially in adolescence where the soiling is particularly unbearable.

The basic management of the bowel problems in a child with the above neurological problems is identical to that of the ordinary child. In addition, examination and special investigations should confirm the main area of pathophysiology and indicate the most appropriate treatment regime. The essential of management of children with spina bifida is to ensure that the rectum is kept empty. In some cases the stoma wash out tube or a balloon catheter may be helpful. In others continence may be obtained with the help of biofeedback training. In some cases there have been dramatic improvements as a result of the new surgical interventions. Children with cerebral palsy can be helped by diet and the sensible use of stool softeners as well as training to develop effective defaecatory patterns. They may need specially adapted lavatories.

CHAPTER 12   Social and emotional problems

It is common for children with a soiling problem to be 'difficult' in varying ways, since soiling results in such a social problem for the child concerned, and is so damaging to his self-esteem. Many become blasé about their problem—having little option but to develop a tough skin about it. Most have desperate strategies to try and avoid discovery when they have soiled. (Morgan 1981, p. 83).

Throughout this book we have emphasised that a soiling problem does not come in a neatly packaged parcel, but brings with it a whole range of associated problems which may be either primary or secondary to the original soiling. In this chapter we will look at some of these issues in greater depth, demonstrating how soiling can permeate every area of the child's development and in extreme cases can place the child at serious risk of physical abuse. Much of the evidence comes from the author's study (Buchanan 1990). The following quote was made to the author by a 'recovered' soiler after many years of treatment:

> For a child, if you are labelled 'difficult', without those around having the knowledge as to why you are being 'difficult', it creates severe social problems for you. You may have been considered 'difficult' before you developed the soiling problem—be that as it may—but once you have a soiling problem, you are likely to be a whole lot more 'difficult'. Being 'difficult' implies that it is somehow your fault. You could stop being 'difficult' if you wanted to. The ray of hope, but as a soiling child you are unlikely to know this, is that you will be much less 'difficult' when you finally get to grips with your soiling. If only your mother knew this, . . . so 'being difficult' was not your fault after all!

What then is the concern? As children gain control of their bowels, everything will improve. Time, however, does not stand still in child development. The anxiety is that, in the crisis of a soiling problem, the child will suffer irreparable harm. There are four areas of concern. Firstly the child may develop severe difficulties with his relationship with his parents; secondly he may develop problems with his relationships at school which may affect his progress at school; thirdly in an

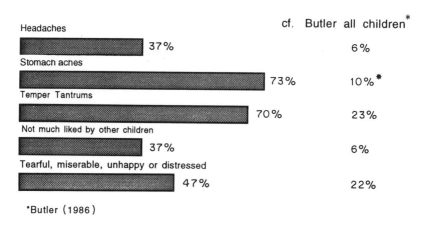

Headaches   cf. Butler all children[*]

37%   6%

Stomach aches

73%   10%[*]

Temper Tantrums

70%   23%

Not much liked by other children

37%   6%

Tearful, miserable, unhappy or distressed

47%   22%

*Butler (1986)

Figure 30. Some associations with a soiling problem (Buchanan 1990)

effort to survive, as Roger Morgan has identified in the above quotation, he may develop behaviour difficulties; finally and more seriously, when all the stresses are put together, the soiling child may be at quite serious risk of physical abuse.

Problems Associated with Soiling

Not feeling 100% and behaving
accordingly

As we saw in Chapter 10, many children with soiling problems feel unwell for much of the time. Although this may result from the physical retention problem, the behavioural expression of this may affect the relationships the child has with those around him.

The findings from the author's study suggest that whatever has caused the initial soiling problem, the soiling child is not a happy one, with headaches and stomach aches, many times more frequently than the national average (Figure 30). Saddest of all is his isolation. Other children just do not like him, And this, at a time of his life when friends are not only important but essential to his development.

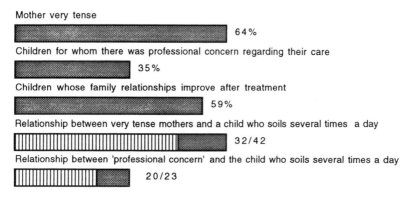

Mother very tense

64%

Children for whom there was professional concern regarding their care

35%

Children whose family relationships improve after treatment

59%

Relationship between very tense mothers and a child who soils several times a day

32/42

Relationship between 'professional concern' and the child who soils several times a day

20/23

Figure 31. Parental and family relationships (Buchanan 1990)

Poor relationships

Perhaps more worrying still is the association between soiling and the child's poor personal relationships (Figure 31).

Figure 31 illustrates the very real tensions within the family of a soiling child. These tensions appear to be worse when the child soils several times a day. The more often the child soiled, the more likely was there to be concern for his physical safety. When a child's soiling had improved, almost all of the original 'tense' mothers were less 'tense'. But this could still have meant that the child had spent a large part of his early childhood at the butt end of a very cross parent. Poor family relationships were not the only worrying problem. Soiling appeared to be associated with schooling problems (Figure 32).

Figure 32 illustrates several concerns. Firstly there is the child who misses periods of schooling because of his problem or because he is attending treatment. Secondly some children have an especially difficult time in school because of their problem. Thirdly there are relatively high numbers of soiling children who are reluctant to go to school. The research also showed that if the child who soiled also had low ability this compounded his unwillingness to go to school. What was especially worrying was that many children, even when they had overcome their soiling problem, continued to underachieve in school. As we will see in Chapter 14 underachievement at school can have long term consequences on the life opportunities of children.

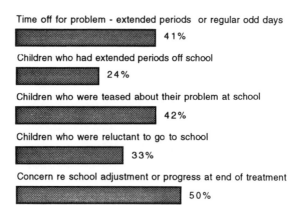

Figure 32. Schooling and peer group relationships (Buchanan 1990)

Behaviour

In the United Kingdom, it is interesting that under the definition of a 'child in need' in the Guidelines and Regulations of the Children Act 1989 (HMSO; Children Act Vol. 2 1991), children whose behavioural development is of concern are identified as a priority group requiring supportive services. These children 'in need' are in addition to children with a disability and those whose health and development are at risk. This is perhaps a recognition that the child can in the long term be just as disabled by behavioural problems as by physical difficulties. With children who have a soiling problem, Levine et al (1980) have shown that behaviour problems in soiling children generally improve when their soiling disappears. This is welcome news for the child and his parents, but it does not prevent the damage the child can do while his behaviour is problematical.

The figures presented in Figure 33, which are again from the author's study need to be interpreted with care but are given because of the possible interest. Forty-one per cent of all parents coming to the agency for help specified that their child had a behaviour problem in addition to their soiling problem at the initial assessment interview. Over half of all parents felt soiling was not the chief problem for their child at the initial assessment. It has to be remembered that many of these children had had a soiling problem for many years before coming for help, and may have already been to one or more agencies seeking the elusive cure. A third of the children, in the author's study, who were treated

Behaviour at initial assessment

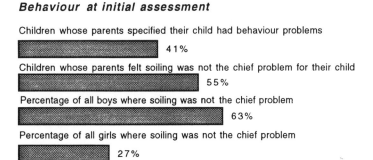

Children whose parents specified their child had behaviour problems

41%

Children whose parents felt soiling was not the chief problem for their child

55%

Percentage of all boys where soiling was not the chief problem

63%

Percentage of all girls where soiling was not the chief problem

27%

Figure 33. Some possible effects of a soiling problem: behaviour (Buchanan 1990)

by the hospital still had behaviour problems at the end of treatment. In the 'whole child' treatment group only 3% had behaviour problems at the end of treatment. This was because specific efforts were made to alleviate behavioural difficulties.

There was a strong suggestion from the study that boys' behaviour, more so than girls', became worse as the soiling continued. There was a tendency for the boys to demonstrate more anti-social behaviour as they grew older.

There was evidence that the behaviour problems were indeed more debilitating than the soiling for some children. Anti-social behaviour problems, rather than the soiling, resulted in children being suspended from school, and neurotic behavioural problems resulted in children of normal intelligence having to go to special schools because they were quite unable to function in a normal school environment. The strong message was that if it is not possible to 'cure' the soiling, the behaviour problems need help in their own right.

Risk of physical abuse

As we have seen soiling children are an unhappy group with head-aches, stomach aches, temper tantrums, tearful miserable, unhappy or distressed behaviour, eating problems and poor height/weight being many times more common than in children in the general population. In fact quite apart from the soiling itself, because of other factors, commonly associated with soiling, these children are difficult and unsatisfactory children to rear. But of course soiling itself produces its own stresses.

> At a recent training day for social workers on 'Identifying the Child at Risk of Physical Abuse', I took the trainees through the early history of a soiling child, and asked them to imagine that this was their child. The scenario starts with the news that they have just been promoted at work with a substantial pay rise. This means that they can afford the mortgage on their new house. The following week, little Johnny age four is sent home from the nursery . . . he can come back when he is 'toilet trained'. No other childminding facilities can be found and mother has to give up her job to look after him. Eventually, the family lose the house as they cannot afford the mortgage. In the following years the family remain in rented accommodation. Mother spends long hours attending the hospital appointments getting more desperate about Johnny's soiling. Two small sisters are born, who do not soil and do not behave badly. Johnny can't cope at primary school, so he ends up in special school. Eventually, after years of treatment, Johnny now aged 12 and still soiling, is suspended from his special school for attacking another child, and parents advised to see a psychiatrist 'to help with their family relationship problems'. Just before you set out for the appointment, Johnny shits himself all down his legs, through his new trousers and over the car . . . The social workers were then asked, if that was *your* child how would *you* respond. The point was made. Even social workers might hurt their children (Buchanan 1990).

In addition to the stress of the soiling we also know that some soiling children come from quite difficult social situations, with pre-existing difficult parental relationships, and social stresses. How then do you assess the risk to the child? Table 9, based on work by Jackie Roberts (1988), highlights risk factors that indicate those children who may be physically abused. As can be seen there is a relationship between many of these factors and soiling children. The implication is that a soiling child is further at risk because of his soiling problem.

Jackie Roberts' indicators of physical abuse were based on her study of abused children coming to the Park Hospital in Oxford (Roberts 1988). The indicators are listed, firstly those present in the parents, and secondly, those present in the child. The second column gives the percentage of those soiling children in the author's study who were known to have the indicators. The third column gives the percentage, where available, of the number of children in the general population. These figures are from Butler's study (Butler & Golding 1986).

As we have already seen, there is a very real relationship between the extent of the child's soiling and the tension of the mother. In the author's study at least 10% of the children were known to have been on the Child Protection Register, maintained by Social Services. This risk needs to be borne in mind in any treatment and management programme. The very isolation of not knowing any other parents who are experiencing the same stresses increases the risk of physical abuse.

What is the Role of Stress, Personality Type, Depression and Learned Helplessness?

In the literature in Chapter 3, there was a strong suggestion that there was a relationship between high levels of stress in the child's environment and soiling (Burns 1941, 1958, Bellman 1966, Benpard 1971). Because of this, social stresses surrounding the soiling child were closely assessed in the author's study. Efforts were made to establish whether the family were experiencing any of a whole range of stresses. Among these were marital problems, housing problems, financial difficulties, unemployment, health or mental health concerns, pressures from the wider extended family such as illness and/or bereavement. In the studies around a quarter of the families of the soiling children at referral admitted to more than three social stresses. In addition most families were able to identify a social stress either in the family or for the child that they felt was responsible for their child's soiling.

It was interesting that, when it came to the end of treatment, there was no significant difference in treatment outcome between families who experienced a lot of social stress and those who experienced very little. This of course may have been related to efforts made by the therapist to reduce the stress levels on the child. However, Butler (Butler & Golding 1986) who was looking at a whole population of children noted 'one of the unexpected findings in this study was the apparent lack of association with situations thought to be stressful to the child. The literature certainly suggests that traumatic events are likely to promote encopresis, but we found no evidence for this in our study.'

Table 9. Risk factors of physical abuse and percentage of soiling children with factor

Risk factors (Roberts 1988)	Buchanan (1990) % in soiling children	% General population (Butler & Golding 1986)
Parents		
1. Unhappy childhood. Abused as child	No data	
2. Parents under 21	No data but most older	
3. Psychiatric problems in parents	Chronic illness (plus mental illness) 33%	
	Very tense mothers 64%	
4. Bereaved parents	No data/but death in family associated with soiling (Bellman 1966)	
5. Alcohol and drug abuse	No data	
	Bellman (1966) found an association	
6. Ill health	Chronic illness in family 33%	
7. Poor marriage/single parent	Marital problems 39%	3.9–5.8%
	Single parent 13%; Reconstituted† 20%	
8. Diffuse social problems	Financial problems 41%;	(6.0% *1988)
	Unemployment 16%	
9. Social isolation	No data but all parents of soiling children isolated	

Children

1. Born too soon. Low birth weight, premature	Low birth weight 17% Intensive care 27%	6.9%
2. Sick or handicapped Difficult child to rear	Stomach ache or vomiting 73% Medical developmental problems 20% Eating problems 53%	10.0% 37.0%
	Convulsions 27% Low ability 26% Low weight 37% Speech disorders 27%	 + (10.0%) 10.0%
3. Born different wrong sex	No data	
4. Born unwanted	No data	
5. Interaction/parent/child	Professional concern re care 35% (note worse more times child soils) Behaviour problems 41% Tearful miserable, unhappy or distressed 47% *Incontinent:* Bedwetting 42% Soiling 100% Day wetting 17%	 22.0%

+ Percentile charts.

* Local unemployment rate at time of study.

† Families living with new partners (one parent and one step parent, or one parent and one mother/father figure).

Of course, what Butler could not measure were the internal dynamics of individual families, and what may be stressful for one may not be for another. Certainly in the author's experience reducing stresses *as perceived by the child* was a very important part of treatment.

The Personality of the Child

The author's study offers another slant on the dilemma. The personality of the soiling child may offer a clue. In her study, children were assessed on the Rutter 'A' schedule. This is a method for identifying the level of maladjustment in children. Having assessed the child it is then possible to score whether the child's maladjustment is more of an anti-social type or a neurotic type. In the author's study 40% of the children scored highly on the Rutter Neurotic scale, while only a fifth scored highly on the Anti-social scale. These were, as mentioned, the older children who had experienced many years of treatment for their soiling. (There may be a relationship between physically invasive type therapies and the development of anti-social behaviour.)

However, Levine says 'acting-out or sociopathic behaviours are not frequently found in children with encopresis; they are more likely to isolate themselves to varying degrees and show excessive dependency' (Levine 1982). Generally speaking, except for the few older long term male soilers this was the author's impression, and is supported by the Rutter assessments on the children (Buchanan 1990).

We have another clue from the author's study from the numbers of children who were classified 'often worried' on the Rutter assessment schedule: 37% of the soiling children were labelled by their mothers as 'often worried', compared with 5.5% of children in the general population (Butler & Golding 1986). Of course, realistically these children have something to worry about, and a soiling problem may create or exacerbate neuroticism, but even so, it is possible there may be a particular personality type which is more vulnerable to soiling problems, and this personality type is likely to be more distressed by constipation and the pain of defaecation and less able to deal with them. The chief stressors for this type of child will be a very personal experience, and may be quite unrelated to other more obvious stress factors around.

The Role of Depression

Another controversial area which we touched on in Chapter 3 is the role of depression in soiling children. The loss of a parent (Olatawura 1973, Bemporad 1978) is a common antecedent to a soiling problem. Bellman (1966) also noted this in his study. Could it be these children suffer from a passing depression, one long enough to disturb their natural body rhythms, so bringing about constipation? The relationship between constipation and depression has long been recognised. The certain fact about soiling is that it is a very depressing condition and the effect it has on those around you cannot make you feel any better about yourself. If you are a more 'neurotic type' personality it is likely to make you feel worse about everything, and feeling bad about everything may well make you more constipated and less able to break out of the cycle. Tied into this, you are being ridiculed, shamed and blamed for something you 'did not cause and over which have little if any control' (Levine 1982). You have become one of the world's 'learned helpless' (Seligman 1975), and having no way out you become depressed. Seligman would say that this depression is not the sort of depression that responds readily to psychotherapy. What the child needs is someone to show him what he can do to help himself; what the soiling child needs to do is to take control of his own bowels and body. This simple factor may be the reason for the positive results from many behavioural studies. Once the child believes he can 'win' or at least start on the road to winning, this helps lift the gloom surrounding himself and this could have an effect on his constipation problem. This relates to Beck's cognitive behavioural work with depressed patients where he helps them question the 'automatic' hopeless thoughts and replace them with positive thoughts (Beck 1970).

Whether the child's personality type or any depression he may be experiencing is a factor in the causation of the soiling, or comes as a result of it, is open to discussion. But Clayden (1992), in his long experience of treating children with constipation, has recently highlighted the importance of 'intrinsic' psychological factors. Of course for the soiling child, it is immaterial what caused his problem (unless of course it is sexual abuse). What we need to remember is that what he wants is a way out of the vicious circle that permeates every aspect of his life—a vicious circle which can, as we will see in Chapter 14, have a lasting effect on his life opportunities.

SUMMARY

In this chapter evidence is presented to demonstrate the range of social and emotional problems associated with soiling disorders; the child with headaches, stomach aches, who does not feel well and behaves accordingly; the child with poor parental and family relationships; the child who has difficulties at school; and finally in the extreme the child whose parents become so stressed that the child may be at risk of physical abuse. The possible role of intrinsic psychological factors in the aetiology of soiling is discussed; in particular the relationship of stress, personality type, depression and learned helplessness.

CHAPTER 13   Soiling and sexual abuse

Dr Hobbs, who wrote the controversial paper 'Buggery in childhood: a common syndrome of child abuse' (Hobbs & Wynne 1986, Lancet ii: 762–96), was recently asked how many of his sample of abused children had presented with soiling. He replied that he did not know but suspected when the true facts were known 'This would be another area where we would have to rewrite Paediatric Text-books'. (Buchanan 1990)

Problems may arise if the mesh of the net is too narrow or too wide. If we have a system in which it is so tight that not a single case of abuse is missed then it is almost certain that innocent people will be wrongly accused. If the mesh is too loose some cases of abuse will be missed, but it is unlikely that innocent families will be disrupted. It is for society to choose in which direction we should lean, and thereby potentially err. (Clayden 1988a)

These two quotations highlight the dilemma. Of all the issues which surround the soiling child and his/her family, the possibility that the child may be a victim of sexual abuse is the one that causes the professional most anxiety. In recent years the British social worker cannot, if one is to believe the media, get it right. Either children are left in abusing situations for extended periods having been placed there by social workers (the 1991 scandal in the UK of the Berkshire special boarding school where the headmaster had been sexually interferring with a large number of the pupils) or social workers have apparently lost all sense of balance by removing children through dawn raids on the vaguest of suspicions that they may have been victims of ritual sexual abuse (the British 1991 Orkneys child care scandal). The Cleveland child care episode in 1988 demonstrated that even respected paediatric consultants could face ruin at the hands of the media. The subject is endlessly newsworthy. It is, however, interesting to reflect that in the 1970s society did not want to accept that parents 'battered' their children. Here in the 1990s, the fact that some parents undoubtedly do sexually abuse their children is equally unpalatable.

The real difficulty is that the knowledge on child sexual abuse, and the consequences, despite the great volume of literature, is still in its infancy. When in the 1970s in Britain, the realities of 'the battered baby syndrome' were first made known, many professionals who were involved at that time might say retrospectively that too many children were taken into care, too few efforts were made to keep children with their families, and some of these children were probably more damaged by their 'care' experiences than the physical abuse they might have received at home. Recently Colin Pritchard, Professor of Social Work at Southampton University, has noted that in the UK while child deaths from physical abuse appear to have gone down, adolescent and young people's suicide rates appear to have gone up. Many of these young suicides had previously been 'in care' (Pritchard 1991). The corollary may be that the emotional cost on the individual of being protected as a child (removed from home, brought up in care) may lead to a later vulnerability to depression and possible suicide.

This information may be especially relevant for professional people in the throes of learning to work with sexually abused children. Although there is considerable evidence of the damage done by sexual abuse (Jehu 1989), there is less evidence about those who survive abuse with less overt damage. A serious issue must be whether the psychological damage from sexual abuse is greater than the psychological damage of system abuse from disclosure of the sexual abuse? There is much we need to know.

Soiling and Sexual Abuse—a Note of Caution

If knowledge about child sexual abuse is in its infancy, knowledge of the relationship between specific conditions and sexual abuse is only at an embryonic stage. The concern is that what knowledge there is may give a distorted view. With the large number of short training programmes on child sexual abuse, professional social workers are likely to be more familiar with the signs and symptoms of sexual abuse than they are familiar with the associated problems of a child with a soiling problem—hence the possible bias to misdiagnosis.

Misdiagnosis is of course another form of 'abuse', and this professional 'abuse' could be as damaging and in some cases more damaging than the suspected sexual abuse. It is also important to remember, and this will be illustrated graphically later in this chapter, that many soiling children can demonstrate signs or symptoms of possible sexual abuse which they have acquired quite innocently as a result of their soiling problem. Having highlighted this problem, it is still important that the possibility of sexual abuse should remain on the agenda.

Sexual abuse is rarely a life-threatening situation, and most clinicians who suspect a child may be the victim of sexual abuse can allow themselves the luxury of time in coming to their diagnosis. It is also probable that there are different degrees of physical and emotional damaged inflicted by sexual abuse, although knowledge in this area is still limited. These differences may be related to such factors as the age of the child, the type of abuse, the power relationship within the abuse, and also to factors as nebulous and immeasurable as how the child feels about the abuse. Some children, knowing the likely consequences of a disclosure, may choose to live within an abusing situation, judging this to be the lesser of the evils. Hopefully there may come a time when they can be helped to make a less desperate choice.

In this chapter we will take a balanced view of some of the issues surrounding soiling and sexual abuse. We will look at what *is* known about the risk factors, the indicators, the danger of misdiagnosis and we will examine the author's own findings (Buchanan 1990). If this chapter helps practitioners to be aware of the possible association between soiling and sexual abuse, and yet acknowledge that there is still much we do not know, and that in not knowing, there is much damage we can do to children and their families, it will have achieved its purpose.

The Beginnings of Knowledge

Despite the fact that incest has been a crime since the Middle Ages, it is only recently that the potential scale of sexual abuse of children has been recognised (Finklehor 1979, Mrazek & Kempe 1981).

Awareness that there may be a relationship between soiling and sexual abuse is even more recent. With hindsight, we now know the evidence was there. Was not Freud in his essays on sexuality in children and anal erotism (1905, 1917) opening our eyes to the possibility that children presenting with soiling may have been sexually abused?

In Bellman's learned and lengthy discourse on soiling published in

1966, sexual abuse is not even considered. Indeed at that time the possibility that some children might have been sexually abused was hardly on the child care agenda.

In an earlier paper by the author (Oliver & Buchanan 1979), an association between soiling, sexual abuse and physical abuse was noted in three generations of one multi-problem family. It was observed that in these very disturbed families, the boundaries between the private and family functions of the different generations often become blurred. Although it was known that soiling problems in children and sexual abuse of children often co-existed in the same households, it was not possible to make the leap that the soiling might have been caused by sexual abuse.

This leap was made with the publication of the Hobbs & Wynne paper 'Buggery in childhood: a common syndrome of child abuse' (1986). The relationship between some cases of soiling in children and sexual abuse was now recognised, but with this recognition came mighty controversies (Cleveland Report 1988).

Definitions of Sexual Abuse

Studies on the incidence of child sexual abuse vary from 1 in 10 (MORI Poll 1984) to 1 in 3 (Russell 1983) depending on the definitions used. Sexual abuse of boys is felt to be less common than sexual abuse of girls. Hanks et al (1988) feel that the incidence of sexual abuse of boys may be underestimated, and this may be due to our 'deeply embedded societal mores'. Certainly boys appear less likely to disclose and adults less likely to suspect abuse of boys.

Central to the number of children diagnosed as sexually abused is of course the definition of sexual abuse. Kempe (1980) used a very wide definition:

> The involvement of dependent, developmentally immature children and adolescents in sexual activities that they do not fully comprehend, to which they are unable to give informed consent or that violate the social taboos of family roles (Kempe in Kempe & Helfer (eds) 1980, p. 198)

The Danger of Misdiagnosis

Hanks et al (1988, pp. 142–6) stated that the symptoms presented by children who are being sexually abused were many and varied:

The association of both physical and behavioural changes is especially characteristic . . . the cardinal (physical) symptoms of injury are pain, soreness, swelling and bleeding. Difficulty with the passage of urine and bowel movement are encountered . . . secondary or late-onset wetting and soiling in a child who has previously been clean or dry are especially important.

One symptom, however, on which they placed special emphasis, reflex anal dilation (RAD), is now known to be misleading. The Cleveland Report (1988) warned that extreme care needs to be taken in the diagnosis of sexual abuse, especially where the evidence is based solely on physical findings. Clayden (1987, 1988a) and Stanton & Sunderland (1989) have shown that the symptom RAD can be elicited in children with a history of significant constipation, and in these cases the symptom is related to their physical condition, and in some cases to the treatment procedure of anal dilatation. Clayden has also noted that children who have experienced coercive physical treatment for their constipation such as enemas or suppositories can produce symbols in drawings that are highly suggestive of violation or sexual assault (Clayden 1988a).

In 1989, the author published a paper highlighting the danger of misdiagnosis (Buchanan 1989a). The following hypothetical case study illustrates the concerns.

A social worker takes a girl suspected of being sexually abused to see a paediatrician. Having recently moved to the area, early medical records are unavailable. But this child has in fact a history of severe constipation from birth, has been treated with suppositories and anal dilatation (medical stretching of the anus), has had recurrent urinary infections (commonly associated with chronic constipation in girls, Levine & Bakow 1976), and now presents with severe behaviour problems and a poor relationship with mother. Without the early medical records, one strong possible diagnosis is that the child has been sexually abused. *But this diagnosis could be very wrong.*

In the author's survey, it was decided to focus on this 'clustering effect' of behavioural, social and medical symptoms seen in the 30 soiling children who took part in the author's experimental treatment group. The symptoms focused on were all symptoms that could have been indicative of sexual abuse, or equally well could have been acquired quite innocently as the result of the soiling problem. Table 10 looks at three aspects. Firstly those children with behavioural symptoms—in

Table 10. The danger of misdiagnosis. The clustering of sexual abuse symptoms in 30 soiling children, all of which could have been acquired as a result of their soiling problem (Buchanan 1990)

	Sex	*Behaviour	*Social	*Medical
1	M	+	+ + +	+
2	M	−	+	+ +
3	F	+	+ + +	+ + + +(a)
4	M	+	+ + +	+ +
5	M	−	+ +	+ +
6	M	−	+	+ +
7	M	+	+	+
8	F	−	+ +	+(a)
9	F	−	+	−(a)
10	M	−	+	−(a)
11	M	+	+	−
12	F	−	+	+ +
13	M	+	+	−(a)
14	M	+	+	+
15	M	+	+ +	+ +
16	M	−	+ +	+ + + +
17	M	+	+ + +	+
18	M	+	−	−
19	F	+	+ +	+ +
20	M	+	+	−
21	F	−	+	+ + + +(a)
22	M	+	+	+
23	M	+	+	+ +
24	M	+	+ +	+ + +
25	M	−	+ +	+
26	M	+	+ +	+
27	M	+	+	+ +
28	M	+	+ +	+(a)
29	M	+	−	+(a)
30	F	+	+	+

*For specific symptoms see text.
(a) Identified as possibly at risk of child sexual abuse by further survey.

this case children who had a Rutter 'A' score of more than 12 (this suggests a degree of behavioural maladjustment) (Rutter 1965). Secondly those children with social indicators, such as a very tense mother, poor marital relationships (or poor father figure/mother relationships), known professional concern regarding their care. Thirdly those children who had medical conditions or treatment procedures relating to their soiling problems which could be misinterpreted without a proper history, such as severe constipation, passage of abnormally large stools, recurrent urinary infections, treatment with suppositories or enemas, treatment by anal dilatation, history of very 'sore' bottom from constantly sitting around in soiled pants.

A cross under the appropriate column indicates the presence of one of the symptoms.

The table illustrates quite graphically that for many of the soiling children there is a 'clustering' of symptoms which might suggest a diagnosis of sexual abuse. Although there was no surety that some of the children had not been sexually abused, if any of the above children came to a court of law, it would have to be said that all the above symptoms could have been acquired as a result of soiling.

Possible Indicators of Sexual Abuse in Children who have Soiling Problems

The previous discussion has highlighted some of the controversies. In the author's original study in only three cases out of thirty was the possibility of sexual abuse considered (Buchanan 1990).

These three cases were all girls. In each case the girl was admitted into hospital or the local adolescent unit for further investigations for soiling, with the additional brief that sexual abuse should be considered. In all three cases investigations were negative or inconclusive.

Because of concern that some sexually abused children may have been missed in this study, a further retrospective screening process was undertaken.

Experience suggests that there may be three possible triggers for soiling following sexual abuse. Firstly fine bowel control may be damaged by buggery; secondly the post trauma of the assault may trigger psychological mechanisms resulting in soiling; and thirdly some of the children may use soiling as a defence against unwanted sexual advances. In coming to some specific diagnostic criteria the task is to link what is known about sexual abuse to what is known about soiling.

Developing an 'at risk' checklist

Finklehor (1979), who has extensively reviewed child abuse literature and undertaken large scale retrospective studies of adults admitting sexual victimisation in childhood in the USA, has developed a checklist which highlights the girls he has found to be more likely to suffer sexual victimisation.

There are eight 'vulnerability factors' in this list. These are: a girl who has a stepfather; a girl who has lived without a mother; a girl who is not close to her mother; a girl whose mother never finished high school; a girl whose mother is sex-punitive (that is, witholds sex from partner as a punishment for misdemeanours); a girl whose mother receives no physical affection from father; a family whose income is under $10 000 per annum; a girl who has two friends or less in childhood (Finklehor 1979). In Finklehor's study, 80% of those girls 'victimised' had four or more of the above factors present. Unfortunately, Finklehor has not developed a similar checklist for boys, but has summarised the most important findings noted in sexually abused boys. He notes that estimates drawn from men in the general population suggests 2.5–8.7% of men have suffered sexual victimisation as children. These figures indicate that on our present knowledge two or three girls are victimised for every boy. Although boys are commonly victimised by men, they are more likely than girls to be victimised outside the family, and in conjunction with other children. Boys are also more likely than girls to come from poor single-parent families and they are also more likely than girls to be victims of physical abuse, but they are less likely to be reported to the police, or other protective agency.

Finklehor's ideas were used to develop a checklist to highlight soiling girls and boys who may be more vulnerable than other children to sexual abuse (Table 11). Two additional risk factors were added for the boys which were factors seen in other boys who had disclosed sexual abuse in the author's clinical experience.

Consistency of soiling

Hanks et al (1988) and Hobbs (1989, personal communication) suggest that it is important to separate out children who soil as a result of severe constipation from those who are 'soft' soilers. In Hobbs's

Table 11   Children who may be vulnerable to sexual victimisation

Girls' checklist: possibly at risk (score 4 or more; score 1 for each factor (Finklehor 1970))	Boys' weighted checklist: possibly at risk (score 4 or more; score as outlined)
(i) Stepfather (ii) Ever lived without mother (iii) Not close to mother (iv) Mother left school without taking any exams* (v) Sex-punitive mother (vi) No physical affection from father (vii) Family on Income support* (viii) Two friends or less in childhood	(i) Parents on DHSS benefit (score 1)* (ii) Single parent (score 1) (iii) History of neglect/abuse (score 1) (iv) History of poor supervision/ different caretakers (score 1) (v) Social contact with known paedophile (score 3)† (vi) Shared bed: boy/male adult. Adolescent boy/single mother (score 2)†

*These were adapted to British equivalents.
†These were risk factors from the author's experience.

experience most child sexual abuse children are soft soilers although he has known sexually abused victims who are constipated.

This, however, is a controversial area, and other authorities, notably Clayden (1989, personal communication), would dispute this. We have already discussed how hard it can be to diagnose constipation effectively. In Clayden's experience you do not have to be a 'hard' soiler to suffer from constipation. Soft soiling is commonly associated with constipation. He too, has seen children with severe constipation who have been sexually abused. But even so, the consistency of the soiling may, with other factors, be an indicator.

Children who were previously clean

Similarly Hobbs (1989, personal communication) feels that a child who has previously been clean and then suddenly starts to soil 'invites explanations'. These would be children who had never soiled. Of course, we know there are many reasons why a child starts soiling; and this may be as innocent as attending a school with poor toilet facilities. On its own this would not be an indicator of sexual abuse but clustered with other factors it could be.

Indicators from inappropriate sexual
behaviour/family histories/medical
indicators

Since Cleveland we have to be very careful not to rely on a single indicator but on a range of social, medical and behavioural indicators. In the author's study, the following questions were asked:

1. Were there any definite sexual indicators in the child's behaviour? (For example, simulated intercourse, inappropriate sexual knowledge.)
2. Were there any particular factors in the child's social circumstances which might place the child at particular risk? (Known family history of child sexual abuse (CSA), history of rape, homosexuality in family member or person living with family.)
3. Were there any 'hard' medical indicators of CSA (injuries in genital area, venereal disease, pregnancy).

Results from using all the above indicators
in a retrospective study

In the author's study, the 30 children in the treatment study were screened against the above factors, to see if any of the children came up with a *range of indicators*. This screening highlighted the three children who had already been identified as at risk; it also highlighted a further five children where possible sexual abuse should have been considered. The first was a 13 year old girl who suddenly starting soiling age nine, and was a 'soft' soiler. The second was a six year old boy who was a 'soft' soiler but who lived with a man who may have had paedophilic tendencies. The third was an intelligent boy of 10 also a 'soft' soiler previously clean whose problem improved when he moved away from some neighbours who had made him very twitchy and nervous. The fourth case was a poorly supervised four year old who lived in an abusive family setting. He may have been at risk because of poor supervision and because he lived in an area where a known paedophile operated. Finally the last child may have been at risk because he shared a bed with his much older adolescent brother. When the family were rehoused the boys had separate bedrooms, and his soiling improved but this may have been due to psychological factors. The survey suggested that the above factors may be a useful tool in highlighting soiling children who may be more likely than other soiling children to be victims of sexual victimisation.

All methods have major limitations. The concern is that if they are used in isolation they become yet another tool to increase the danger of misdiagnosis.

The Dilemma

This then is the dilemma for the clinician. On the other hand there is the need to protect children from sexual abuse, on the other hand is the danger of wrongly accusing families with all the resultant distress.

What is desperately needed is a comparative study of definitely sexually abused children who had soiling problems, and soiling children who (as far as it is possible to ascertain) had not been sexually abused, if such a study were possible. Until this is done, all we can do is to follow the advice of the Cleveland Report (1988).

> If there is a suspicion of child sexual abuse in the mind of the professional, the dangers of false identification ought not to be forgotten. Therefore, when a suspicion arises the professional may elect to:

> Take no further action.
> Hold a watching brief.
> Make further informal inquiries.

It follows from this that where there is a soiling problem the professional involved should have an expert knowledge not only of sexual abuse but also of the associated problems of soiling.

SUMMARY

This chapter highlights a dilemma. On the one hand there is a growing knowledge of the extent and the symptoms of child sexual abuse, but on the other hand with soiling children there is a strong danger of misdiagnosing sexual abuse, as many of the symptoms can be acquired quite innocently as a result of the soiling problem. Methods on how to improve diagnosis of sexual abuse in soiling children are discussed, but it is recognised there is a danger that these too if used in isolation may result in further misdiagnosis.

CHAPTER 14   The future for the soiling child

Although soiling or wetting, especially night encopresis, have a profound psychological effect on both parent and child, they have never been considered as major reasons for health expenditure. These disorders are not thought to have far-reaching overt health consequences but the long-term psychological effects have largely been uncharted.
(Butler & Golding 1986, p. 64)

In this chapter we look into the crystal ball. All parents want to know what the future holds for their soiling child. It is not enough for them to know that he/she will get better; they want to know when and what the long term effects are likely to be. Clinicians too need to know the factors which may indicate a prognosis. Every child is an exception, but it is easier to make clinical decisions if there are some signposts on the roadmap.

Until recently, the long term consequences of a soiling problem had largely been uncharted, although as we saw in Chapter Nine, Dr Clayden includes a useful diagram on the length of time his patients needed to take stimulant laxatives (Figure 18). In the author's study (Buchanan 1990), a special focus was made on the future for the soiling child. In this chapter we will outline some of these findings. In many cases numbers involved are small and no firm conclusions should be attached to them, but they are given for the possible direction they may suggest.

There are three areas of interest. Firstly we will look at factors influencing treatment outcome. Secondly we will look in depth at children who 'relapsed' back into soiling having been clean, and the results of a further five year follow-up study undertaken by the author on all 66 children and the implications from these findings. Finally, in the vein of Professor Rutter and others who have stimulated an interest in 'pathway studies', that is plotting potential routes from childhood disorders into adult life (Rutter 1989), we will take a less scientific look

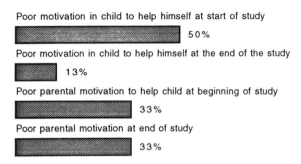

Figure 34. Motivation in soiling children (30 children under a 'whole child' treatment) (Buchanan 1990)

into the crystal ball, and consider possible life span issues for the soiling child.

Factors Affecting Treatment Outcome

'Motivation', especially the child's 'motivation', is a factor suggested by Taitz et al (1986) and Richman (1983) as influencing treatment outcome. In the author's 'whole child' treatment group, encouraging the children to help themselves, or become 'motivated' to help themselves and their soiling problem, was a focus of therapy. It was felt that you could not dismiss children as 'not motivated' when not being motivated might well be a result of 'learned helplessness'. In the author's study, motivation was assessed by two therapists (Figure 34).

Fifty per cent of the children had little or no motivation to help themselves and their soiling problem and were effectively resistant to any treatment approaches at the start of treatment. Figure 34 suggests that the 'whole child' therapist was able to overcome the child's resistance in most cases. What was significant is that where it was not possible to overcome the child's resistance, there was little or no treatment success. *Motivating the child therefore was indeed essential for a good treatment outcome.* The therapist was less successful in overcoming parental resistance. The parents who had poor motivation at the beginning of the study were not all the same parents who were poorly motivated at the end. Some parents changed as they felt treatment was/was not progressing. Most poorly motivated parents were poorly motivated in that they were not supportive to their child and his efforts

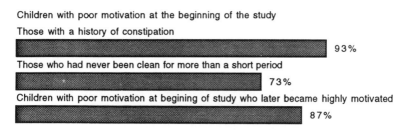

Children with poor motivation at the beginning of the study
Those with a history of constipation

93%

Those who had never been clean for more than a short period

73%

Children with poor motivation at begining of study who later became highly motivated

87%

Figure 35. Factors affecting motivation (Buchanan 1990)

at helping himself, or were not consistent, or not especially interested. These parents, however, were not associated with treatment failure, but treatment may have been less successful because of their attitude, and longer treatment may also have been necessary. There was, however, a strong association between a parent who actively undermined the child's efforts and limited or no treatment success.

There was a very significant association between a history of constipation and the child's initial motivation (Figure 35). Managing a child's constipation had an important bearing on motivation. A child was unlikely to remain motivated to help himself if constipation was not effectively managed. Initially where the child had never experienced being clean, there was difficulty in inspiring in him the belief that there was some purpose in trying. Surprisingly, high stress levels in the home were not necessarily associated with poor child motivation. But all the children in special schools for slow learners were poorly motivated at the start of the study and remained poorly motivated at the end of the study. No pattern between age and motivation or sex and motivation could be identified.

Another factor that has been cited as related to treatment outcome is the socioeconomic background of the child's family (Taitz et al 1986). Figure 36 compares treatment outcome by socioeconomic status of the parents. It also compares the findings with those of the Taitz study (1986).

The numbers in the author's 'whole child' treatment group were very small, but are given here to indicate that children with a soiling problem living in families in low socioeconomic groups do not necessarily have to have a poor treatment outcome. Taitz's (1986) families had of course to make their own way to a hospital appointment, whereas the author's study was home based. It may be more accurate

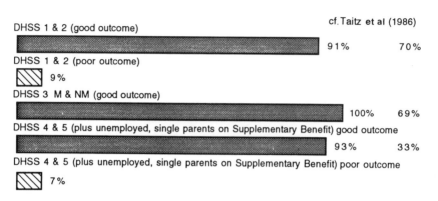

Figure 36. Occupational background of parents and treatment outcome of 30 children (Buchanan 1990)

to say that not having a car, and not being able to afford a taxi to get to the hospital, is related to poor treatment outcome, rather than socioeconomic background.

Figure 37 relates treatment outcome to various social factors seen in the total group of 66 children treated in the various settings. Children for whom there was professional concern about their care did less well than those for whom there was no concern, although these results were not significant. Having a 'very tense' mother also appeared to affect outcome, but again these differences did not reach a significant level. Having more than three social stresses in a family surprisingly had less effect on outcome.

The combination of having a 'very tense' mother and having a present or past history of constipation was, however, associated with poorer treatment outcome. Only 50% of these children had any treatment success.

One of the most important prognostic factors was the child's ability level, and this was a factor in whatever treatment approach was used (Figure 38).

Children who Relapse

One of the unexpected findings of the author's treatment study was the number of children who became clean and then reverted to soiling —what was called 'relapse'. A relapse back to soiling can be a devas-

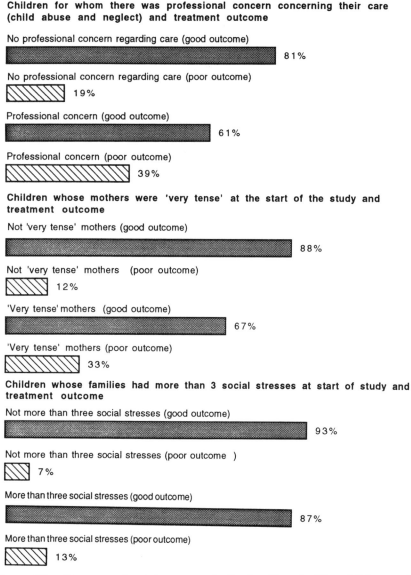

Children for whom there was professional concern concerning their care (child abuse and neglect) and treatment outcome

No professional concern regarding care (good outcome)

81%

No professional concern regarding care (poor outcome)

19%

Professional concern (good outcome)

61%

Professional concern (poor outcome)

39%

Children whose mothers were 'very tense' at the start of the study and treatment outcome

Not 'very tense' mothers (good outcome)

88%

Not 'very tense' mothers (poor outcome)

12%

'Very tense' mothers (good outcome)

67%

'Very tense' mothers (poor outcome)

33%

Children whose families had more than 3 social stresses at start of study and treatment outcome

Not more than three social stresses (good outcome)

93%

Not more than three social stresses (poor outcome)

7%

More than three social stresses (good outcome)

87%

More than three social stresses (poor outcome)

13%

Figure 37. Presence of social concerns in the families of soiling children and treatment outcome (Buchanan 1990)

tating blow for a child and his family who may have thought their problem was behind them. The literature did not cover this well, although recently Clayden has published some interesting findings (Clayden 1992). According to Levine (1982) the 'remission rate is

Average or above average ability

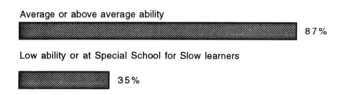

87%

Low ability or at Special School for Slow learners

35%

Figure 38. Child's ability and good treatment outcome

high but so is the relapse rate'. Berg et al (1983) said 'although successfully treated cases sometimes had further bouts of soiling they *usually* cleared up quickly', but he made no study of this. There was no literature on how many children relapsed after significant clean periods, or what caused the relapses. Indeed the author's interest in relapse came by chance, and it was only because she was in direct contact with the families that she was able to question the validity of her statistics. In her study, at the end of the 'whole child' treatment, the soiling of 90% of the children was considerably reduced. More precisely 77% of children in the 'whole child' treatment group were soiling once a week or less. On follow-up at six months after the end of treatment, 70% were soiling once a week or less, and on follow-up at one year 70% were also soiling once a week or less. These appeared highly satisfactory results, especially when one looked at the number who had been *totally* clean for over two months. But what the figures did not show is that the figures did not represent the same children. When the records of individual children were examined it was discovered that only about a fifth of children became clean and stayed clean for ever. All the others had shorter or longer relapses. Because part of the treatment was to train children to cope with relapses, most had managed without too much ado, and in most cases without further treatment.

Because of this unexpected finding, further efforts were made to establish what children relapsed and why.

Figure 39 considers this factor. It separates those children who relapsed back into soiling behaviour from the non-relapsing children. Only 30 soiling children were involved, so no definite conclusions can be reached from such a small sample. The figures are only given as an indication of three factors that might appear to separate relapsers from non-relapsers. Firstly most non-relapsers were age six or under. None were in the 8–10 year bracket. The other few non-relapsers were 12 +

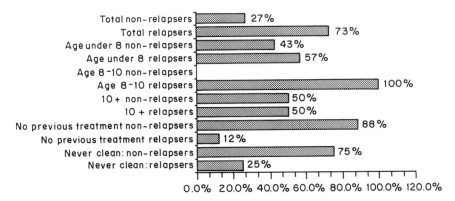

Figure 39. Children who 'relapsed' into soiling having been clean (Buchanan 1990)

and maybe had grown out of their problem. Most non-relapsers had had no previous treatment, and most had never been clean before asking for help. Efforts were made to see if the groups differed in presence or absence of constipation, early birth history and social class. None of these factors showed any major difference between the groups, but this may be because of the small size of the sample. This suggests that relapsers and non-relapsers are broadly sim... children. Maybe the non-relapsers were able to overcome their problem before too many secondary problems set in. The figures also suggest that if the soiling child 'misses the boat' before the age of eight (possibly younger) soiling will be a problem which will come and go over the middle years of childhood with all the resulting difficulties.

The Natural History of Soiling Problems

In the author's study, the above findings raised questions that were too important to be ignored. It was therefore decided to undertake a further final survey of all the study children. This took place five years after the start of the research project. Every child guidance agency in the area, and in particular where the child lived, was approached and their index cards checked. The two main child psychiatric centres which had grown up over the period were also approached and their index cards checked. Permission was also given for the hospital records of all the 66 children to be checked. This survey did not pretend to be

Table 12. The final assessment—five years on (66 soiling children)

Present age (mean)	Age referred (mean)	Age last known treatment for soiling (mean)
Children treated at hospital (18 children)		
14 years	6.0 years	9.2 years
Children treated by the child psychiatric clinic (18 children)		
18.4 years	7.9 years	9.8 years
Experimental group 'Whole child treatment group' (30 children)		
11.5 years	7.5 years	9.0 years

Buchanan (1990).

complete. Some children might have left the area; it was discovered that one child had died. The hospital, however, was the central hospital for the area and although specialist cases may have been sent out of the area to Oxford or even London, it is unlikely that they would have been so directed without first going through the local hospital. Hospital records at the hospital were traced for all the 66 children.

It was hoped that with the length of time that had elapsed between the start and the end of the study, a better picture would emerge of the natural history of a soiling problem. Table 12 summarises the situation of the 66 children five years on.

It was hypothesised that this final survey would produce some surprises. What it did show was that over a third of children who were treated by the child psychiatric clinic later needed further treatment and most chose to go to another agency. Also over a third of the children treated by the hospital also needed further treatment and many of these children went to another agency for this help.

Although 23% of the 'whole child' treatment group needed further help most returned to the original agency.

This movement between the agencies supported the hypothesis that there were some children who moved from agency to agency to seek the elusive cure. If patients are dissatisfied with their original treatment centre, they may want to be referred somewhere else for a new look at their problem, but this at least initially must be more time-consuming for the professional who has to go over the whole history again. There is also evidence that families were sometimes confused by the different interpretations of their child's problems given in different agencies. The survey also supported the hypothesis that for many children soiling is a long term problem, whatever treatment route is taken.

The study showed that when *all known treatment is recorded*, that is the time from the initial referral to a consultative agency to the last known treatment for soiling at a consultative agency, there was an average of 3.5 years of treatment for each soiling child.

It has also to be remembered these averages are made up of some children who needed many years of help. Indeed there was one child who was known to have been treated by the hospital for over seven years.

Implications for Treatment

That soiling is by its nature a relapsing condition was an important finding. This means that treatment has to look beyond the short term cure and plan for a long term problem which for many soiling children will be with them throughout middle childhood.

The implications for treatment are, as we have seen in Chapter 12, that many of the associated difficulties can be even more disabling to the child than the initial soiling problem, and that in order to limit the damage to the child they need treatment in their own right: The following analysis of the life span issues for the soiling child dramatically illustrates this point.

Life Span Issues

In an interesting article in the *Journal of Child Psychology and Psychiatry* entitled 'Pathways from childhood to adult life', Michael Rutter (1989) reviewed principles and concepts of development in relations to life span issues.

Findings from these 'pathway' studies showed the need to consider:

> Development in its social context; timing of experiences; intrinsic and experimental factors; continuities and discontinuities; parallels and differences between normal and abnormal development; heterotypic and homotypic continuities; key life transitions; risk and protective factors; indirect chain effects; mediating mechanisms; age as an index of maturational and experimental factors. (Rutter 1989)

The key issue is that a child's behaviour and experiences in childhood serve to shape the environment experienced in adult life. Thus a soiling problem in a child, if poorly managed, can have consequences for the child well beyond the actual period of the soiling problem. The legacy of 'having been' a soiling child can carry through into his adult life and with some children profoundly affect their life opportunities. Figure 40 shows a projected pathway from childhood to adult life for the soiling child.

This figure is of course a very simplified pathway, and some factors are not contingent upon soiling, but the point is that they inter-relate with the soiling problem to produce a poor prognosis for later life.

It is known for instance that poor school attendance can lead to early school leaving and lack of scholastic qualifications leading to unskilled work or a poor employment record (Gray et al 1980). Again there is an association with frequent temper tantrums in childhood, making it more likely that this explosive type of behaviour would lead to an early exit from school with poor educational attainments and lower occupational status in mid-life (Caspi, Elder & Herbener 1990). There is also an association with difficult behaviour in childhood and lack of control in adult life and 'ill tempered parenting' (Caspi, Elder & Herbener 1990). It is well known that children with a range of severe anti-social behaviours in childhood are associated with a variety of poor outcomes in adult life (Graham 1986).

In our soiling children, anti-social behaviour was only associated with some children who had had many years of treatment for their soiling problem. More typically the soiling child was a sensitive personality who scored highly on Rutter's Neurotic scale. There is an association between childhood shyness and late entry into a stable career leading to lower occupational achievement (Caspi, Elder & Herbener 1990). It is quite possible that some of the soiling children whose self-esteem was severely affected by their problem fell into a similar pattern.

If one looks closely at the pathway chart there are many other problems associated with soiling which could have long term repercussions for the child. Relationship problems with parents could lead to family breakdown and consequential events; undiagnosed sexual abuse can lead to later psychiatric problems (Jehu 1989); the high risk of physical abuse could lead to physical damage and/or separation from the family.

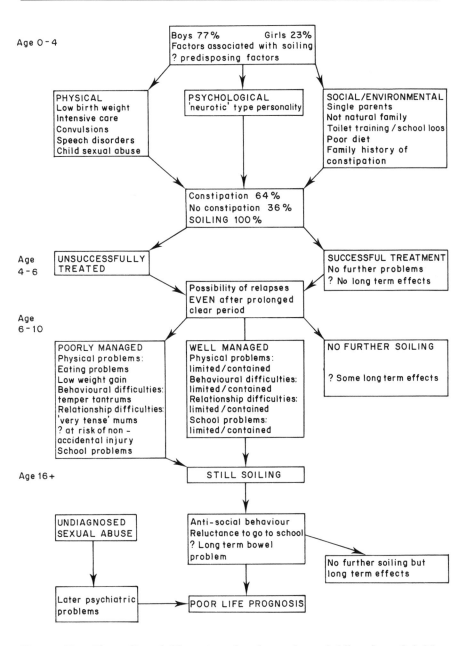

Figure 40. The soiling child: projected pathway from childhood to adult life (Buchanan 1990)

SUMMARY

In this chapter we have looked at the prognosis for the soiling child, and have drawn a possible life path from childhood to adulthood following the example of the pathway studies by Professor Rutter (Rutter 1989). When one thinks of the future for the soiling child, Rutter's 'Pathways from childhood to adult life' can make depressing reading, but in his article he makes the point strongly that the routes are not inevitable. At every stage along the route there are possible mediating mechanisms, for continuities or discontinuity. This is especially relevant for the soiling child. Many of the factors associated with soiling, for example low birth weight, being born to single parents, have in themselves given the child a certain vulnerability to later life stresses (Butler & Golding 1986), but the treatment and management of the later soiling problem and its associated difficulties can increase or decrease these stresses and so affect the pathway into adulthood. This then is the real challenge for those trying to help the soiling child.

AFTERWORD Setting up treatment centres

AFTERWORD Setting up treatment centres

. . . create a system or be enslav'd by another Man's (Blake (1757–1827) *Jerusalem* f10 line 20)

In this final section, we move from what is known and what we have learnt about soiling children and their families to thinking about creating the treatment centres and systems which will meet their needs. New knowledge makes ever increasing demands on existing systems. Systems which may have been set up to meet quite different perceptions of need can prove inflexible in bringing the benefits of new knowledge into practice. In this afterword we will look at some ways of adapting existing treatment centres or developing new systems to meet the needs of the soiling child.

When thinking about soiling children, it is important to note that their needs are not that different from children with other chronic childhood disorders such as asthma, diabetes and epilepsy. The link between 'psyche' and 'soma' in all these groups is well recognised. Indeed, in an interesting book by Lask & Fosson (1989), it is suggested there are many conditions where 'children talk *with* their bodies'.

'Stress and distress can produce virtually any physical symptoms, and the physician should certainly not discount psychological factors as a possible cause whatever the symptoms' (Lask & Fosson 1989, p. 54). All such conditions benefit from treatment approaches and systems which focus on the 'whole child', and in meeting the specialist needs of soilers, it may also be possible to set up integrated or parallel systems for some of these other groups.

Setting up a system is also about allocating scarce resources. But if the new system also benefits a wide range of children suffering from other disorders, the new system may in itself bring about savings.

The Need for a Higher Medical Priority for the Treatment and Management of Soiling

However, quite apart from the needs of other children, soiling children themselves merit a higher medical profile.

Soiling is not a life-threatening condition. Most soiling in children is self-limiting. Leukaemia, the most common malignant disease in childhood, only occurs in 1 in 30 000 children under the age of 14 (Hull & Johnston 1981) but it accounts for half the children dying from malignant disease. Malignancies are second only to accidents as the most common cause of death in childhood.

But as Hull & Johnston (1981) say 'a death of a child over the age of one year is rare'. Deaths in childhood range from a figure of 65/100 000 at 1–4 years to 28/100 000 at 10–14 years (Hull & Johnston 1981). Acute infections, which used to be a major cause of death in childhood, are usually controllable. Children who fall ill suddenly are brought directly to the hospital emergency and accident department. The corollary is that most patients seen by the paediatric consultancy service have less acute conditions. 'The commoner problems include recurrent respiratory infections, asthma, failure to thrive, small size, suspected developmental delay, convulsions or suspected convulsions, nocturnal enuresis and constipation' (Hull & Johnston 1981). What is interesting is that in all these conditions, possible psychosocial components in the disorder are well recognised. In many cases too, with these conditions, the expectation is not so much that the physician will 'cure' the disorder, but will, by effective management, improve the quality of the child's life, and maybe limit possible longer term damage. This is perhaps one of the purposes of the specialist clinics that have been set up in paediatric departments: asthma clinics, diabetic clinics, epileptic clinics, clinics for growth problems and developmental clinics. The secondary benefit of these clinics is that they provide an opportunity for groups of parents and children with the disorders to meet up, which is in itself therapeutic and costs nothing.

Although the physical health risks from soiling and constipation may be less acute than, say, asthma or diabetes, in other aspects they are very similar. Soiling is not a life-threatening condition, but it carries physical and psychological health risks for the child, and his family. (In fact, in the author's study, one child died age 16 as a result of drowning but there was a suspicion that there may have been suicidal intentions (Buchanan 1990).) Early expert care can reduce the long term health risk for the child. Most soiling in children, as we have mentioned, is self-limiting. But other self-limiting conditions happily are also very common in childhood. Many children 'grow out' of asthma, the tendency to have fits, or enuresis. However, during the 'growing out of it' period they need careful medical management.

Although most soilers also 'grow out' of soiling, some of them may suffer long term physical damage as a result of their childhood disorder, and in extreme cases a soiling disorder could make them more vulnerable to bowel carcinomas in adulthood (Read 1986).

Soiling, as we have seen, is a common disorder, but it has traditionally been the 'Cinderella' of paediatrics, and child psychiatry. Indeed it is not a topic that naturally recommends itself to ambitious young researchers. However, when we remember that children's intestinal tracts are 'the mirror wherein is reflected the status of bodily activities in general', (Bargen 1946, in Walker 1985), might we be missing something by giving soiling disorders such a low medical profile?

The Present Treatment for Soilers

The present treatment for soiling children, certainly in the UK, and probably in most countries, is at the very least lacking in overall planning, at worst not helping the soiling child nor Health Service budgets. Soilers are heavy users of resources. Taitz in the UK has estimated that disorders of defaecation account for up to 10% of his consultation time (Molnar et al 1983). In the UK, leukaemia affects 1 in 30 000 children, diabetes 1 in 1 200 children, convulsions 1 in 25 children (Hull & Johnston 1981). Soiling affects 1 in every 33 five year olds and 1 in every 100 children aged 10, 11 or 12 (Butler & Golding 1986, Rutter, Tizard & Whitmore 1970). As we have seen, the mean length of treatment is around four years, and the mean age of the last consultative appointment is about nine years, whatever treatment agency the child attends (Buchanan 1990).

Many children go from consultative agency to consultative agency looking for the elusive cure. No attempt has been made to estimate the hours of treatment the soiling child receives at the hands of his general practitioner. When there is evidence that easy access to expert medical care at an early age can reduce treatment time and give the child a better prospect of total cure, it is right to ask is there not a better way of managing the problem?

A soiling child's treatment trip

Let us consider a typical treatment trip for a soiling child in a local community in the UK. Initially the mother has to overcome a number of obstacles before receiving expert help. Firstly she has to overcome her natural reticence, shame and guilt about her failure to toilet-train her child. She then seeks help from her health visitor (in other countries perhaps her local child clinic), or her general practitioner, or she is persuaded to seek help by the child's nursery or school. From her primary care agency she receives a range of advice. As Graham notes 'parents are sometimes confused by conflicting advice given to them by professionals, unaware of previous opinions offered' (Graham 1986).

When her primary care agency is unable to help, she seeks a referral to a consultative agency. This may involve telling her respected general practitioner that she is dissatisfied with his service; or going into the child's school and talking to the headmistress. Mother is then directed to the consultative agency: psychiatric or paediatric. Here, the treatment package can be very different depending on the agency, although as we have seen the treatment needs of most soiling children are similar. Once at the treatment centre, the effort of attending regular appointments, or even the stress engendered by some appointments, particularly some types of psychiatric therapies, may be too great.

Mother may then drop out of treatment—it is really easier to put up with the child's soiling. But in all probability, there will be a further crisis and she will re-present later at the same agency, or to go back to her primary agency to seek a referral to the other type of agency. Once again she will receive a totally different treatment package. In the meantime, the child gathers a host of secondary problems.

This is surely not a road that promotes easy and early access to expert treatment. As we know, the assessment of some aspects of a soiling problem can be difficult; the role of constipation, the possible chance that the child may be sexually abused. Under the system described, a child could be grossly constipated, or sexually abused, for some years before the correct help was at hand.

No story is of course totally one sided. There are benefits to the above system. Most treatment, whatever treatment is given, is effective at least in the short term. When children drop out or do not re-present it is tempting to think they have dropped out because they no longer have any symptoms. What research has shown is that for many children this is not so.

The dual treatment route—paediatric care or psychiatric care—does give the families an alternative centre, which may be able to reassess the problem and approach it from a new angle. Whether the benefits of this outweigh the confusion that can be engendered by the different approaches is doubtful.

At present the main expectation in the consultant's mind appears to be that he will effect a 'cure' of the soiling symptom. Because the consultant has what can be a false expectation, when the child continues to soil, or relapses after a period of treatment, it is easy to feel that his present treatment is ineffective and he needs 'the other sort'.

Families too feel let down when there is no 'cure'. With the high rate of drop out, particularly from the psychiatric agencies, and the difficulty in getting a referral, the child is left with the symptom and its consequences.

But does the soiling child need continuous access to medical treatment? To limit the access is of course the most cost-effective solution, especially when the condition is self-limiting and not life-threatening. This is an option. Indeed the long term costs may be as much the responsibility of the social and educational services as medical. However, despite the obstacles, soilers do present and re-present at medical agencies and it is hard to deny them help. It is doubtful whether the multi-agency treatment is cost effective. This type of approach is not meeting the soiling child's needs. As well as being ineffective, it may also be a very expensive service.

The Better Solution: a Multi-disciplinary Approach—Led by the Parents and Patients?

The difficulties of multi-disciplinary work are well known. Dr Roy Meadow, Professor and Head of Paediatrics and Child Health at Leeds in the UK, notes in his foreword to the book by Lask & Fosson, *Childhood Illness: the Psychosomatic Approach*, that where paediatricians are interested in the holistic approach, interdisciplinary difficulties and misunderstandings often destroy the effectiveness of any such treatment approach. 'The respective specialists then work within their own familiar territory and fail to communicate with others' (Meadow in Lask & Fosson 1989). The importance of Lask and Fosson's approach is that they demonstrate that medical specialists, in this case a child psychiatrist and a paediatrician, can work together for the benefit of children. Their book suggests that for this to happen, the child psychiatrist has to understand the way the paediatrician works and his knowledge base, and similarly the paediatrician has to understand the way the child psychiatrist works, his knowledge base and what he has to offer. One of the major difficulties is that each specialism has developed its own specialist language, and this factor is even more pronounced across disciplines. It is not so much the specialist words that cause the difficulties, but words which have another meaning in common English parlance. Another difficulty is learning about the 'culture of the other'. For example, paediatricians, educational psychologists and social workers have, through their professional training, common areas of interest but also different agendas and priorities in working with children and their families. The paediatrician is primarily concerned with the physical health of the child; the educational psychologist the educational progress of the child; and the social worker, in this media conscious age, the physical and emotional 'safety' of the child in his social setting.

While immersed in the arguments of multi-disciplinary work, it is easy to forget that at the very centre is the patient, in this case the soiling child and his family, and that they not only can, as Dr Clayden outlined in Chapter 9, but *should* have the main role in liaising and communicating between different therapists. Indeed this role is in itself 'empowering' and therapeutic; it is a 'partnership' between 'the helpers' and 'the helped', led by the 'helped'.

This places in proper perspective the further dilemma: who holds overall responsibility for the 'care' management of the child. I believe, and child psychiatrists may disagree, that the professional responsibility for the case is most appropriately held by the paediatrician, but of course in reality it is the child and the parents who take responsibility for deciding which of the treatment options they choose to take. Under Dr Clayden's scheme, this becomes more meaningful when letters/records to other professionals are communicated openly, carried by those it involves—the patient and his parent. Because professionals have to communicate in a language that the parent can understand this avoids communication difficulties between disciplines. In some cases, parents and children, having seen the contents of the letter, may decide not to pass the information on. This, too, is their choice. The exception may be in some cases of suspected child abuse, but recent practice in child care has demonstrated that here, too, openness is usually the best approach. Working in multi-disciplinary 'partnership' with patients and parents is not only good practice but indirectly may result in financial savings.

A Specialist Clinic for Soiling Children

Dr Clayden at St Thomas's Hospital has for many years run his Intestinal Motility Clinic for children with constipation, soiling and other gastrointestinal problems, on a multi-disciplinary basis, but most local hospitals will not be able to afford this service. Using both his experience and the author's, Table 13 attempts to highlight the aims of a local service set up to meet the needs of soiling children.

It is of course one thing to list aims, but another thing to work out how these may be met. But to reiterate an earlier point, the aims of a system to meet the needs of soiling children would not be all that different to those of a system to meet the needs of children with some other disorders. In setting up one system it may be possible to integrate it into a better system for treating all children whose disorders have a strong psychosocial element.

Even so, we need to look for further savings. For those with tight budgets, Table 14 may give ideas on how to set up a better service for soiling children without the expense of the ideal.

Where Should the Specialist Clinic be Based?

In developing the idea of a single treatment agency for the treatment and management of soiling children, two possible agency bases suggest themselves. These would be possible here in the UK but hopefully they would also, perhaps with minor adaptations of site and

Table 13 Aims of agency/clinic which would meet needs of soiling children

Overall
1 An effective local system for the treatment and management of soiling children
2 The most cost effective system

Agency
3 Easy access, early access, to local treatment agency. ?direct from primary health care providers, not just general practitioners
4 Single specialist agency in local community
5 Standardised assessment approach, packages of treatment tailored to individual children
6 Self-referral back to specialist agency for relapsers
7 Expert medical care available for assessment at start of treatment, and easy access to expert medical care during treatment. Expert medical care familiar with symptoms of sexual abuse as well as soiling
8 Paramedical support (behaviourally trained social worker or nurse, or other) based in same agency as the expert medical care, able to visit children in their own homes, also familiar with indicators of sexual abuse
9 An agency that stays with the problem through the crises and relapses, and is able to alleviate some of psychosocial stresses around the child, and limit the damage of secondary problems
10 An agency which may be able to initiate a parents' support group

personnel, be possible in other countries. On the one hand is the idea of a paediatric clinic staffed by one or two paediatricians with a specialist interest in soiling, supported by a social worker/specialist nurse based in the hospital who also has a specialist interest and some behavioural training. On the other hand is the community-based school health clinic modelled on or even linked with the enuretic clinic as an 'incontinence clinic'. Here the home visiting of the soiling children would be serviced by the school nurses who would have to set up and supervise the behavioural programmes.

The paediatric clinic has advantages over the community-based incontinence clinic. Firstly many chronic soiling children are already known to the paediatric clinics. They are already taking up considerable paediatric time. With early and easy access there is the possibility that some treatment time could be reduced, but this would be balanced out by the increasing numbers of children coming to the agency who were previously seen at psychiatric clinics. In the UK and elsewhere, paediatric outpatient clinics are already established for a number of disorders. Figure 41 looks at possible systems for children who soil.

The paediatric clinic for soiling children

Apart from the resource implications of setting up any new paediatric clinic, a further difficulty with this option might be funding the appropriate worker to support the 'whole child' approach. In the UK, social workers in hospitals are financed by Social Services. In the present climate Social Services have their own set of priorities, which may not place a soiling child particularly high on their agenda, even with the known risks of physical and possible sexual abuse. However, under the Children Act 1989, a soiling child could be identified as 'a child in need'. Section 17 of Part III 'gives local authorities a general duty to safeguard and promote the welfare of children in need and to promote the upbringing of such children by their families . . . by providing an appropriate range and level of services: (The Children Act 1989, *Regulations and Guidance Volume 2*). Under Section 17, local authorities may feel it a good use of money to fund a part-time social worker. The needs of other children visiting the paediatric outpatient department, such as diabetic children, epileptic children, asthma sufferers, who would also be identified as 'children in need', could be linked in with the social worker's case load. The worker could also be involved in setting up parents' support groups. A specialist social worker is only one option. Dr Clayden feels that nurse specialists also have potential value. Although their training is less focused on the social and emotional needs of children, they do have greater skills in administering medication and undertaking minor physical treatments.

What population therefore would be necessary to establish a specialist paediatric clinic? Estimates from the author's study, based on the numbers of soiling children that paediatricians in Reading, UK (which has a population of 200 000) currently see, suggested there should be sufficient soiling children to run at least one clinic a month and possibly three in a two month period. If, however, estimates are based on the population figures, and the known prevalence of soiling problems (Rutter et al 1970, Butler & Golding 1986), the figures suggest that there are potentially more than enough soiling children in the community of 200 000 people to run clinics more frequently.

The most appropriate place for the soiling clinic would be the local hospital, which already holds clinics for other paediatric problems. One clinic a month, or two in a two month period, would probably meet the medical needs of the soiling children but it would need the support of

Table 14. Elements of the whole child treatment package: Essential elements and less essential elements.

Treatment element	Special conditions
Essential	
(1) Focus on 'whole' child	None
(2) Assessment by and access to expert medical care	None. Many families will not travel long distances
(3) Demystification, child responsible for own bowel management with help if necessary: child trained into regular bowel habits. The expectation that relapses are common, built into treatment at early stage. Child trained in survival-at-school tactics	Child sexual abuse disclosure may give different priorities. However, even after cessation of on-going CSA, child may need this approach to regain continence. If CSA suspected but evidence inconclusive this approach still useful in maintaining contact with child. Note: continued soiling does not necessarily mean CSA is on-going
(4) Possibility of using a behavioural programme to teach child regular habits and break into any learned helplessness	As above Behavioural programme *must* produce positive results, otherwise must be changed to where success is guaranteed
(5) Reducing of psychosocial stresses on child. Efforts to limit the secondary effects of problem	Must be good for child in all cases. But some stresses cannot be alleviated; others may not be identifiable without home visit
(6) An approach that stays with the problem, through the crises, and relapses	Some families may request second opinion. This is their choice but if the original agency makes the referral, histories can be sent
Important but not essential	
(1) Behaviourally trained nurse specialist visiting the home setting up the behavioural training programme	All behavioural programmes are better set up in the situation where they operate, but they could be set up at the treatment agency. These carry risks of 'black stars'; also some families may miss follow-up, so child misses reinforcement. School nurses, clinical psychologists are equally effective in setting up programmes

Table 14. Continued.

Treatment element	Special conditions
(2) Home visiting to assess psychosocial stresses and to limit secondary problems	Family may not wish to have worker visiting home. But this may be because initial referrer has not explained role. Without home assessment, important problems can be missed; e.g. with child who lived in caravan with outside toilet.
Less essential (1) On-going home visiting over period	This is expensive. Telephone contact may be an option as used by Kaplan in Canada (Kaplan 1985). Many families need more support. This could come from a parents' support group
(2) Social worker undertaking home visiting, setting up behavioural programme and taking key role	Social worker is an appropriately trained professional to visit the home and assess the child, and in cases where physical or sexual abuse is suspected may be essential. Other paramedicals with training are as good at setting up behavioural programmes.

a social worker or other paramedical. This worker, by working with the families, may be able to reduce hospital attendance. This, however, may well be balanced out by the extra children coming to such a clinic. In effect the paediatricians could have a similar workload but would be seeing more children less frequently. The author's research demonstrated that in the past some soiling children spent prolonged periods as inpatients in hospital, an expensive resource. An effective paediatric outpatient department might have the added advantage of reducing the number of children who needed to be admitted, bringing about further savings. This was also the experience of the author's study.

How much time would a social worker or other paramedical have to give to such a clinic? The author estimated in her study that, in an area with a population of 200 000, a social worker would need to spend less than two days a week on such a clinic. This was a generous allowance.

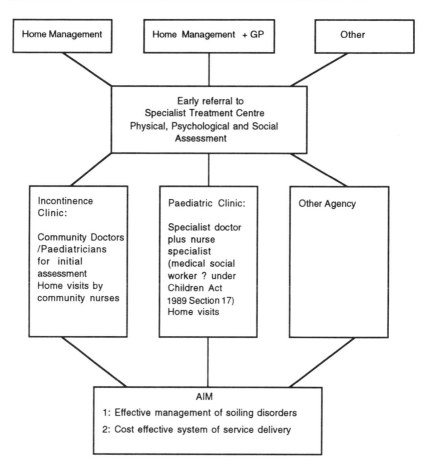

Figure 41. Possible Treatment and Management Systems for Soiling Children.

With telephone and parents' self-help groups her time could be reduced.

If the paediatric clinic was not able to have its own specialist worker, the clinic would still be offering an improved service because the bringing-together of families with similar problems would offer them the chance of mutual support and the possibility of a self-help group being set up. Once a central clinic for the treatment and management of soiling children has been set up it has the opportunity to develop and improve its services.

The community clinic—linked to the enuretic clinic

In Berkshire in the UK, as indeed in other parts of the country, there are effective systematised community clinics for bedwetters. In Berkshire, because of the association between bedwetting and soiling, school nurses already visit a number of soilers, but at present their brief is to stay strictly to the 'wetting' mandate. In discussion with the author, a number of the school nurses suggested they would like to become more involved with soiling problems. They feel they would then offer a more comprehensive service. This then is another system which might be extended to meet the needs of soiling children.

The community clinic has two problems. Firstly, in Reading, in Berkshire, there is not 'a' community clinic as such, although the school nurses operate out of a building close to the hospital, so there is no facility for children and parents to come together. School medical officers work closely with the school nurses, but they see children at school. Many soiling children would be reluctant to discuss their soiling problems in their school, fearing quite wrongly that their friends would hear of their problem. However, some school medical doctors also have part-time posts at the hospital and there might be a possible link with the children going to a paediatric clinic and the school nurses visiting the children in the home. This idea was recently put to one of the joint post school medical/hospital doctors in Berkshire and her opinion was that she would find it difficult relating to, and building up a working practice with, a large number of different school nurses. Even so, the idea is a starter and other areas may find it fits in with their existing systems and is less expensive to run than a paediatric service. Nurses could easily be trained to improve their behavioural skills. They might be reluctant to become involved with social problems. But with their school links they may be able to highlight and help school-based problems, and with their community links they might be more effective at assisting community-based problems than other paramedics.

The Better Option

The discussion has really only begun, and specialists in other areas may have ideas on how the identified treatment needs of the soiling child can be met and funded. The first step is to set up a local specialist clinic. In the author's experience and with the area she knows best foremost in her mind, she feels the paediatric clinic operating on three afternoons every two months, and supported by a behaviourally trained social worker, spending up to two full working days per week on the clinic work and the rest of the week on other paediatric outpatient clinics, would offer an enviable service to soiling children and their families, and for limited cost offer a good return on the money spent. If the social worker spent the remainder of her week servicing other children's clinics also looking at the needs of the whole child, not only may there be savings all round, but this would give a better service for these children and these families. In addition, in the UK, these social workers' services could be paid for by Social Services under their Children Act 1989 statutory duties to provide services for children 'in need'.

Future Tasks: Need for Publicity

In this book our focus has been the individual soiling child and his family. But much larger numbers of soiling children would receive a significant benefit from publicity which lifted the secrecy about soiling in general, and which explained that soiling was a common problem in childhood. As Levine in the USA (1982) has noted, most parents have not heard of another child with the same problem. They have heard of leukaemia, diabetes, asthma. These are all 'OK' problems to mention to your friends, but no one talks about soiling. As a result, many children do not come forward for treatment until the problem is established. The secrecy also places extra stress on the child and family because of the very isolation it causes. There are not many 'talking' taboos left. We can talk about death, sex, child abuse, and in certain circumstances even sexual abuse. But we cannot talk about defaecation and defaecation problems.

More publicity is also needed to encourage schools to consider the condition of their toilets. Although poor toilets may not in themselves cause a soiling problem they are likely to affect an existing problem, and even set off a problem in an already vulnerable child. This problem has already been highlighted by the author in a short paper in *Health and Education*, a small magazine circulated to all schools in the UK (Buchanan 1989b). Similar publicity may be needed in other areas.

Need for Further Research

The spate of child care scandals in Britain in the 1980s was a cogent reminder to all professionals involved in child care that the knowledge base for diagnosing children who have been sexually abused was grossly inadequate. Indeed the Cleveland Report (1988) and the study by the author (Buchanan 1989) demonstrated that children with severe constipation could be misdiagnosed as victims of sexual abuse because of the similarity of symptoms. The idea that the soiling child and his family, with all their existing difficulties, might inadvertently and through no fault of their own also become the victims of professional abuse is grotesque. Therefore one of the most pressing needs for research is to find some specificity for each condition. The present situation is most unsatisfactory. What we still need to know is how sexually abused soilers differ from non-sexually abused soilers.

Another area about which we need to know more is what happens to soilers when they grow up. Fraser (1986) has shown that some childhood soilers carry their disorder into adulthood. How many children does this apply to? Read (1986) has indicated that some adult patients with bowel disorders had soiling problems as children. How great is the risk that childhood soilers develop other bowel problems in adulthood?

We have indicated that relapse is a major problem for soiling children. More research is needed into what children have relapses and how these relapses can be prevented.

Finally, more research is needed into the role of diet and the role of allergy in causing and maintaining a constipation problem.

CONCLUSION

This brings us to the end of this book and to the conclusion of the study on which the book was based, which took place over more than five years. Although, in this work, much was discovered about what causes a child to soil, and although new ways to improve the lot of a soiling child and perhaps make his treatment a little shorter have also been uncovered, there is still much about soiling which remains a mystery. Deep down in every researcher there is a silent hope that by careful empirical study they may metaphorically unlock the secret of the DNA. In this case the secret of the DNA is still elusive and is still there to tease other researchers. At present the reality is that for some children, soiling will remain a long term management problem and it is important then that everything is done to lessen the secondary effects. It is appropriate here to end where we began. Problems with 'me bowels' have after all been with us since time immemorial. Within this time-span, to have entertained a hope that more than a few more pieces would be added to the jigsaw, was a little arrogant. Hopefully, however, with the help of this book, some children and their families may be helped to cry less and to laugh more over their 'bowels'. The full version of the letter quoted at the start of the book sums up the situation well and makes an appropriate finale.

FINALE   'It's me bowels'

(Reprint of a letter from Dr Walker to the *British Journal of Hospital Medicine* 1985, reproduced with permission)

Sir E.R. Beck, in his stimulating contribution 'It's me bowels' (August 1984, p. 85), noted that 'The GP sees many patients with this complaint (bowel disorders) who consume a lot of time and a lot of pills . . .' This is but an echo of what has been said time and again—although primarily in relation to constipation.

In 1911, Sir John Sawyer wrote 'for the physician, the treatment and cure of habitual constipation engage attention more often than other details of remedial art'. In 1886, Cheadle asserted similarly that there was 'no disordered condition of the body which is so frequently the subject of medical treatment as constipation'. Going back further to the 18th century and the time of the purging excesses—not wholly for constipation—an ardent protagonist was Benjamin Rush (King, 1958) who, in his treatment particularly of fevers, insisted that 'the true way to proper therapy was purge, purge and purge some more'. The great Moses Maimonides (Leibowitz and Marcus, 1974) considered it essential that faeces should be soft.

Hippocrates (Adams, 1939) wrote in a similar vein and averred that for good health, defaecation should be 'twice or thrice a day'—a far cry from the present average of once a day or less. Still further back, the early Egyptians (Marti-Ibanez, 1965) used castor oil; they also had recourse to enemas. Furthermore, medical practice had reached such a remarkably high degree of specialisation and hierarchy that a particular specialist physician was designated as 'guardian of the anus' of the Pharaoh.

In view of the intense preoccupation (indeed obsession) with bowel movement by many, can we answer: how important is it to health whether stools are soft or hard, small or large, formed or formless, eliminated infrequently or regularly, with pain or with ease? Almost a century ago, worthies such as Sir Lauder Brunton (Brunton, 1896) discoursed expansively on the relevant toxaemias and other ill effects of constipation. Near the turn of the century, patients with 'intractable' constipation were subjected to mutilating operations whereby various lengths of bowel were removed. Sir William McEwan in his 1904 Huxley Lecture said sarcastically 'There is a present openly expressed discontent about the alimentary tract. Some are persuaded that there is an intestinal whorl too much, and that this whorl requires to be short circuited.'

As late as 1929 an Annotation in *The Lancet* maintained that 'constipation is undoubtedly the cause of much ill health'.

Have we progressed since then? Thanks to Alvarez (1924), the ill effects of constipation are no longer feared. Yet, as Dr Beck instances in his article, the fear has been transferred to other aspects of bowel behaviour. Thus, Thompson and Heaton (1980) elicited symptoms of functional bowel disease in no less than 30.2 per cent of apparently healthy Britons. Using an amended version of these authors' questionnaire locally among rural and urban blacks 4.2 and 12.0 per cent respectively affirmed symptoms of irritable bowel syndrome (Segal and Walker, 1984).

Accordingly, whether in developed or developing populations, problems over 'me bowels' are with us to stay, concerning as they do the intestinal tract which Bergen (1946) regarded 'as a mirror wherein is reflected the status of bodily activities in general' (from emotion to eating and drinking and 'states of disease').

Signed:
A.R.P. Walker/B.F. Walker, South African Institute for Medical Research, Johannesburg, South Africa.

Adams, F. (1939) *The Genuine Works of Hippocrates*. Williams and Wilkins, Baltimore, p.9.
Alvarez, W.C. (1924) *Physiology Reviews*, **4**, 352.
Bergen J.A. (1946) *Journal of the American-Medical Association*, **132**, 313.
Brunton, L. (1896) *Lancet*, **i**, 1483.
Cheadle, W.B. (1886) *Lancet*, **ii**, 1063.
King, L.S. (1958) *The Medical World of the Eighteenth Century*, University of Chicago Press, Chicago. p.147.
Lancet (1929) **i**, 1368
Leibowitz, J.O., Marcus, S. (1974) *Moses Maimonides on the Causes of Symptoms*. University of California Press, Los Angeles. p.111.

McEwen, W. (1904) *British Medical Journal*, **ii**, 873.

Marti-Ibanez, F. (1965) *A Pictorial History of Medicine*. Spring Books, London. p.47.

Sawyer, J. (1911) *Lancet*, **ii**, 810.

Segal, I., Walker, A.R.P. (1984) *South African Medical Journal*, **65**, 72.

Thompson, W.G., Heaton, K.W. (1980) *Gastroenterology* **79**, 283.

REFERENCES

Agnarsson, U., Gordon, C., MacCarthy G., Evans, N. & Clayden, G.S. (1989) Anorectal function in children and adolescents with spina bifida, *Gut* 30: A715.

Ahnsjo, S. (1959) Pre-school children in a children's colony. Thoughts and conclusions connected with a survey. In *The Parents' Role in Child Development*. I.U.C.W., Geneva.

Anthony, E.J. (1957) An experimental approach to the psychopathology of childhood: Encopresis. *Br. J. Med. Psychol.* 30: 146–75.

Arhan, P., Faverdin, C., Devroede, G., Pierre-Kahn, A., Scott, H. & Pellerin, D. (1984) Anorectal motility after surgery for spina bifida. *Dis. Col. Rect.* 27: 159–63.

Barker, L.M. (ed.) (1982) *The Psychobiology of Human Food Selection*. Ellis Horwood.

Barker, P. (1983) *Basic Child Psychiatry*. Granada Publishing.

Barrowclough, C. & Fleming, I. (1986) *Goal Planning with Elderly People. Making plans to meet individual needs. A manual of Instruction*. Manchester University Press, UK.

Beck, A.T. (1970) Cognitive therapy: nature and relationship to behaviour therapy. *Behav. Therapy* 1: 184–200.

Bellman, M. (1966) Studies in encopresis. *Acta Paediatr. Scand. (Suppl.)* 170: 7–132.

Bemporad, J.R. (1978) Encopresis. In Wolman, B., Egon, J. & Rass, A. (eds) *Handbook of Treatment of Mental disorders in Childhood and Adolescence*. Prentice-Hall, New Jersey.

Bemporad, J.R., Pfeifer, C.M., Gibb, L., Cortner, R.H. & Bloom, W. (1971) Characteristics of encopretic patients and their families. *J. Amer. Acad. Child Psychiatry* 10: 272–97.

Bennholdt-Thomsen, C. (1954) Zur Entstehung Kindlicher Verhaltensstorungen. *Deutsch Med. Wschr.* 79: 1326.

Bentley, J.F.R. (1964) Some new observations on megacolon in infancy and childhood with special reference to the management of megasigmoid and megarectum. *Dis. Col. Rect.* 7: 462–70.

Bentley, J.F.R. (1971) Constipation in infants and children. *Gut* 12: 85–90.

Bentley, J.F.R., Nixon, H.H., Threnpreis, T.H. & Spencer, B. (1966) Moderators. Seminar on pseudo-Hirschsprung's disease and related disorders. *Arch. Dis. Child.* 41: 143.

Berg, I. & Vernon-Jones, K. (1964) Functional faecal incontinence in children. *Arch. Dis. Child.* 39: 465–72.

Berg, I., Forsythe, I., Holt, P. & Watts, J. (1983) A controlled trial of 'senokot' in faecal soiling treated by behavioural methods. *J. Child Psychol. Psychiatry* 24(4): 543–9.

Bloch, C.E. (1932) Constipation incontinence. *Acta Med. Scand.* 78: 248.

Bodian, M., Stephens, F.D. & Ward, B.C.H. (1949) Hirschsprung's disease and idiopathic megacolon. *Lancet* i: 6.

Bodian, M. (1952) Chronic constipation in children, with particular reference to Hirschsprung's disease. *Practitioner* 169, 517.

Brocklehurst, J.C. & Khan, M.Y. (1969) A study of faecal stasis in old age and the use of Dorbanex in its prevention. *Gerontol. Clin. (Basel)* 11: 293–300.

Bryce-Smith, D. (1977) Lead and cadmium levels in stillbirths. *Lancet* i: 1159.

Buchanan, A. & Oliver, J.E. (1977) Abuse and neglect as a cause of mental retardation: a study of 140 children admitted to subnormality hospitals in Wiltshire. *Br. J. Psychiatry* 131: 458–67.

Buchanan, A. (1987) Treatment and management of soiling children. Submitted paper, meeting St Bartholomews Hospital. Association of Child Psychology and Psychiatry.

Buchanan, A. (1988) The Treatment and Management of Soiling Children (Can we do better?). Workshop presented at The Child Guidance Trust, Inter-Clinic meeting, Regents College.

Buchanan, A. (1989a) Soiling and sexual abuse: the danger of mis-diagnosis. *ACPP Newsletter* 11(5): 3–9.

Buchanan, A. (1989b) Soiling in school age children. *Health and Education*, HEA Schools Health Education Unit, Exeter.

Buchanan, A. (1990) Treatment and Management of Soiling Children. PhD thesis. University of Southampton.

Buisseret, P.D. (1978) Common manifestations of cow's milk allergy in children. *Lancet* February 11, 304–5.

Bulkeley, R. & Sahami, V. (1984) Treatment of long standing encopresis in a twelve year old boy using behaviour modification within a framework of systems theory. *ACPP Newsletter*, 6: 24–7.

Burns, C. (1941) Encopresis (incontinence of faeces) in children. *Br. Med. J.* 29: 767.

Burns, C. (1958) Childhood encopresis. *Medical World* 89: 529.

Butler, N. & Golding, M. (1986) *From Birth to Five. A Study of the Health and Behaviour of British Five Year Olds*. Pergamon Press.

Cabanac (1971) In Barker, P. *The Psychobiology of Human Food Selection*. Ellis Horwood.

Cameron-Gruner, O. (1930) *A Treatise on the Canon of Medicine of Avicenna*. Luzac & Co., London.

Caspi, A., Elder, G.H. & Hebener, E.S. (1990) In Robins, L. & Rutter, M. (eds.) *Straight and Devious Pathways from Childhood to Adulthood*. Cambridge University Press, New York.

Children Act 1989. HMSO.

Children Act 1989. *Regulations and Guidance Volume 2* (1991).

Christie, M.J. & Mellett, P.G. (eds.) (1986) *The Psychosomatic Approach: Contemporary Practice of Whole-person Care*. J. Wiley & Sons.

Clayden, G.S. (1976) Constipation and soiling in childhood. *Br. Med. J.* 1: 515–17.

Clayden, G.S. & Lawson, J.O.N. (1976) Investigation and Management of long-standing chronic constipation in childhood. *Arch. Dis. Child.* 51: 918–23.

Clayden, G.S. (1978) Hirschsprung's disease. Preserving the child's dignity. *Nursing Mirror*, Oct. 19, 52–5.

Clayden, G.S. (1980) Organic causes of soiling in childhood. *ACPP Newsletter* No. 5, 1–4.

Clayden, G.S. (1981) Chronic Constipation and Soiling in Childhood. MD Thesis. University of London.

Clayden, G.S. (1986) 'He won't use the Pot'. *Update* 15 January, 127–31.

Clayden, G.S. (1987) Anal appearances and child sex abuse (Letter) *Lancet*, 620–1.

Clayden, G.S. (1988a) Reflex anal dilation associated with severe chronic constipation in children. *Arch. Dis. Child.* 63: 832–6.

Clayden, G.S. (1988b) Is constipation in childhood a neurodevelopmental abnormality? In Milla, P.J. (ed.) *Disorders of Gastrointestinal Motility in Childhood*. Wiley, Chichester.

Clayden, G.S. & Agnarsson, U. (1991) *Constipation in Childhood*. Oxford Medical Publications, Oxford University Press.

Clayden, G.S. (1992) Personal practice: management of chronic constipation in children. *Arch. Dis. Child.* 67: 340–4.

Cleveland Report (1988) *Summary of Findings*. HMSO, London.

Coekin, M. & Gairdner, D. (1960) Faecal incontinence in children. *Br. Med. J.* ii: 1175–80.

Conger, J.C. (1970) The treatment of encopresis by the management of social consequences. *Behaviour Therapy* 1: 386–90.

Conners, C.K. (1980) *Food Additives and Hyperactive Children*. Plenum, New York.

Davidson, M., Kugler, M. & Bauer, C. (1963) Diagnosis and management in children with severe and protracted constipation and obstipation. *J. Pediatr.* 62: 261–75.

Davie, R., Butler, N. & Goldstein, H. (1972) *From Birth to Seven. Report of the National Child Development Study*. Longman.

Davis (1928) In Barker, P. *The Psychobiology of Human Food Selection*. Ellis Horwood.

Edelman, R.I. (1971) Operant conditioning treatment of encopresis. *J. Behaviour Therapy Exp. Psychiatry* 2: 71–3.

Egger, J., Graham, P.J., Carter, C.M. & Gumley, D. (1985) Controlled trial of oligoantigenic treatment in the hyperkinetic syndrome. *Lancet* 9 March, 540–5.

Ellis, R.W.B. (Ed.) (1962) *Child Health and Development*. Churchill, London.

Fenichel, O. (1945) *The Psychoanalytic Theory of Neurosis*. Norton, New York.

Fiengold, B.F. (1976) Hyperkinesis and learning disabilities linked to artificial food flavours and colors. *Am. J. Nurs.* 75: 797–803.

Finklehor, D. (1979) *Sexually Victimised Children*. Free Press, New York.

Fowler, G.B. (1882) Incontinence of faeces in children. *Am. J. Obst. Dis. Women Children* **15**: 984.

Fraser, A.M. (1986) *Br. J. Psychiatry* **146**: 370, 371.

Freud, S. (1905) Three essays on the theory of sexuality. *Complete Psychological Works of Sigmund Freud Vol. VII.* Hogarth Press, London.

Freud, S. (1908) Character and anal erotism. *Complete Works of Sigmund Freud Vol. IX.* Hogarth Press, London.

Freud, S. (1917) On transformation of instincts as exemplified in anal erotism. *Complete Psychological Works of Sigmund Freud Vol. XVII.* Hogarth Press.

Friedman, M.H.F. & Snape, W.J. (1946) Color changes in the mucosa of the colon in children as affected by food and psychic stimuli. *Fed. Proc.* **5**: 30.

Frolich, Th. (1931) Contribution to a discussion. *Acta Paediatr.* **12**: 251.

Gathorne-Hardy, J. (1972) *The Rise and Fall of the British Nanny.* Hodder and Stoughton.

Gelber, H. & Meyer, V. (1965) Behavioural therapy and encopresis: the complexities involved in treatment. *Behaviour Res. Therapy* **2**: 227–31.

Grace, W.J., Wolf, S. & Wolf, H.G. (1951) *The Human Colon.* Hoeber, New York.

Graham, P. (1986) *Child Psychiatry. A Developmental Approach.* Oxford Medical Publications.

Gray, G., Smith, A. & Rutter, M. (1980) School attendance and the first year of employment. In Hersov, L. & Berg, I. *Out of School: Modern Perspectives in Truancy and School Refusal.* pp. 343–70. Wiley, Chichester.

Hanks, H., Hobbs, C.J. & Wynne, J.M. (1988) In Browne, K., Davis, C., and Stratton, P. (eds). *Early Prediction and Prevention of Child Abuse.* Wiley.

Haynes, W.G. & Read, N.W. (1982) Ano-rectal activity in man during rectal infusion of saline: a dynamic assessment of the anal continence mechanism. *J. Physiol.* **330**: 45–66.

Health and Community Care Act 1990. HMSO.

Hein, H.A. & Beerends, J.J. (1978) Who should accept primary responsibility of the encopretic child? *Clin. Pediatri. (Phil.)* **17**, 67–70.

Henoch, E. (1881) *Vorlesungen uber Kinderkrankheiten Ein Handbuch fur Aerzte und Studirende.* Hirschwald, Berlin.

Herbert, M. (1981) *Behavioural treatment of Problem Children. A Practice Manual.* Academic Press, London; Grune & Stratton, New York.

Herbert, M., Sluckin, W. & Sluckin, A. (1982) Mother to infant bonding. *J. Child Psychol. Psychiatry* **23**(3), 205–21.

Hersov, L. (1977) Faecal soiling. In Rutter, M. & Hersov, L. (eds) *Child Psychiatry, Modern Approaches.* Blackwell Scientific Publications, Oxford.

Hobbs, C.J. & Wynne, J.M. (1986) Buggery in childhood: A common syndrome of child abuse. *Lancet* ii: 762–96.

Hull, D. & Johnston, D.I. (1981) *Essential Paediatrics*, p.150. Churchill Livingstone.

Hungerland, H. (1936) Chronische Obstipationals Ursache Fur Incontinentia alvi. *Arch. Kinderheilk.* **108**: 43.

Hurst, A.F. (1934) Anal achalasia and megacolon (Hirschsprung's disease); idiopathic dilation of the colon. *Guy's Hospital Rep.* **84**: 317.

Jehu, D. (1989) *Beyond Sexual Abuse. Therapy with Women who were Childhood Victims.* Wiley.

Jekelius, E. (1936) Incontinentia alvi im Kindesalter. *Arch. Kinderheilk.* **109**: 129.

Jones, J. (1988) Bowel training for children with spina bifida. *Professional Nurse,* November, 87–90.

Jolly, H. (1977) *Book of Child Care.* Sphere Books, London.

Jolly, H. & Levine, M.L. (1985) *Diseases of Children.* Blackwell Scientific.

Jowett, B. (1943) *Plato.* Clarendon Press, Oxford.

Kanner, L. (1953) *Child Psychiatry,* 2nd edition. Thomas, Springfield.

Kaplan, B.J. (1985) A clinical demonstration program of a psychobiological approach to childhood encopresis. *J. Child Care* **2**(3): 47–54.

Kazdin, E. & Petti, T.A. (1982) Self-report and interview measures in child and parent evaluations of depression and aggression in psychiatric inpatient children. *J. Child Psychol. Psychiatry* **23**(4): 437–57.

Kempe, C.H. & Helfer, R.E. (1980) *The Battered Child.* University of Chicago Press.

Kempton, J. (1961) Constipation and encopresis: A paediatrician's view. In Mackeith, R. & Sandler, J. (eds) *Psychosomatic Aspects of Paediatrics.* Pergamon Press.

King, F.T. (1913) *Feeding and Care of the Baby.* Macmillan, London.

Knights, B. (1987) Power tactic at Pooh Corner: A clinical strategy for effecting change in encopretics. Submitted Paper Meeting, Association for Child Psychology and Psychiatry. *Newsletter* **9**: 28.

Kohler, W. (1925) *Mentality of Apes.* Kegan Paul, London.

Laird, R. (1973) The excretory habits of piglets. In Kolvin, I., Mackeith, R. & Meadow, R. (eds) *Bladder Control and Enuresis. Clin. Develop. Med.* Nos. 48/49. 22 Spastics International Medical Publications/Heinemann, London.

Lask, B. & Fosson, A. (1989) *Childhood Illness: The Psychosomatic Approach. Children Talking with Their Bodies.* Wiley.

Lehman, E. (1944) Psychogenic incontinence of faeces (encopresis) in children. *Am. J. Dis. Child.* **68**.

Leoning-Baucke, V.A. & Younoszi, M.K. (1982) Abnormal anal sphincter response in chronically constipated children. *J. Pediatr.* **100**(2): 213–18.

Leoning-Baucke, V.A., Desch, L., Wopfraich, M. (1988) Biofeedback training for patients with myelomeningocele and fecal incontinence. *Dev. Med. Child Neurol.* **30**: 781–90.

Levine, M.D. (1975) Children with encopresis: a descriptive analysis. *Pediatrics* **56**(3), 412–16.

Levine, M.D. & Bakow, H. (1976) Children with encopresis: a study of treatment outcome. *Pediatrics* **58**: 845.

Levine, M.D., Mazonson, P. & Bakow, H. (1980): Behavioral symptom substitution in children cured of encopresis. *Am. J. Dis. Child.* **134**: 663.

Levine, M.D. (1982) Encopresis: its potentiation, evaluation, and alleviation. *Pediatr. Clin. North Am.* **29**(2): 315–30.

Lipowski, Z.J. (1986) What does the word 'Psychosomatic' really mean? A historical and semantic inquiry. In Christie, M.J. & Mellett, P.G. (eds) *The Psychosomatic Approach: Contemporary Practice of Whole-person Care.* Wiley.

MacGregor, M. (1961) Chronic constipation in children. In Mackeith, R. & Sandler, J. (eds) *Psychosomatic Aspects of Paediatrics.* Pergamon Press.

McTaggart, A. & Scott, M. (1959) A review of twelve cases of encopresis. *J. Pediatr.* 54: 762–8.

Margolies, R. & Gilstein, K. (1983) A system approach to the treatment of chronic encopresis. *Int. J. Psychiatry Med.* 13(2): 141–52.

Meadow, R. (1989). Foreword. In Lask, B. & Fosson, A. (eds) *Childhood Illness: The Psychosomatic Approach.* Wiley.

Meunier, P. (1984) Physiologic investigation of primary chronic constipation in children. *Gastroenterology* 6: 1351–7.

Molnar, D., Taitz, L.S., Urwin, O.M. & Wales, J.K.H. (1983) Anorectal manometry results in defecation disorders. *Arch. Dis. Child.* 58: 257–61.

Morgan, R. (1981) *Childhood Incontinence: Disabled Living Foundation.* Heinemann Medical Books, London.

MORI Poll (1984) Poll of 2019 Adults over 15. Mori Poll, London.

Mrazek, P. & Kempe, C.H. (eds) (1981) *Sexually Abused Children and their Families.* Pergamon Press.

Neale, D.H. (1963) Behavioural therapy and encopresis in children. *Behaviour Research and Therapy* 1: 139–49.

Nixon, H. (1961) In discussion on megacolon and megarectum. *Proc. Roy. Soc. Med.* 66: 575–8.

Olatawura, M. (1973) Encopresis: A review of thirty two cases. *Acta Paediatr. Scand.* 62: 358–64.

Oliver, J.E. & Buchanan, A.H. (1979) Generations of maltreated children and multi-agency care in one kindred. *Br. J. Psychiatry* 135: 289–303.

Olness, K., McFarland, F.A. & Piper, J. (1980) Biofeedback; A new modality in the management of children with faecal soiling. *J. Pediatr.* 96: 505–9.

Pedrini, B. & Pedrini, D.T. (1971) Reinforcement procedures in control of encopresis. A case study. *Psychol. Rep.* 28: 937–8.

Pinkerton, P. (1958) Psychogenic megacolon in children: the implications of bowel negativism. *Arch. Dis. Child.* 33: 371–80.

Porteus Problem Checklist (obtainable from NFER, Windsor, UK.)

Pototsky, C. (1925) Die Enkopresis. In Schwarz, O. *Psychogenese und Psychotherapie Korperlicher Symptome.* Springer, Berlin.

Preston, D.M., Pfeffer, J.M. & Lennard-Jones, J.E. (1984) Psychiatric assessment of patients with severe constipation. *Gut* 25: A582.

Pritchard, C. (1991) personal communication.

Rachman, S. (1962) Learning theory and child psychology: therapeutic possibilities. *J. Child Psychol. Psychiatry* 3: 149–68.

Read, N.W. (1986) Impairment of defecation in young women with severe constipation. *Gastroenterology* 90: 58–60.

Read, N.W. & Abouzekry, L. (1986) Why do patients with faecal impaction have faecal incontinence. *Gut* 27(3): 283–7.

Read, N.W. & Timms, J.M. (1986) Defaecation and the pathophysiology of defaecation. *Clinics in Gastroenterology,* 15: 937–65.

Registrar General, Great Britain (1960) *Classification of Occupations*. HMSO, London.

Rehbein, F. & Von Zimmerman, H. (1960) Results with abdominal resection in Hirschsprung's disease. *Arch. Dis. Child.* 35: 29.

Richman, N. (1983) Choosing treatments for encopresis. Submitted Paper Meeting. Association for Child Psychology & Psychiatry. *Newsletter* 16: 34.

Richmond, J., Eddy, E. & Garrard, S. (1954) The syndrome of fecal soiling and megacolon. *Am. J. Orthopsychiatry* 24: 391.

Roberts, J. (1988) In Browne, K., Davis, C. & Stratton, P. (eds). *Early Prediction and Prevention of Child Abuse*. Wiley.

Russell, D.E.H. (1983) The incidence and prevalence of intra-familiar and extra-familiar sexual abuse of female children. *Child Abuse and Neglect.* 7: 133–46.

Rutter, M. (1965) Classification and categorisation in child psychiatry. *J. Child Psychol. Psychiatry* 6: 71–83.

Rutter, M., Tizard, J. & Whitmore, K. (eds) (1970) *Education, Health and Behaviour*. Longman, London.

Rutter, M. (1975) *Helping Troubled Children*. Harmondsworth, Penguin.

Rutter, M., Maughan, B., Mortimer, P. & Ouston, J. (1979) *Fifteen Thousand Hours. Secondary Schools and their Effects on Children*. Open Books Publishing.

Rutter, M. (1986) Child Psychiatry: Looking 30 years ahead. *J. Child Psychol. Psychiatry* 27(6): 803–40.

Rutter, M. (1989) Pathways from childhood to adult life. *J. Child Psychol. Psychiatry* 30(1): 23–51.

St Bernadino of Sienna (1388–1444) In Wright, L. (1960) *Clean and Decent*. Routledge & Kegan Paul.

Schauss, A.G. (1981) *Diet, Crime and Delinquency*. Parker House.

Scobie, W.G., Eckstein, H.B. & Long, W.J. (1970) Bowel function in Meningomyelocele. *Dev. Med. Child Neurol.* 12, suppl. 22: 150–6.

Selander, P. & Torold, A. (1964) *Enkopres. Nord. Med* 72: 1110.

Seligman, M. (1975) *Helplessness*. W.H. Freeman & Co, San Francisco.

Shandling, B. & Gilmour, R.F. (1987) The enema continence catheter in spina bifida: successful bowel management. *J. Pediatr. Surg.* 22: 271–3.

Skinner, B.F. (1938) *The Behavior of Organisms*. Appleton-Century-Crofts, New York.

Sluckin, A. (1975) Encopresis: a behavioural approach described. *Social Work Today.* 5(21): 643–6.

Sluckin, A. (1981) Behavioural social work with encopretic children, their families and the school. *Child Care, Health and Development* 7: 67–80.

Sluckin, W., Herbert, M. & Sluckin, A. (1983) *Maternal Bonding*. Blackwell, Oxford.

Smith, N. (1968) Effects of irritant purgatives on the myenteric plexus in man and the mouse. *Gut* 9: 139–43.

Stanton, A. & Sunderland, R. (1989) Prevalence of reflex anal dilation in 200 children. *Br. Med. J.* 298: 802–3.

Taitz, S., Wales, J., Urwin, O. & Molnar, D. (1986) Factors associated with outcome in management of defecation disorders. *Arch. Dis. Child.* **61**: 472–7.

Thorling, I. (1923) Einige Typen von Incontinentia alvi bei Kindern. *Med Revue* **40**: 97.

Todd Report (1968) The Royal Commission on Medical Education. HMSO.

Tripp, J.H. & Candy, D.C. (1985) *Manual of Paediatric Gastro-enterology.* Churchill Livingstone.

Vaughan, J. (1961) Constipation and encopresis. A children's psychiatrist's view. In MacKeith, R. & Sandler, J. (eds) *Psychosomatic Aspects of Paediatrics.* Pergamon Press.

Walker, A.R. (1985) 'It's me Bowels'. *Br. J. Hosp. Med.* **33**(2): 118.

Wallace, A. (1888) Incontinence of faeces for three years. *St. Bartholemew's Hospital Rep.* **24**: 260.

Watson, J.B. & Rayner, R. (1920) Conditioned emotional reactions. *J. Exp. Psychol.* **3**: 1–14.

Webster, A. & Gore, E. (1980) The Treatment of Intractable Encopresis: A Team Intervention Approach. *Child Care Health and Development* **6**: 351–60.

Weissenberg, S. (1926) Uber Enkopresis. *Z Kinderheilk.* **40**: 674.

Whitehead, W.E., Parker, L., Masek, B.M., Catalder, M. & Freeman, J.M. (1981) Biofeedback treatment of fecal incontinence in patients with myelomeningocoele. *Dev. Med. Child Neurol.* **23**: 313–22.

Whitehead, W.E., Parker, L. & Bosmajian, L. (1986) Treatment of fecal incontinence in children with spina bifida: comparison of biofeedback and behaviour modification. *Arch. Phys. Med. Rehabil.* **67**: 218–24.

Whiting, B.B. (ed) (1963) *Six Cultures. Studies in Child Rearing. Laboratory of Human Development.* John Wiley & Sons, New York.

Williams, N.S., Hallan, R.I., Koeze, T.H. & Watkins, E.R. (1990) Restoration of gastrointestinal continuity and continence after abdominoperineal excision of the rectum using an electrically stimulated neoanal sphincter. *Dis. Col. Rect.* **33**(7): 561.

Wright, L. (1960) *Clean and Decent.* Routledge & Kegan Paul.

Yule, W. (1984) Child behaviour therapy in Britain: 1962–1982. *ACPP Newsletter* **6**(1): 15–20.

APPENDIX   Information booklet for children and parents

The following pages contain the booklet which we hand out routinely to the children attending our special clinics. This has been rigorously edited and criticized by a large number of these children. The language is aimed at 10–12 year olds but it can be read to younger children. This attempt to demystify the subject has succeeded in many cases and has led other children to frame questions around particular concerns in the text. When the booklets are given out a reminder of the individual nature of the problems in that particular child is given.

Readers are invited to photocopy this section of the book for their patients' use, if they feel this may be helpful. This will not infringe the Copyright Laws unless a charge is made for a copy or an attempt is made to publish the booklet without the permission of the authors and Oxford University Press.

SOME INFORMATION ABOUT CHRONIC CONSTIPATION IN CHILDREN

Introduction

We are often asked to explain what is happening inside a child with chronic constipation. This is not easy to answer for two reasons:

(1) No one knows exactly how we learn to control our bowels, nor how that end of the body works.

(2) Every child has an individual form of constipation. Each one has a particular mixture of all the factors which make up the problem.

In this booklet, we try to explain many of the possible factors, and your own individual problem will be caused by some, but not all of these. We hope to find out which are the main ones as you come to the clinic appointments. We will then give you our theory of why the problem is there and suggest the best way of solving it.

Contents

SOME PRACTICAL HINTS

(1) We know that repeated hospital visits are difficult, what with travelling and waiting, so we try to reduce these to a minimum. We know that most children will need to come for at least one year and so we try to spread these appointments out. At first they will be approximately monthly but very soon about three monthly. It is important to be able to keep in touch between these appointments, so we can make small alterations, etc. We try to run a telephone service where we can return your call, or arrange an earlier appointment. Clinics try to be flexible about dates and times, so please alter an appointment, especially if it clashes with something good happening at school. (We sometimes have to alter clinic dates as well.) Some play facilities are available in the clinics, but it is well worth bringing your own toys and books (especially for the grown ups!).

(2) You will probably be given diary sheets to record the medicines given and your progress. Please bring these to clinics and ask for new ones when you are there.

(3) Try to discuss with your local family doctor what is going on if you get the chance. We will write to him at times. He may be asked to prescribe your medicines, as most hospitals cannot give out enough to last the length of time between Out-Patient Clinic visits. It is best to take the empty bottles along to the surgery so the doctors can read the labels, in case they have not received letters from us.

(4) We are happy to write to school doctors or anyone else helping your family, with your permission.

(5) When clinics are arranging special tests or even an In-Patient stay, these arrangements may be complicated. Try and telephone to confirm these dates, if you haven't had official confirmation the week before.

A3

The words we use

It is often embarrassing talking about bowel problems. One added difficulty is the large number of words used for the subject. Here are some of them and their medical terms:

Defaecation—opening the bowels, having a pooh, passing motions, big jobs, doing No. 2, big toilet, going to the loo/lavatory/toilet.

Faeces—stools, poohs, No. 2s, big jobs, plops, bowel motions, (plus those Anglo-Saxon words which may offend some of our readers!).

Most families have their own word for it and it is important we all know what it is when discussing problems.

HOW THE BOWEL WORKS

What are stools?

When we eat, our teeth crush up food until it is soft and we swallow it. When we swallow food, it starts on its journey down a tube (about 26 ft long) from your mouth to your anus (bottom). This long tube (your bowels or gut) gets wider in places, e.g. the stomach. As the food passes along, all the useful parts are absorbed into the blood in the tiny blood vessels running beside the bowel. The blood then carries these 'goodies' to other parts of the body where they are stored, or used to give you energy to run about, to build strong bones, or to make you grow. Gradually all the useful parts are absorbed, leaving just the waste. The last part of the bowel (called the large intestine or large bowel, or colon) allows this waste to move slowly through, and the water is absorbed. You can imagine how important this is in hot countries, especially in deserts. Thus the stool becomes less watery and more formed.

Stools will be different if we eat different things. Some foods leave lots of waste by the time they reach the large bowel—these are called 'high fibre' foods, e.g. apples, peas, potatoes, lettuce, cereals. Some foods contain very little fibre—such as cheese, milk, sweets. If there is too little fibre reaching the large bowel, then stools (poohs) can become rather hard. Fibre helps stools to remain large and soft. If we don't drink enough water or other drinks, the large bowel will do its best to absorb as much water as possible from the stool—it thinks it's in a desert! Thus the stool gets very hard and dry, becoming difficult to pass.

A4

How do we pass stools?

Stools reach the far end of the large bowel (called the rectum). When the stool enters, the rectum seems to feel it arrive there. A message is sent up the nerves to warn you a stool has arrived and you will need to find the loo soon. Another message is sent down to the muscles keeping the anus closed. This message makes the muscles relax slightly and the stool can move further down. When the stool touches the special skin inside the anus, our feeling of wanting to go gets more urgent. These muscles are not directly under our control: they are part of the automatic system which moves food along this tube, from your throat to your anus. Luckily we have some muscles at our bottoms which we can control ourselves, so when the urgent need to pass a stool comes, we can just about hold on for the time it takes to find a loo.

Everybody is different when it comes to the feeling they get from their bottoms, and how easily they can hold on until they find a loo. This difference is the clue as to why some people get constipated (that is, having difficulties in passing stools) and some do not.

Before going into details about this we must know how we learn about the feelings in our bottoms, and what to do about them:

How do children learn to control their bowels?

When babies are fed, as their little stomachs get full, a message is automatically sent down to the rectum. It is as if the stomach were warning the large bowel to empty so as to make room at the top end for milk. For this reason, babies often have stools after feeding. When babies get a feeling from the rectum that it is full, the stool is ready to come out, they automatically relax their bottom muscles, grunt, and push out the stool.

As they grow older, their parents learn to notice when the child (from around the age of two years) is getting this feeling. Quite often the toddler stands quietly as if concentrating and may even go a little red around the eyes, or pale around the nose and lips when s/he is about to go. If the parents manage to put the child on the pot, then the stool will go in the pot and the toddler will see it and notice how pleased Mum and Dad are. He or she will gradually learn that those early feelings coming from the bottom are a sign to sit on the pot which parents get pleased about. It takes months for most children to learn this and sometimes there are problems.

A5

WHY DOES CONSTIPATION HAPPEN?

As we said at the beginning of this booklet, no one child has exactly the same problem as another. There are sorts of constipation which happen more at one age than another. Babies and toddlers may find that their stools are hard to pass. This is often because the child is not having enough water to drink in the day. The stools get dried up and hard. Each day stools are smaller than usual and so it may take two or three days longer for the rectum to fill enough to set off the grunting and straining. Some minor illnesses like a cold or the 'flu will increase the body's need for water and so the stools become harder and less frequent. In some children, when they pass these hard, delayed stools, it hurts. If they are old enough to remember this, the next time they are about to go, they get frightened it will hurt again and so hold on as hard as they can, with their muscles. Unfortunately for them, they have to go some time. By the time they do go—maybe after several days—the stool is very hard and large. This produces pain and once again they learn that defaecating is a bad idea. At a young age they don't understand that they can't just put off going.

A routine develops of being OK for a couple of days, then a day or more of getting feelings of wanting to go. This makes them afraid they will go and so they stand around (or hide) and strain all their bottom muscles to stop going. They often get angry or irritable because they are not feeling too good, what with the feelings coming from their bottoms and the fear that a hard stool will come out and hurt them. Eventually it does come and, if it is hard, it will hurt again, so they are proved right. Naturally the parents are worried that the child must have a motion. They know that all the days of delay are making the stool even harder and larger. They try to help by putting the child on the loo or pot. The last thing the child wants to do is to have a motion and so jumps straight off. As you know, this is bound to lead to a battle; both sides are right, but they have a different understanding of what is going on. Put into words they might say:

CHILD: "Stop it—you are trying to make me have a pooh which will hurt my bottom. You are trying to hurt me!"

PARENT: "Sit there—don't hold on to your pooh or else it will be painful for you another day. Go now—it will be worse later."

A6

Like many battles, a lot of other fights happen as well—'Do as you are told', 'Go away', 'We know best', 'I want to choose for myself'. The battles get hotter when the parents get worried that constipation is making the child ill and they therefore fight harder to save him or her. Fortunately, it is very rare that constipation is dangerous in a child over two years old, but the going off food and looking ill is a worry.

Why does this only happen to some children of this age?

There are several reasons again, and usually the reason for a particular family is a mixture of factors. The size of the rectum varies from child to child—just like there is a difference in how tall you are, or how long your nose is, or what size shoes you take. Some children are born with, or develop, a large rectum. This allows the stools to be stored for a longer time. It may be that a baby with a slightly large rectum will develop a larger one as s/he grows up with constipation. It is probably true that the longer you can hang on to the stools, the larger the rectum is.

Another reason is that some children and parents are more sensitive to worries about stools. Some are more likely to have battles over things like eating, getting dressed, going to bed, etc. If these children are unlucky enough to have a hard stool at some stage, then a battle may develop over this. There is nearly always a bit of this and a bit of that in how constipation develops.

What happens when constipation goes on for a long time?

(We will come to treatment and ways of helping, soon.)

Some children seem to have constipation which goes on and on. Often this is complicated by soiling loose stools into the clothing. This becomes an urgent reason for getting the bowels sorted out, as the soiling can cause great embarrassment. When constipation has been going on for a long time, the rectum is usually large and filled up with hard or soft stools. We can feel how much has built up by abdominal examination (feeling the tummy).

A7

Diagram of the last part of the large bowel

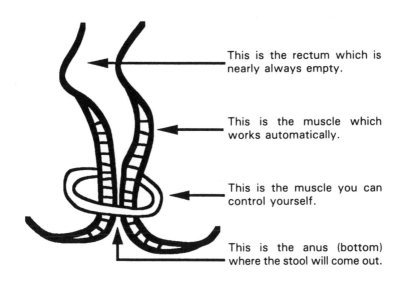

This is the rectum which is nearly always empty.

This is the muscle which works automatically.

This is the muscle you can control yourself.

This is the anus (bottom) where the stool will come out.

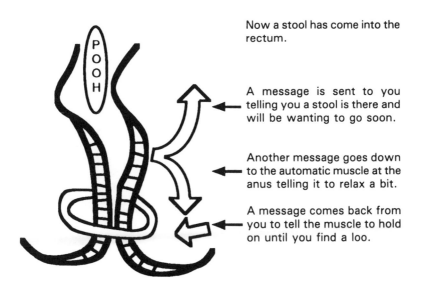

Now a stool has come into the rectum.

A message is sent to you telling you a stool is there and will be wanting to go soon.

Another message goes down to the automatic muscle at the anus telling it to relax a bit.

A message comes back from you to tell the muscle to hold on until you find a loo.

A8

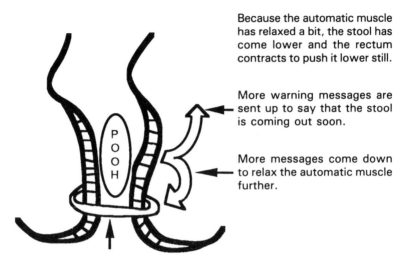

Because the automatic muscle has relaxed a bit, the stool has come lower and the rectum contracts to push it lower still.

More warning messages are sent up to say that the stool is coming out soon.

More messages come down to relax the automatic muscle further.

Your messages to hold on tight with this muscle stop when you find the loo and sit down and relax. (This muscle can only hold on for a short time when the message from the rectum completely relaxes the automatic muscle.)

The rectum contracts and helps push out the stool. You get a feeling that you should push down into your bottom by holding your breath or grunting.

Both the automatic muscle and your controlling muscle are relaxed and the stool comes out easily

These muscles contract afterwards to close the anus again.

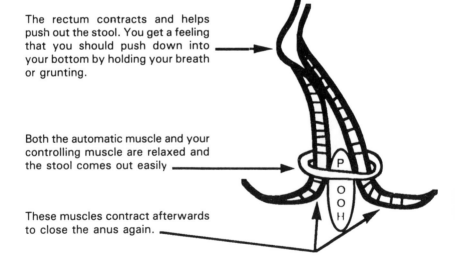

Diagram of the last part of the large bowel in chronic constipation

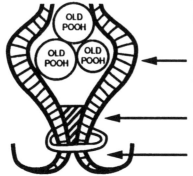

This is the enlarged rectum, pretty full of old stools.

Because it is used to holding heavy stools, the walls are thickened.

There is a little loose stool which passes around the harder stools.

The automatic muscle at the anus is also thickened.

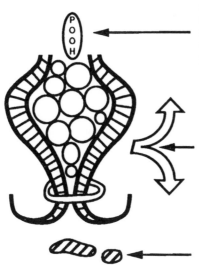

When a new stool comes into the rectum, it is so loaded it doesn't seem to notice its arrival and so no messages are sent up to warn you that another stool has come in.

The rectum churns the old stools about and sometimes sends messages up: but it says that the rectum is quite loaded, but it is not urgent. Sometimes a message is sent down to the automatic muscle, which relaxes only enough to let out some of the soft fluid stools. These seep out, without any feeling and stain the pants.

Because no clear messages are coming up from the rectum, this muscle which we can control ourselves does not squeeze and stop the fluid soiling.

A10

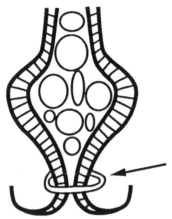

After about 1 to 3 weeks, the rectum gets very loaded, then it starts to give messages which often feel like pain in the tummy. Eventually the automatic muscle gets enough message to relax and let out the giant stool.

The muscle you can control is eventually unable to stop the large stool coming out and it gets so urgent a rush to the loo is needed.

Even after all this, there is still some left, which will be the old stool at the centre of the next giant stool.

Thank goodness that's out but, oh dear, not another blocked loo!

A11

The vicious circles

The first vicious circle is that the distended and enlarged rectum allows a large collection of stools, which makes the rectum grow larger, and so on:

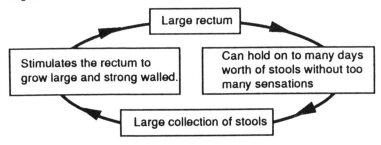

The next vicious circle is that the children who have a dislike of stools (they even dislike the smell of stools, more than children who have not had these problems), so they try as hard as they can not to make stools. This means the stools build up inside and only the fluid, loose stool leaks out. This causes soiling which causes more embarrassment and the child hates stools even more.

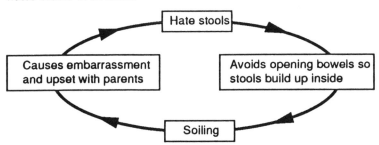

Another vicious cycle is that the muscle wall of the rectum becomes thickened when it is persistently loaded (as if it were an athlete doing weight training). The thickening and strengthening of the muscles also involves the automatic muscles of the anus. This means it takes more messages from the rectum to make it relax and, even then, its thickness does not allow the ordinary sized stools to come down easily.

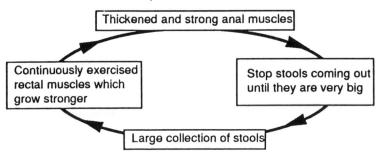

A12

Another circle we discussed earlier is the child who is afraid that a large stool will hurt, and so avoids passing it until it becomes large enough to cause pain:

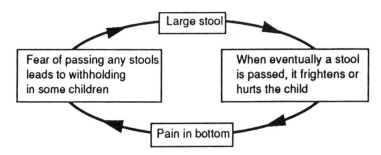

If this becomes a battle area between parent and child, this cycle gets worse.

Another cycle which occurs in chronic constipation, and which will be looked at in the next section, is our diet (what we eat).

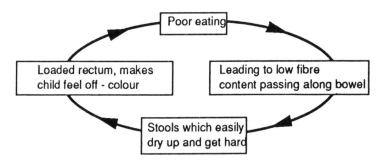

There are many other circles like these, which happen in some children and not in others. These are often connected with the emotional effects of this difficult problem. Again, we must emphasize that every child is different, and not all these cycles happen in every child.

This all sounds very difficult, but keep reading, because we will now show you how many ways we have to help.

A13

WAYS TO HELP?

1. Food

Some foods have the wrong effect because they tend to slow down the movement of the bowels or fill the child up, so they don't want to eat very much. Milk and sweets (especially sweet milky tea or coffee) do this.

Any food which leaves fibre when it passes through the bowel will help keep stools soft. If the large rectum needs to work on large stools, then high fibre foods will help. The stools will fill up the large rectum within a few days staying soft and so be less likely to hurt.

Food such as these contain lots of fibre:

Cereals like oatmeal porridge, All Bran, Shredded Wheat, Shreddies and Weetabix. Apples and pears with skins, soft fruit, grapes, etc., baked jacket potatoes (skins should be eaten), wholemeal bread, digestive biscuits.

Adequate fluid intake—6–8 cups of liquid a day (everything counts—tea, juice, etc.),

Fruit and vegetables (cooked or uncooked)—root vegetables have higher roughage. The only problem with making changes in the diet is that many of the fibre foods are not very popular with children. This may lead to more disagreements—over meals.

Luckily we have some medicines which provide this sort of roughage, and help keep the stool soft, such as:

Methyl cellulose—Cologel, Celevac, Cellucon.

Bran tablets—Fybranta, Isphagula, Regulan, Metamucil.

Other roughage medicines—Fybogel, Isogel, Inolaxine, Normocol.

Medicines which contain special sugars called 'long sugars' do not get absorbed from the bowel, but stay in the waste from food. When these sugars reach the large bowel, they get eaten by the good germs which we all have there. It may seem unpleasant to you that inside us there are a lot of germs, but these are very useful and some make vitamins to keep us healthy. The others help to keep our stools soft and probably help to keep harmful germs away. Lactulose is the name of one of these sugars and you find this in medicines such as Duphalac and Gatinar.

A14

2. Routines

The body seems to like keeping to regular rhythms—e.g. times of meals, going to bed, waking up, and having a motion. When we have trouble with passing stools apart from keeping the stools soft by having plenty of roughage, we can help by trying regularly. The most likely time to be successful is after eating (just like the babies mentioned on page A5). If you try after every meal, you may find that you occasionally succeed at a particular time in the day. It is worth staying on the loo for ten minutes or more—even if you don't feel like going—especially at those times, and it is worth having a stock of comics there. Sometimes you might pass a small stool and jump off but, if you wait, quite often another comes (try timing when the second one comes!).

3. Medicines

When constipation has been going on a long time, we must find some medicine to help send the stools along faster and make the rectum contract more. Many people use Senokot, mainly because the amount you need can be changed quite safely, and most children like the taste of the syrup. It can also be given as granules or tablets. We advise you to take it only once per day and it is best taken in the evening. It takes quite a long time to work—about 12 to 24 hours. This is because it doesn't work until the good old germs in the large bowel have had a chance to eat some of it. When it starts to work, the muscles in the large bowel start to work more. The stool gets moved about and you sometimes feel this as a feeling that you sometimes want to pass a stool, but often as a funny feeling or even as a slight ache. If you feel any of these, try to pass a stool. When you have had a motion, the Senokot seems to make sure the rectum is really empty and this should help stop what happens in the diagram on page A11.

A15

Senna is a plant which has been used for years to help overcome constipation; here is an old fashioned drawing of the plant from 1646:

Nowadays the pods from the plant are purified and the Senokot you have is much easier to take. Everyone is individual, and some people do not like Senokot, so we have other medicines which work in a similar way: Normax, Dulcolax.

A16

If you look back at the diagram of the loaded rectum on page A10, you can see that sometimes the large stools clog up at the end of the bowel. Before we can start to use medicines like Senokot, we have to use something to get rid of the hard old stools. If we don't, then powerful medicines like Senokot will just cause discomfort. We try to soften up these stools and 'dissolve' them with Docusate. This medicine has the same effect on stools as washing up liquid has on greasy plates: it helps to loosen the hard stools so they can be passed. Sometimes the stools are so hard they take too long to dissolve and then an enema may be given. This means a small amount of medicine is squirted into the rectum through a small tube passed through the anus. This loosens everything up, makes the rectum very active and helps the stool come out. Usually we don't have to use enemas, but many children have had one by the time they come to a clinic, which is why we tell you about them. Sometimes picosulphate is used to clear out the old stools instead. This is taken by mouth and works in about 6 hours.

It is important that all your medicines are taken regularly. This helps get the body into a rhythm. We often start patients with a week or two of Docusate and then go on to regular Cologel (to keep the stool soft) and use Senokot at night (to keep the bowel moving regularly, and help the rectum shrink down a bit). As you get better, the dose of Senokot can be reduced, perhaps to every other day, and you will gradually need less and less. If you were having 20 mls (four teaspoonfuls) every night, then it is best not to stop this suddenly, but over a couple of weeks, reduce to 15 mls (three teaspoonfuls) or 10 mls (two teaspoonfuls). To help you (and us), the diary sheets give you a space to tick how much you have had. If you take Senokot tablets, one tablet is the same as 5 mls of syrup.

Some children find Cologel difficult to take because, if it warms up it goes thick (a bit like glue!). If you keep it in the fridge, it will stay runny. Another medicine we use is Lactulose, which toddlers and young children take 5 mls of twice a day, and older children take 10 mls twice a day. It is best to keep these going on longer than the Senokot, probably for three to six months, even when you are getting better. This is to stop the constipation happening again, while the rectum is gradually shrinking down to a better size.

A17

4. Special tests

Sometimes we need to do tests to find out exactly what is causing your bowel problem. Usually we get an X-ray picture of your abdomen (tummy) to see where the stools are: we will show you this X-ray. If your bottom problem is quite complicated, and is not getting better, we may carry out other tests.

One test is to put a little balloon in your bottom—you just feel something cold and then you lie there while the machine records things and prints it out on paper. We will show you this tracing and try to explain how your bottom works. This takes about 20 minutes and all you usually notice is the cold feeling as the balloon goes in, or occasionally a feeling that you would like a motion, or nothing at all. What we see looking at the recording, is how well the automatic muscle relaxes. Most children who are old enough to read this (e.g. over seven years old) find the test a bit odd, but certainly not distressing. It is difficult to explain this test to younger children, who are often very frightened of things to do with bottoms and stools, so we do this test under an anaesthetic.

Another test which is sometimes done is a special X-ray called a barium enema. Here a small amount of special liquid is squirted into the anus and X-rays are taken: this shows the shape of the lower bowel. You may have had this test done in the past.

There is one condition we are very careful to look for in all constipated children and this has the name of Hirschsprung's disease. Hirschsprung was a doctor in Denmark during the last century: he described two children who had very severe loading of their rectums. It was later found that the automatic muscles do not relax properly in Hirschsprung's disease. This is because the messages from the bowel above cannot pass to the bowel below because the nerves in the bowel wall are not properly formed. This problem mainly affects babies but, just rarely, we see children who have had trouble with this since they were babies. These children do not get better by taking medicines alone. Our balloon test shows that the automatic muscle of the anus does not relax in children with Hirschsprung's disease. To be sure not to miss any constipated children with this disease, we sometimes do a rectal biopsy. This is usually done under an anaesthetic—a tiny piece of the rectum wall is snipped off and looked at under the microscope. We then count the number of nerves there. If there are too few, an operation is needed to put the constipation right.

A18

As we said earlier, the problem of constipation is not just the shape of the rectum or the anus. Sometimes small physical problems are made worse by worries. So other tests are available to help find out if you have any difficulties at school: a psychologist may see you, or if you are having problems with your speech, a speech therapist.

5. Special help

Sometimes, problems with the bowels upset children and their parents so much that this upset makes the problem last longer. This is another circle which we need to break. We try and help by providing social workers, child psychiatrists, and art therapists. They help in many cases by relieving some fears and misunderstandings. Sometimes children keep their feelings inside them and they need to let them out in order for them to be dealt with. Sometimes the battles going on between the parents and child need someone from the outside to bring about a peace treaty! Often children feel that they will never get better and they need encouraging and praising. Some of them are still not sure that having a motion is a good idea, and they need help to try and be reassured that it is. A stay in the children's ward may help, because they see other children with similar worries. Most families feel they are the only ones with this bowel problem. This is probably true of their neighbourhood, but hospitals see children from quite a large area of England and sometimes from abroad, so there is nearly always someone else in the ward with this problem.

6. When do we need to bring children into hospital?

We have mentioned that sometimes we have to do tests which require anaesthetic, so children have to come into hospital for this. Sometimes we want to see just what the pattern of passing stools is. Occasionally, we cannot clear the stools from the loaded rectum and we need to clear them out under an anaesthetic. We also have learned, from treating children with Hirschsprung's disease, that stretching the troublesome automatic muscle of the anus, under anaesthetic, helps in some cases. We find that giving children with chronic constipation an anal dilatation, as it is called, weakens the automatic anal muscle. You remember that it is the muscle which cannot relax properly and will only let the stool out when the rectum is really loaded. By stretching it under anaesthetic we weaken it and from then on the rectum can empty when it is less loaded. So children find they can go more easily and without pain. One extra value of doing this, is that under anaesthetic we can do the balloon test or a rectal biopsy. We can also check how large the anus is, whether it is in the correct position and at the same time, remove any stools loading the rectum.

A19

This can be done just as a Day Case (staying in for one day only), but we often find a few days stay, preferably with Mum, is better. When children are on the ward, we can see that the medicines are the right ones for them, and that they are happier going to the loo. We may give them a chart on which they can put a star every time they pass a stool in the loo. Often they have had these charts before, but have been unable to go and are disappointed. Now they will be able to go, and will get some stars. After they go home they are advised not to stop their medicines too soon, in case loading should come back and undo some of the good that has been done.

Another bonus for the parents on the children's ward is that they meet other parents whose children have similar problems. Again, please remember that all children are different.

Sometimes children need more than one anal dilatation, or even a small cut into the troublesome muscle (this is called a sphincterotomy). Fortunately, this does not lead to any difficulties with holding the stools normally. The soiling is usually the first problem to disappear with any of these treatments. All the different tests and treatments take time to be performed. Some of the arrangements for these are complicated and may even have to be changed at short notice. We try hard to fit our plans in with yours, so as not to interfere with your holidays or arrange for a test to be done in hospital on your birthday. Please let us know in plenty of time if the dates are not right for you so we can give you another. If you forget to come to an out-patient visit, please telephone and make another appointment—we don't want you to get lost. Sometimes we have to change your appointment, or even delay your coming into hospital, because the wards are full of unexpected emergencies. We realize this is disappointing and are sorry if it happens.

It always seems a long time for children to get over their problems with their bowels. Please don't expect a treatment to work quickly or to be able to come off a medicine after just a few weeks. Most children need to come to their out-patient clinics for at least one year.

When you eventually come off medicines, you won't need to attend routinely but we are still happy to hear from you and happy to give further advice in the future. You may be sent letters or forms to fill in many years after you stop coming, which will ask how you are. These help us find out more about these bowel problems. So if you change your address when you have stopped coming to the clinic, please let us know of your new address. (If you can remember your hospital number, this will also be of help).

A20

If you have managed to read through all this, you will probably have quite a few questions! Please ask them next time you come to your out-patient appointment. It sometimes helps if your parents write any questions down, so you don't forget to ask them when you see us.

G. S. Clayden
V. Agnarsson
London

INDEX

disorders, 153
Survival packs for school, 125
Syrup of figs, 8
Systems for treatment and
management of children who
soil, 216
better option, 217–218

Taitz, S., 5, 59, 64, 66, 192, 193
Talking with their bodies, children,
205
Tearful, miserable, distressed and
soiling, 168
Telephone, use of in management,
131–133
value of, 125
Temazepam sedation with enemas,
115
Temper tantrums and soiling, 168
Temperamental factors and onset of
soiling, 91
Tense mother and treatment
outcome, 194–195
Tests in medical assessment, 89
Thorling, I., 47
Threadworm, 30
Timing of problem in assessment,
100
Todd Report, Royal Commission on
Medical Education, 70
Toilets and soiling
adaptations in cerebral palsy, 164
in constipation, 24
fears of, behavioural
management, 119
feelings about, 98, 99
home, 39
role of, 104, 108–9
school, 39
school toilet refusal, 60
schools, need to encourage better
provision in, 218
Toileting routine, establishing, 120

Treatment
behavioural approaches, coming
of, 77–80
behavioural studies, 57
common expectation of, 73–74
comparison, to other disorders,
207–208
development of modern paediatric
approach, 53
early ideas on, 52
need for high medical priority for,
206–207
principle studies of, 62
route of child who soils, 208
studies by family therapists, 58
studies on, for severe
constipation, 55–56
use of family therapy, 81
use of social workers, 58
Treatment, whole child approach
in case studies, 137–144
coming of, 59
ethos of, 71, 88
length of treatment in final
assessment, 198–199
medical priorities in, 113
outcome, factors affecting, 192–
195
packages of care in, 73–83
possible multidisciplinary
approach, 209
process of, 112–114
recognising child's feelings about
previous, 98–99
results from, 65
stress of, in case study, 140
Tripp, J. H. and Candy, D. C., 29,
48
Tuberous sclerosis, 90
Tumour, abdominal, 29, 31

Ulcerative colitis, 95